FLORIDA STATE
UNIVERSITY LIBRARIES

SEP 3 1997

TALLAHASSEE, FLORIDA

INTERNATIONAL POLITICS
AND GERMAN HISTORY

INTERNATIONAL POLITICS AND GERMAN HISTORY

The Past Informs the Present

EDITED BY
DAVID WETZEL AND THEODORE S. HAMEROW

Westport, Connecticut
London

Library of Congress Cataloging-in-Publication Data

International politics and German history : the past informs the
  present / edited by David Wetzel and Theodore S. Hamerow.
      p.   cm.
  Includes bibliographical references and index.
  ISBN 0–275–95749–7 (alk. paper)
  1. Germany—History. 2. Germany—Foreign relations.
  3. International relations. 4. World politics. I. Wetzel, David.
  II. Hamerow, Theodore S.
  DD112.I57   1997
  943.08—DC21   96–39840

British Library Cataloguing in Publication Data is available.

Copyright © 1997 by David Wetzel and Theodore S. Hamerow

All rights reserved. No portion of this book may be
reproduced, by any process or technique, without the
express written consent of the publisher.

Library of Congress Catalog Card Number: 96–39840
ISBN: 0–275–95749–7

First published in 1997

Praeger Publishers, 88 Post Road West, Westport, CT 06881
An imprint of Greenwood Publishing Group, Inc.

Printed in the United States of America

The paper used in this book complies with the
Permanent Paper Standard issued by the National
Information Standards Organization (Z39.48–1984).

10 9 8 7 6 5 4 3 2 1

To
Gordon A. Craig
Again

Contents

Introduction
David Wetzel and Diethelm Prowe   1

1. Does the History of International Politics Go Anywhere?
   Paul W. Schroeder   15

2. The Diplomatic Revolution of Our Time
   Paul Gordon Lauren   37

3. Monarchy, Court, and Society in Constitutional Prussia
   David E. Barclay   59

4. Karl Lamprecht: A Historian's History
   Roger Chickering   75

5. "Der Bund für Bürgerrechte": Transnational Relations and the Problem of Democratization in West Germany, 1949–1954
   Hermann-Josef Rupieper   87

6. German Unity and Military Professionalism: The Officer Corps of the German Armed Forces Confronts the Legacy of the *Nationale Volksarmee*, November 1989–January 1993
   Donald Abenheim   103

7. Reflections on the German Question
   Gaines Post, Jr.   127

Afterword: Gordon A. Craig and the Old-Fashioned Way of Doing History
David Wetzel and Theodore S. Hamerow   147

Selected Bibliography   161

Index 171
About the Editors and Contributors 179

INTERNATIONAL POLITICS
AND GERMAN HISTORY

Introduction
David Wetzel and Diethelm Prowe

Historians have been writing diplomatic history for a long time, indeed ever since they penetrated the archives of state. Leopold von Ranke spent the most productive days of his life poring over the state papers of the republic of Venice. Albert Sorel wrote a masterpiece, *Europe and the French Revolution* (1875), which showed even in its title that the two events were linked. C. K. Webster reached the same supreme level in his study of *The Foreign Policy of Castlereagh* (1925). These historians and others like them set out to write history out of the foreign office archives. But they had a more important task. They claimed to be able to write about contemporary events with the same detachment as if they were treating more remote periods. The claim may have been justified, but it would be foolish to pretend that the sudden interest in contemporary events was detached or "scientific." It was forced on them by the First World War and particularly over preoccupation with the question of "war guilt." Had Bismarckian peace endured, it is doubtful whether the twentieth century would have shown as much concern with diplomatic history.

The years between the settlement of 1919 and Hitler's victory in 1933 were the great days of the "pure" diplomatic historian. People wanted to understand the contemporary world; historians assured them that they could do so if all diplomatic secrets were revealed. The result proved disappointing. For the most part the documents confirmed what the historians had in mind before they started to write: The Germans demonstrated that they had not caused the war; Soviet historians continued to blame capitalist imperialism; and the cynical were convinced that all statesmen had lurched from one blunder to another.

Thus began the great doubts about diplomatic history. It was not merely that historians had missed some revelation, or were being denied some material. They were asking the wrong questions. They had to turn from the

Foreign Office, to the profound forces that shape the destinies of mankind. The slide worsened after the Second World War and has persisted to the present day. Diplomatic history is nowadays ignored or even despised in the high councils and organizations of professional historians. Historical journals are dominated by trendy forms of social history, from Marxist analyses of class struggle, Western imperialist exploitation, Third World dependency, and the formation of race and class consciousness to the "new social history" of the French *Annalistes*, and gender, race, ecological, and subaltern studies.

This prejudice, for that is what it is, sometimes makes our critical judgments unbalanced, if not naive. Moreover, the trend confronts us with a paradoxical situation. The apparent retreat of diplomatic history from the core of historical scholarship and education comes at a time when its popularity with the lay audience, from whom historians must after all derive legitimacy, is at an all time high. Paul Kennedy's *The Rise and Fall of the Great Powers* (1987), Henry Kissinger's *Diplomacy* (1994), and most recently Gerhard Weinberg's brilliant book, *A World at Arms* (1994) have been best sellers. More important, the world political reality demands attention to and better knowledge of international history today. As Paul W. Schroeder points out, "The revolutionary transformation of the world scene and the international system occurring since World War II, especially in the last decade" has also, "far from ending international history, . . . revalidated it, and revalidated in particular the historical approach to understanding it." And, in fact, even on the edge of the historical profession, the field has broadened and changed remarkably in the last decades. The chapters in this book are testimony to this fact.

Historians of Germany have been particularly engaged with this development of international political history for two reasons. First, international politics has been central in that country's history in the last two centuries. The German political sense of national identity was born during the Napoleonic wars. Johann Gottlieb Fichte's "Addresses to the German Nation" and Ernst-Moritz Arndt's national poetry were responses to the international political challenge of the French Revolution and Napoleon's armies. Otto von Bismarck's unification of Germany by blood and iron was almost entirely the result of his exploitation of a favorable international situation. The nation's ambitious grasp for world power and its humiliation in World War I and the volatile interwar European politics and economics induced it to follow Hitler into his criminal gamble of conquest, mass murder, and collapse in the Second World War. And, as the chapters by Hermann-Josef Rupieper and Gaines Post, Jr. suggest, Germany has owed its democratization and its opportunity for economic growth and reunification substantially to international politics, first under American tutelage. Reunification, finally, was once more achieved by taking advantage of a brief favorable opening in the international power constellation.

Introduction

Second, German historians have played a pioneering role in the historiography of international politics. Was it not Leopold von Ranke, who in the age of unification and Bismarck, modeled classical diplomatic history on the principle of *Primat der Aussenpolitik* (primacy of foreign policy)? Was it not Karl Lamprecht, the tragic hero of the chapter by Roger Chickering, who led the first rebellion against that principle? Was it not Fritz Fischer who picked up this revisionism and led his thunderous assault against traditional German historiography over the origins of World War I? It was only natural that West German historians, in a state so essentially conditioned by cold war international politics, have continued to develop and broaden international history.

This volume thus explores questions of international politics as they relate primarily to German history in the broadest international and political-constitutional sense. It is no coincidence that the authors of these essays are also linked by another factor. They have all been closely associated as students or colleagues with the *Nestor* or dean of German historians, Gordon A. Craig, who, as a virtuoso of diplomatic, military, as well as intellectual, literary, and cultural history, has been a pioneer of the history of international statecraft in the broadest context. Of the seven chapters in the volume, four—those by Schroeder, Lauren, Rupieper, and Abenheim—deal directly with issues in diplomatic history and international politics; while the other two—by Barclay and Chickering—illuminate related political and cultural transformations. The concluding chapter by Post crosses memory with international politics and shows how both merged into a German political culture on the path to unification. The Afterword, by David Wetzel and Theodore S. Hamerow, examines the career, works, and philosophy of Gordon A. Craig himself, and argues that the kind of history Craig has written is not only elegant and trenchant, but of enduring relevance and certainly fit to retain its proper place in the study of the past.

The first chapter by Paul W. Schroeder addresses the fundamental questions about the history of international politics. He not only argues that the study of international history has been anything but stagnant; his own chapter demonstrates the vitality and currency of the best diplomatic history. In the face of the new world order left by the demise of the Soviet Union and the end of the cold war, he asks where international politics is going. Has there been progress in international politics?

From the course of European, and more recently, world history of the last three hundred years he derives "a certain amount of rational hope and emancipatory power in facing the future in international politics." He argues that international politics has in that time made undeniable progress. The recognition of a European state system in 1648, the emergence of a balance of power in the eighteenth century, and most important—the changed mentality and the system of procedures laid down in the relations of the Great Powers between 1813 and 1815–significantly stabilized international relations in Europe and reduced the number of wars. This nineteenth-century transformation was conceived in the 1780s, when the British economy was the first to achieve self-sustaining growth, and the French Revolution began the process of clearing away the *ancien régime*. But its actual birth was long delayed by the Napoleonic Wars. It could gather strength only when peace came and the immense new resources in finance, management, science, and technology that were now available could be put to constructive use. That, in turn, could not have been accomplished without the diplomatic revolution that Schroeder describes.

Schroeder first introduced the concept of such an epochal transformation in the arena of international politics in his highly acclaimed, massive study of *The Transformation of European Politics, 1763–1848* (1994), which T.C.W. Blanning heralded "a watershed in the historiography of eighteenth and nineteenth-century Europe."[1] The transformation was as essential as the birth of a new concept of domestic politics that emerged with the French Revolution, as described by Lynn Hunt and others. What made this turn in international political culture so enduring—notwithstanding the catastrophic backlashes of the two world wars and Leninist-Stalinist and fascist revolutions—was that this shift brought to the fore a different kind of international actor, the trading state, which increasingly depended on and therefore sought to secure economic strength. In this chapter Schroeder carries his innovative concept to the whole of modern diplomatic history—toward the present and back to the beginning of modern European diplomacy, the Treaties of Westphalia at the close of the Thirty Years War in 1648. He argues that the post-Napoleonic turn endured beyond the Vienna System and its midcentury crisis marked by the 1848 revolutions and the Crimean War. By the later nineteenth century this long-term "progress" in international politics led to the emergence of growing numbers of international organizations and, more recently, to international integration, heralding an accelerating, irreversible evolution or revolution that may possibly represent the most fundamental transformation ever.

The conception of the broad sweep of modern diplomatic history that Schroeder presents here differs from the traditional "event history," as the French *Annalistes* so contemptuously characterized political and diplomatic history of the Rankean and positivist tradition, not only because he looks beyond the case-by-case analysis of dramatic international events to the development of systems of international relations over time. He also challenges the perspective taken by recent leading histories on great power interaction—Paul Kennedy in *The Rise and Fall of the Great Powers*, Gordon A. Craig and Alexander L. George in *Force and Statecraft* (1990), and Kenneth Waltz in *Theory of International Politics* (1979) most of all. In Schroeder's view, such histories are based on the assumption "of an essentially unchanging, cyclical struggle for power or of the shifting play of the balance of power."[2] Schroeder is instead interested in a systemic analysis of "the fundamental changes in rules, norms, expectations, and collective assumptions," as he puts it in Chapter 1. He shares with M. S. Anderson's recent synthetic work, *The Rise of Modern Diplomacy* (1993), a great respect for the increasingly complex network of classical diplomacy, "which, with all its faults, was one of (Europe's) more important gifts to the world."[3] But he sees the different stages in the evolution of international politics not so much as reflections of changing cultural assumptions of the eras of faith, the Enlightenment, or industrialization, and so forth, as Anderson does, but as a process with its own internal dynamics of cultural progress because European statesmen ultimately learned from their defeats, disasters, and set-backs—in the face of changing economic and military realities—and set out to build institutions, which in turn shaped and limited the culture of international political interaction. Craig and George, who share Schroeder's and others' admiration for the remarkable breakthrough and success of the Vienna System, attribute this achievement to a particular time-bound confluence of factors that met "the requirements of a viable international system," namely an appropriate number of states, commonly accepted goals and procedures."[4] Schroeder, in contrast, discerns in the Vienna System and its later nineteenth-century successor a post-Napoleonic cultural turn, which was the climax of an economic-military development (rise of the modern trading state) coupled with a progressive learning process by statesmen, which—not withstanding the terrible backlashes of the twentieth century—inexorably favored increasing international cooperation and integration in the long run: "The Vienna era pointed toward a future now being realized." The diplomatic historian can now discern the outlines of future structural changes in international politics—led, ironically, by Ranke's intellectual heirs in Germany.

Paul Gordon Lauren echoes Schroeder's thesis of fundamental change, but he sees the changing character of diplomacy rooted in the technological and mass political changes of the revolutionary twentieth century. Whatever critical lessons international statesmen learned from the increasingly destructive clash between an emerging trading state and mounting violence at the end of the eighteenth century, the accelerating sociotechnological changes of the waning nineteenth century stripped classical diplomacy of its accustomed control over international politics, Lauren argues, building on Gordon A. Craig's famous essay "The Revolution in War and Diplomacy."[5] The rise of international integration and community, which Schroeder posits as an important foundation for the Vienna System, grew into a colorful global multitude of actors, which was enthusiastically greeted by democrats like NAACP leader W.E.B. Du Bois in the United States. It also burst the capacities for international coordination, cooperation, and integration. While Schroeder regards this burst of disorientation and ensuing military and racist holocausts as a temporary backlash of terror, Lauren regards these shifts as fundamental and irreversible. He points above all to the expansion of geographical scope, the vast increase in the number and kinds of actors in diplomacy, the decline of cultural homogeneity, the revolutionary impact of modern technological advances particularly insofar as they affect the relationship between warfare and diplomacy, and the dramatic growth in the number of subjects addressed by the diplomats of our time.

Lauren stresses five fundamental effects on the nature of diplomacy, which have largely undermined its effectiveness. The most potent and far-reaching transformation of all is the collapse of reticence and privacy in negotiation. The intrusion of the media into every phase and level of the negotiation process has irreversibly changed the character and spirit of diplomacy. Closely related is a second conspicuous change in the diplomatic process, namely the widespread practice of summitry, made possible by the growing speed in transportation and communication. This has placed negotiation into a public political sphere, severely limiting the bargaining flexibility of classical diplomacy.

Thomas Jefferson, as President of the United States, wrote the following memorandum to his secretary of state: "We have heard nothing from our ambassador in Spain for two years. If we do not hear from him this year, let us write him a letter."[6] This splendid utterance reflects the leisured atmosphere of an age in which the title "ambassador plenipotentiary" was much more than a fiction. In our age it is possible to make a telephone call to the embassy concerned and glean whatever information is needed in a few minutes of time. There is another, deeper, reason why summitry should not be regarded as an unmixed blessing. The sweeping argument has been that the practice involves the prestige of the negotiating parties at a level at which compromise is most difficult. Philippe de Comines in the fifteenth century wrote: "Two great princes who wish to establish good personal relations should never meet each other face to face, but ought to communicate through good and wise emissaries."[7] A more moderate criticism is that summit meetings lead, if not to danger, then at least to superficiality and a flair for dramatic tendency. Unable to solve intricate problems in a few harassed days, statesmen put their names to communiqués that give the impression of success while the more obdurate, central, and intractable issues are swept under the carpet of delay. In 1957 none other than Henry Kissinger, then a theoretician not a practitioner, stated: "Summits are the evasion of concreteness, the reliance on personalities, the implication that all grand problems can be settled with one grand gesture."[8] There can be no denying the fact that summit meetings have increased in frequency and that this is best illustrated by the experience of the United States. Throughout American history up to 1939 fewer than thirty visits had been paid to Washington by the heads of foreign nations.[9] In this age a similar number takes place every year.

Introduction

One effect of the rise in summitry has been a third major change in diplomatic practice, namely, a decline in function of the ambassador and the erosion in the dignity and efficacy of foreign offices through constant interference of political leaders and their corresponding reduction to technical apparatus. As Gordon A. Craig has observed, whatever changes have taken place in diplomacy since the late nineteenth century, the professional ambassadors are the losers on all fronts, usurped as they are by their political masters in the celebrating and dramatizing of international friendships. Miniature foreign ministers spring up in prime ministers' offices; and in the United States a new layer of intervention interposes itself between the policy makers and the embassies—the personal representatives of the president. Gone is the *esprit de corps* of diplomacy and with it a common sense of responsibility and values, Lauren argues quite in contrast to Schroeder, who regards this sense of common international responsibility as an achievement of the nineteenth century that has been undermined, but appears to bear new fruit in the contemporary world.

Fourth, the explosion of the multitude of issues and interest groups from commerce to human rights and the global environment has vastly increased the number and kinds of materials that must be read and mastered by those charged with the conduct of foreign affairs. Finally, the widening academic study of international relations has its impact on diplomacy. Governments have gotten into the habit of calling for academic analysis and advice to advance their position on pressing issues of policy that are being debated at home. This has necessarily expanded the diversity and variety of perspectives among international actors sprawling far beyond the government foreign offices to a variety of nongovernmental institutions and organizations, with loyalties more determined by individual perspectives and training across governmental and private organizations than by traditional diplomatic services. This has fudged the lines of interstate relations. Even individual rights of citizens in other states have become part of an increasingly complex web of international relations.

David E. Barclay's chapter parallels Schroeder's in that he, too, seeks the origins of critical changes in statecraft in the monarchial Europe of the nineteenth century. Like the monarchs at the Vienna Congress, King Frederick William IV of Prussia had learned from the uncontrollable violence of revolution. Albeit with profound revulsion, he accepted an "artificial" system of procedures governing his relations with the popularly elected representatives and his ministers by taking an oath to a written constitution in 1850. The monarchs remained at the center of the Prussian state, indeed gained in visibility and prestige, just as the crowned heads of Europe continued to guide the destinies of Europe under the Vienna System, but they submitted to self-imposed guidelines in order to preserve those very rights and privileges. The monarchial order within the state and in the international order from now on had to be justified, above all, as the best guarantee of peace and justice.

To understand Prussia during this time, Barclay tells us, we must get over the notion that the decade of reaction following the Olmütz Accords of 1850 was an arid and uninspiring time. Far from it. During this period an important series of complex changes, readjustments, and reorientations defined the growing differentiation between the state and crown. The process led in the long run to monarchical dominance and enabled the monarchy to escape parliamentary control and accountability—a development that Barclay shows was not as dark and unhappy as is sometimes supposed. By the 1850 constitution, which he was pledged to defend, the king recognized the principle of ministerial responsibility and parliamentary control over the budget, giving important powers to the liberal opposition, which could affect even the army.

Yet the new order, which circumscribed and fixed royal rights and responsibilities, boosted monarchical authority and monarchical institutions. The size and significance of the court grew rather than diminished in a period of great royalist imaginativeness, vibrancy, and creativity between 1848 and 1888. No one recognized this more than Otto von Bismarck, minister-president of Prussia since 1862, who was, of course, an extraordinary court politician. He himself once remarked that he was destined to be a courtier, not a politician or a diplomat, and he had a deserved reputation for flawless etiquette and refinement at court functions. Neither Frederick William IV nor William I, and still less William II, were fully satisfied unless they were always in motion and constantly, through one means or another, managed to keep themselves in the public eye. In the period Barclay describes, the Prussian monarchy was the center of prestige, power, material advantage, and public acclaim—much more so than has been recognized. Ubiquitous, energetic, and inspired, it was, in a word, the focus of multiple worlds.

Even though this world increasingly worshipped national power and a monarch who derived much of his popularity from a longing for world power, that same late-nineteenth-century Wilhelmine Germany could generate enough diversity to allow a revolt against the dominant academic elite's belief in state power as the primary mover of history and international politics. In Chapter 4, Roger Chickering describes the fundamental challenge to Rankean primacy of foreign policy history launched by the commercially highly successful historian Karl Lamprecht in a spectacular war of words that echoes in the *Historikerstreit*, which was to rage in Germany ninety years later. With the publication in 1891 of the first volume of his *Deutsche Geschichte*, Lamprecht set out to write a *Kulturgeschichte* or total history of the German people, which emphasized those aspects of human life that the reigning consensus was content to leave out: the history of lifestyles, diet and cuisine, mannerisms, tastes in clothing, the family, sexuality, education, the process of law, popular religion and philosophy, money, art, architecture, and, in Chickering's words, "a host of other topics that have since occupied social and cultural historians."

The effect of all this was to land Lamprecht immediately in a tremendous battle with the most senior and respected historians in Germany—Max Lenz, Hans Delbrück, and younger ones like Hermann Oncken and Friedrich Meinecke—who were now forced to confront an array of methodological issues that they had hitherto taken for granted. These men feared that Lamprecht's undertaking would lead them away from the hard, verifiable archival evidence to theory, which to them, as to Goethe, had always been gray. It had seemed to them safe, less pretentious, and perhaps more useful to illustrate general belief through the medium of specific examples, leaving to the reader to draw his own picture of their implications.

In the end Lamprecht lost, and his scholarship was discredited. He was left, as Charles McClelland noted recently, with "the distinction of being the most vilified historian in modern Germany."[10] Chickering explores the tensions of Lamprecht's early life that gave rise to the eccentricity of his personality, the professional oblivion that followed the *Methodenstreit*, and to what extent the reactions of Lamprecht's colleagues were simply hysterically defensive against his conception of social history, which they regarded as a form of local history unworthy of their attention. Yet Lamprecht remains a pioneer in his efforts to integrate intellectual, economic, and political developments and in the mark that he left on the German university as an institution.

Hermann-Josef Rupieper combines Chickering's focus on the challenge to traditional German political culture and institutions with the broader perspective on international politics addressed by Schroeder and Lauren. Rupieper's underlying issue is the role of international political action, particularly by nongovernmental institutions, in influencing the internal political transformation of another country. Building on his benchmark book, *Die Wurzeln der westdeutschen Nachkriegsdemokratie: Der amerikanische Beitrag 1945–1952*, he explores the contribution of one American nongovernmental organization (NGO), the American Civil Liberties Union (ACLU), in the democratization of (West) Germany, and the limits such organizations faced in trying to establish parallel associations in Germany, even with the encouragement of U.S. government representatives. He shows how these efforts shaped attitudes and policies in the postwar years and provided the structure for a return to democracy following the collapse of the Hitler dictatorship.

American organizations like the ACLU, the AFL-CIO, the League of Women voters, and others described by Rupieper did more than contribute an additional technique to the existing resources of diplomacy. They were inspired from the beginning by a desire to make a significant difference in democratization. They believed in the feasibility of cooperation and provided a transatlantic link that, in Rupieper's words, "was crucial for the understanding of U.S. occupation policy and its effect on West German society." As private institutions, they worked outside official channels but contributed nonetheless to the attainment of official goals.

In the case of the ACLU, it was its president, Roger Baldwin, who played the role of a NGO international emissary. Baldwin concentrated his efforts on building support for what he believed would be a German counterpart to the organization. His assumption was that a transfer of this classic institution of American democracy would be necessary to create a consensus for democracy and respect for individual liberties in West Germany. Though few Americans disagreed with the importance of this, the creation of the *Bund für Bürgerrechte*, as the German civil liberties union was dubbed, proved difficult and complex. Baldwin sought to win his case by careful diplomacy of his own, enlisting the cooperation of key Germans who had fled Hitler, while taking care not to antagonize military leaders of the Allied occupation. His success was, as Rupieper notes, by no means complete. The critical problem was "the lack of a tradition in Germany upon which a supra-party organization could be built." Still, the initiative left a mark. Rupieper's closing words merit quotation: "In the transatlantic network that developed between the United States and the Federal Republic of Germany, cooperation between the ACLU and the West German élites was a small part, but an important one, in the shaping of post-war society on both sides of the ocean."

Donald Abenheim addresses an issue in the history of international relations that Schroeder, Lauren, and Rupieper identified as an increasingly important one: institutional integration. He combines an analysis of institutional dynamics with international politics. To be sure, the case of the coordination and absorption of the East German army in the erstwhile West German *Bundeswehr* will presumably remain a rare one for two reasons: The integration entailed two previously opposing armies, and as part of a national reunification, it quickly became a national, rather than an international political issue. Still, such integrations have occurred and can be expected to occur in the future in such places as Korea and China–Hong Kong. Moreover, the size and nature of the German army had major international implications throughout the reunification process, which was only possible due to major shifts in the international constellation. There is no reason why international politics will not similarly reach into future cases of military integration in a world where traditionally domestic issues like environmental policies and civil rights have become international concerns, as Lauren points out in Chapter 2.

Abenheim's chapter provides a general survey of extraordinary range and depth about the background to the unification of 1990 and its impact upon the *Bundeswehr*. The task facing West German army leaders was no less than to tackle the very legacy of Stalinist military ideas. For over forty years, the Federal Republic of Germany had felt the threat or at least bitter enmity of the Soviet and East German forces with their omnipresent border guards ordered to shoot and kill. As late as 1988 few people had as much as an inkling that Soviet power would suddenly disintegrate. The division of Europe and of Germany was taken for granted; and as Abenheim shows, this was certainly the attitude in the West German Ministry of Defense. Communist propaganda had given the East German Nationale Volksarmee (NVA) a wholly undeserved reputation as an awesome fighting force in the West. East German leaders contributed to this benighted state of affairs by enshrining the NVA, in Abenheim's words, "with a nimbus of fake Prussian tradition, prissy socialist martial virtue, and a stultifying cult of secrecy." Thus lulled by their own propaganda, Eastern military planners were taken completely by surprise by the events of 1989.

The integration of the two armies had to be a compromise, carefully navigating between the need for a loyal army and dealing fairly with the human beings in uniform. In the process of merging the NVA into the *Bundeswehr* 70 to 80 percent of the former leadership corps was to be eliminated. Post–cold war muckrakers in the public like journalist Günter Gillessen called for the elimination of all personnel of the former East German military apparatus. The Ministry of Defense chose a "middle path that offered limited hope of permanent service to some, as well as support and retraining to many more for as long as ten years." The whole operation was clearly one of the most difficult in completing the unity of 3 October 1990. The dilemmas were not, Abenheim notes, unlike those after 1945: What to do with the soldiers of a discredited régime? In the end it has worked remarkably well, without the conspiracies and convulsions many feared, mindful of the last integrations of defeated armies in de Gaulle's France after the Algerian War and in post-Franco Spain.

Finally Abenheim's case study of post-1989 reintegration appears to lend support to Schroeder's assertion of broadly continuous systemic change in international politics. The seeds of Schroeder's post-Napoleonic turn have seemingly germinated once more at the place in the heart of Europe, where the lessons of defeats and ultimately disastrous confrontation were most inescapable in the eras preceding both the creation of the Vienna System— following the increasingly destructive wars of the eighteenth century and the French Revolution—and the post-1989 European integration following two world wars, Holocaust, and cold war: in the divided Germany of the conflicted, self-destructing Holy Roman Empire and of the most threatening nuclear cold war confrontations respectively. Like Metternich's German Confederation and, to a lesser extent, post-1871 Bismarckian Germany, Helmut Kohl's reunified Germany of 1990 has experienced those lessons of destructive conflict that seem to demand integration most acutely. A "trading state" in Schroeder's definition like few others, contemporary Germany appears to be pursuing just such a policy of broad integration, as Schroeder's analysis would predict; and this is where, as Schroeder tells us, historians have been "seeing the history of international politics increasingly conceived and written as the story of long-term structural change." Whether or not this trend will be enduring enough to justify "a certain amount of rational hope and emancipatory power in facing the future in international politics," as Schroeder believes, similarities between his post-Napoleonic turn leading to the Vienna System and the present post–cold war integrative trends in Europe are highly suggestive—including even the post-1815 and post-1989 regional fires and the broadly shared assumption that it is the business of international politics to intervene in the internal affairs of smaller states violating common values of government and civic societies.

The seventh chapter, by Gaines Post, Jr., puts the history of international politics into the context of personal international memory and reflection. Two concepts, history and identity, have been at once complicated and enriched by the process of unification. Whose history? Whose identity? are two questions that hover over the minds of those who until recently were part of two distinct and antithetical cultures, "as well as over the minds of historians everywhere for whom the future of Germany's past has abruptly changed." Memory, Post argues, is the bridge, the answer; or it can be.

Post begins on a personal note. He shows how the memory of his own experiences—intimate recollections over thirty years—shaped his understanding of German history. These experiences—stretching from his boyhood in Madison, Wisconsin, during the Second World War to June 1996—are affectingly related; and they illustrate how three generations of Germans tried several variations on the theme of national identity.

It is, of course, wrong to equate national identity with national history. As Charles S. Maier has pointed out, we need to know history to understand identity, but history will not suffice. Identity must be formulated in terms of underlying characteristics that change with time. If history alone were sufficient to understanding national identity then behavior would be predictable, it would follow settled patterns, it would obey certain rules. Two generations are alive that remember the Nazi past, as Post points out; and he belongs to the younger of these generations, too young to have fought in the Second World War, but old enough to make it the emotional point of reference of his life. The same is true of the makers of German policy; for them, too, the German question must break down into small personal experiences that sometimes affect their public decisions in major ways. Post believes with Thucydides that two kinds of experience deepen personal awareness: actual participation in events under study and participation once removed through oral testimonies, memoir literature, and autobiographies. In both kinds of experiences the historian serves as a mediator between history and public memory, showing how memory and historical reconstruction interact and shape each other. These experiences he applies to the German union of 1990—"an immense historical divide where memory will shape the future while reshaping the past."

Post views the future of German history with mixed feelings. In Chapter 7 his final words merit quotation: "Although this didactic power of history is universal, there is something singularly compelling about the German question. Twentieth-century Germany has come to symbolize matters of the heart that define what it means to be human.... For Germans and non-Germans alike, every generation's private memories offer public evidence for what it means—or might mean—to be German. Unification has given Germans the unparalleled opportunity to sift through this evidence to identify Germany's better nature."

The subject of the Afterword by David Wetzel and Theodore S. Hamerow has devoted his life to the study of the questions Post raises. Gordon A. Craig is the preeminent historian of Germany in our time. Wetzel and Hamerow examine Craig's background and outlook and show how his consuming interest has been narrative history, political history. Power is the essential theme of political history. Craig's type of history describes the way people strive for power and use it in their own societies. It tells of personal battles for ascendancy, the maintenance and exercise of rule, the achievement of power through organization, and all the details which appear, as it were, on the front page of the historical newspaper. A good many people now think of Gordon Craig's type of history as a very old-fashioned way of looking at the past—a boring form of study and not very civilized. Wetzel and Hamerow have no time for such attitudes. In their view, historians who can muster no interest for the active political life of past societies have no business being historians at all. The marvelous thing about Gordon Craig's books is that he knows how to tell stories, real stories, flesh and blood stories, though far from simple stories. The books that have flowed from his pen do not pretend to concern themselves with a particular analytical problem but with multiple pieces of human history. Craig's achievement has been, Wetzel and Hamerow argue, to bring knowledge and interpretation into the narrative framework. The essential demand of all historical material is, after all, that it be used to recreate life, to understand and describe the life that produced these extant relics, and therefore to demonstrate the main manifestation of life, which is movement. This is the guiding thread that runs through all of Gordon Craig's work. Nor is this all. Through his books Craig has shown that history is a self-sufficient and self-contained discipline, important for its own sake.

NOTES

1. Review in *The Journal of Modern History* 68, 2 (June 1996): 437.
2. Paul Schroeder, *The Transformation of European Politics, 1763–1848* (Oxford, 1994), xii, xiii.

3. M. S. Anderson, *The Rise of Modern Diplomacy, 1450–1919* (London, 1993), x.

4. Gordon A. Craig and Alexander L. George, *Force and Statecraft: Diplomatic Problems of Our Time* (New York, 1995), x–xi, 30–35.

5. Gordon A. Craig, "The Revolution in War and Diplomacy," in Gordon A. Craig, *War, Politics, and Diplomacy* (New York, 1966), and in Jack J. Roth, ed., *World War I: A Turning Point in Modern History* (New York, 1967).

6. Quoted in Dumas Malone, *Jefferson and His Time*, vol. 4, *Jefferson the President* (Boston, 1972), 43.

7. Philippe de Comines, *Mémoires*, ed. Joseph Calmette, 3 vols. (Paris, 1924), 1: 87.

8. Henry Kissinger, *Nuclear Weapons and Foreign Policy* (New York, 1957), 365.

9. Robert A. Dallek, *The American Style in Foreign Policy: Cultural Politics and Foreign Affairs* (New York, 1983), 112.

10. Charles McClelland, review of *Karl Lamprecht: A German Academic Life* by Roger Chickering, *American Historical Review* 99, 4 (October, 1994): 1344.

1 Does the History of International Politics Go Anywhere?

Paul W. Schroeder

The question in the title suggests a certain skepticism about the possibilities of development and progress in international history (diplomatic history, if you prefer). Such skepticism is not new or uncommon. Charles S. Maier's survey in 1980 of the previous decade of American work in this field clearly indicated by its title, "Marking Time," that he saw no new directions emerging in it.[1] The article, though it attracted considerable attention, was only a gust in a wind that has blown fairly steadily for decades. Since the late-nineteenth and early-twentieth centuries, international history has declined steeply and irreversibly from the position it had once held as king of the historiographical hill, and has also been specifically attacked and rejected, at least in anything like its traditional form, by some of the most influential currents of twentieth-century historiography: by Marxists, because it supposedly ignored the real roots of international politics in socio-economic structures, class struggle, and relations of production; by *Annalistes* because, like traditional political history in general, it was a history of mere short-term epiphenomenal events, ignoring the deeper rhythms and broader structures of total history or serial history; and by practitioners of *Gesellschaftgeschichte*, because it missed the driving force of history, the processes of industrialization and modernization, and their attendant consequences for society as a whole.

Even these criticisms, common in the 1950s and 1960s, were not wholly new, of course. There were serious rebellions in Germany and elsewhere against the Rankean principle of the *Primat der Aussenpolitik* long before Fritz Fischer and his followers led their celebrated revolt against it a generation ago—for example, by Karl Lamprecht and his *Kulturgeschichte* at the turn of the century and by Eckhart Kehr with his insistence on the *Primat der Innenpolitik* in the 1920s and 1930s. Nor will international history cease to be considered old-fashioned, shallow event history by some now that the historiographical vogues of earlier decades have themselves become old orthodoxies and a bit passé. Practitioners of currently fashionable brands of historiography (cultural history, gender history, new social history, history of everyday life, history from the bottom up) will doubtless have their own reasons for considering international history traditional, superficial, and not very profitable, and might well condemn it as sexist, elitist, and racist in the bargain. No field is more open to the charge that it is the record of oppression, aggression, and exploitation by dead white European males.

The current fate of international history in the United States, however, is probably not to be criticized overtly and rejected, but to be ignored quietly. One striking piece of impressionistic evidence about its decline in popularity and influence, the belief that it is not on the cutting edge of scholarship and unlikely ever to be, is the questionnaire that the American Historical Association (AHA) has in recent years distributed to all its members on renewing their memberships, requesting them to list their main fields of specialization. The list provided is comprehensive—sixty-five specific historical fields, categorized by geography, chronology, and subject matter. Included are old standard fields like the history of ideas and new ones like the history of women or gay/lesbian history. U.S. historians have nineteen separate fields from which to choose, including Black, Chicano-Latino, Native American, and U.S. Diplomatic-International (proof that those who compiled and approved this list were aware that there is such a thing as international history). Any member of the AHA, however, whose field is the history of international politics in Europe and the wider world over the last five centuries—whose historiographical forebears, that is, include Leopold von Ranke, Albert Sorel, Edouard Driault, Raymond Guyot, R. H. Lord, William Langer, Charles K. Webster, Pierre Renouvin, Garrett Mattingly, Richard Pares, and a host of other giants; whose current or recent colleagues in the field include such names as Gerhard Weinberg, Charles S. Maier, Paul Kennedy, Klaus Zernack, Michael Roberts, D. C. Watt, Christopher Thorne, Jacques Duroselle, Raymond Poidevin, Andreas Hillgruber, Klaus Hildebrand, Gordon A. Craig, G. de Bertier de Sauvigny, and many others—any such specialist in European and world international history may indicate this preference in a sixty-sixth space, marked "Other."

This doubtless sounds like a querulous complaint about international history being excluded from the spotlight, and a demand that other historians give it more attention and respect. It is not. If, as I think, there is an imbalance here in American historiography, it seems to me only one among several indicators of a kind of trendiness rampant in the so-called profession. As will be argued, this particular phenomenon is local and probably transient, not worth worrying about, and hardly worth talking about. Nor is this a defense of international history against the usual criticisms—that it is superficial, that its subject matter is a kaleidoscopic jumble of events, that it can tell us nothing really new, that it is a record of what one clerk said to another clerk, and so on. For one thing, this kind of defense has already been effectively made.[2] For another, the critics are fairly easy targets for counterattack. If, for example, it is true that the traditional diplomatic approach to international history often misses the forest for the trees, it is equally true that the Marxist at least as often misses the forest for the roots, the *Annaliste* misses the forest for the total global landscape, and *Gesellschaftsgeschichte* misses the forest for the lumber industry. Critics who continue to complain that international history is superficial and relies on a narrow range of questions and sources show how little they understand the ways international history has changed since Ranke's day—and Ranke was anything but a narrow historian. No diplomatic historian worth the name today contests the interdependence of foreign and domestic politics and the vital role of social and economic forces in international history, and all at least try to write international history accordingly. Neither do international historians still share the assumption behind Ranke's *Primat der Aussenpolitik*, namely, that the formation of nation-states and their quest for power and independence was *the* central theme of history and the driving force behind it. They only contend that international history remains worth doing in part because this remains one important theme and driving force in history, and because many other themes and forces—social, cultural, economic, domestic-political—are inextricably tied up with international politics.

None of this critique and defense is very important, however, because, as already mentioned, the apparent decline of interest of American historians in European and world international history may not be a significant phenomenon. It is certainly not worldwide; only France and the United States seem to show it and even in these countries the tide may be turning. If biography and political history can make a comeback in French historiography, as they have already done, can international history be far behind? In some countries, moreover, the study of international history has always flourished and continues to do so—Great Britain, the Netherlands, Austria, Canada, and especially Germany (of this, more later). The history of American foreign policy is a highly organized enterprise, complete with its own society, SHAFR (the Society for the History of American Foreign Relations) and its special journal, *Diplomatic History*. A new journal founded in Canada less than two decades ago, the *International History Review*, has achieved a worldwide reputation as the leader in the field. Any survey of publishers' catalogues, moreover, will show that certain questions in the history of international politics, including the origins of both world wars, the cold war, and various other twentieth-century crises and conflicts, perennially capture the attention not merely of professional historians but also of a broad public.

If some historians slight the history of international politics, moreover, the same certainly cannot be said of scholars in cognate fields. Many scholars in such flourishing disciplines as international politics, strategy and security studies, studies on war and peace, and military history recognize the importance of international history for their work, and try harder to draw broad lessons and insights from it than historians often do. In fact, much of what political scientists write on international politics is quite simply international history—and historians who do not agree with the methods they use or the conclusions they reach ought to feel challenged to do it better.

It is ironic, moreover, to find international history relatively neglected in American historiography precisely at a time when both historians and other scholars have realized once more how central a role is played by the state in society, and how vital the influence of wars, military establishments, and international competition and conflict is on state development and societal evolution and transformation. It is even more ironic that this should happen at a time when the relevance and importance of international history for current and future world developments becomes more obvious every day. The revolutionary transformation of the world scene and the international system occurring since the Second World War, especially in the last decade, far from ending international history, has revalidated it, and revalidated in particular the historical approach to understanding it. The current changes and upheavals in the former Soviet Union, the former Yugoslavia, the rest of Eastern Europe, Germany, and Western Europe, and the Near and Middle East, and the problems and challenges that these create, cry out for analysis in historic perspective, in terms of their historic roots. To solve or manage the problems they create also requires an understanding of the historic evolution of the international system and its current possibilities and limits. Though it would take too long to argue this point here, headlines serve to illustrate it almost every day.

In other words, the international historian should not waste his/her time worrying about the status of the field of international history, the attitudes of other historians toward it, or its place in the historiographical pecking order. It needs no defense in terms of its importance, its relevance to vital issues, or its intellectual depth and challenge; if some historians ignore or despise it, the more fools they.

However, the international historian, having stopped worrying about how much attention and prestige the field enjoys, might start worrying about something else: how the field of international history should be conceived and dealt with. Instead of asking the usual historian's question, "Is the history (meaning the historiography) of international politics going anywhere?" that is, "Are new methods being developed and exciting discoveries being made, putting it on the cutting edge of historical scholarship?" he or she might ask the question, "Does the *history* of international politics go anywhere?" That is, is there a direction to the history of international politics itself? Has international politics, considered as an historic practice, a societal institution, an organized, distinctive pattern of relationships within human society, moved in a particular direction over the course of time, developed in a particular way? The conventional criticisms of international history, as noted, are not very important or difficult to answer. The question of whether the history of international politics goes anywhere, in contrast, is an important and challenging one. It probes the essential nature of international politics and asks whether it lends itself to useful historical treatment, whether its history can be written at all in the same way the history of other great themes is written. It faces the possibility, assumed by some to be a fact, that international politics involves actions and principles that are inherently chaotic, irrational and incalculable in any broad, encompassing sense, and that its history overall must also be chaotic, kaleidoscopic, and irrational.

Why does this make a difference? History, according to Herbert Butterfield's well-known definition, is the study of the changes of things that change. It analyzes how human life and institutions have evolved, how this became that. Even an apparently static analysis of some historic phenomenon concentrating on a particular incident or place at a particular point serves to illuminate change over time, serves at least potentially as a single snapshot in an ongoing motion picture of evolution and change. If the history of international politics is not that of a developing, changing human practice or institution, but instead of a collection of many separate actions impinging on or colliding with each other; if that collection of actions and events we call for convenience's sake "international politics" remains unchanged in its essential nature and characteristic patterns over time, changing only in terms of instrumentalities and externalities; then one *should* doubt the centrality and importance of international politics in history. Then the political scientists may be right who claim that only the methods of social and behavioral science, not the "historiographical mode," can make the history of international politics produce useful generalizations. Then the historians may also be right who, while admitting that events in international politics have often made a difference in history, especially on account of war, do not see these as central factors in human development, but rather as contingent and accidental factors having an impact similar to that of collisions with asteroids on the evolution of life on earth, or of epidemics on the history of medicine.

This point has been put simply and well by Sir Richard Pares, a distinguished historian whose work included considerable international history. In a lecture in 1953 entitled "Human Nature in Politics," Pares argued that all politics could be rational only to a very limited degree, because politics consisted of the interplay of many conflicting ambitions, the simultaneous pursuit of many partial goods, and the overlapping and mutual interference of "many wills and reasons [which] bear, not on the same point, but on hundreds and thousands of different points." The nature of history, especially of politics, as "the product of thousands (perhaps, nowadays, millions) of different wills, none wholly dependent upon any other; of thousands or millions of different reasons, none wholly amenable to any other," explains "why conduct which is, in the main, reasonable so often brings about results which are not reasonable." The basic irrationality of politics, Pares continued,

> is truer of some kinds of activity than of others. Above all it is true of international relations, which are, by definition, the relations of independent wills, each one regarded by its subjects as embodying the highest and most general good which is practically conceivable; a good which is so general as to be self-subsistent. This is why diplomatic history, more than any other kind of history, is 'one damned thing after another,' from which one can deduce no laws or principles, but only generally applicable techniques.... If international relations could be abolished by the establishment of a world state, the greatest single impediment to the exercise of reason and foresight in domestic politics would be removed.[3]

This is a persuasive view of international politics and, by extension, of its history. It fits our intuitive impressions and appears supported by a good deal of social and psychological theory as well. The picture it draws of an international system inherently conflictual and incapable of durable rational control because the sovereign units that comprise it pursue independent, irreconcilable purposes is in accord with all realist international relations theory, including the neorealism or structural realism of Kenneth Waltz and his school.[4] This view also explains and justifies the way in which Pares, like many international historians, wrote the history of international politics—essentially as an irrational play of forces and wills, kaleidoscopic in its changes, without long-range direction, changing not in the nature of the game but only in the rise and fall of powers, the number and importance of the participants, and the level and character of the violence employed in playing it. It would explain equally well why even social and political scientists who take history seriously in trying to build and test their models and develop theories of international politics may use it as a quarry of useful examples and as a source of data for patterns of behavior remaining basically unchanged over time.

If Pares is right, the history of international politics does not and cannot go anywhere; it only turns faster and buzzes louder at some times than at others. He does not deny the possibility and reality of directional change and evolution in domestic politics or social institutions in general. Indirectly, at least, he affirms it, stressing only the limits of change and the factors that retard and distort it, chief among which is international politics. He knew, for example, that between the late-seventeenth and early-twentieth centuries the British domestic political system evolved from something close to absolutism into full parliamentary democracy. But like many others, he denied that international progress has gone anywhere in any similar fashion, or can.

International historians more than others should think about whether the history of international politics goes somewhere, shows direction and development, or whether its pattern in history is essentially repetitive, cyclical, and nondirectional. First, as already noted, this addresses the central assumption behind much study of international politics, both in history and social science. It confronts the basic assumptions of realism: the structural anarchy of international politics, the necessity and inevitability of a resort to self-help, the inescapable operation of balance of power. The question therefore goes to the intellectual heart of the issue.

It also addresses the more serious side of the criticism of international history as an easy, superficial, less useful kind of history. Pares's verdict on diplomatic history as "just one damned thing after another," for example, is not a confession that he found eighteenth-century international history simple to research and write; his own work in the field is notable for its complexity and profundity. It rather expresses his conviction that it was impervious to rational control, that international politics was, as he says, though tactically complex, emotionally simple and unvarying. Like war, it was about winning and losing and would always be so. If international politics remains an unchanging struggle for power and advantage, then the historian seeking to analyze and explain historic change ought to concentrate on the things that do change—society, domestic politics, economic life, collective mentalities, ideologies, and so forth. These somehow must be the real sources of change and development even within international politics. This kind of thinking, to some extent, lies behind the constant search for the domestic, economic, and political factors that supposedly determine foreign policy, or current arguments that mature democracies do not fight each other, or explanations of the long peace since World War II as the result of the change in weapons' technology which produced a nuclear stalemate between the two superpowers. International politics, in other words, does not change history; other things in history change international politics.

This assumption that the game of international politics does not change must also deprive international history of much of the attraction of other fields of history. New fields and varieties of history emerge and gain followers in good part by showing, or purporting to show, how various aspects of human existence—which were once deemed fixed by biology, physiology, so-called human nature, or some other supposed unchanging structure—can really be seen to be results of historical development, products of change, and producers of it. This has happened with psychohistory, the history of gender, women, class, political culture, childhood, death, family, sexual practices, and other subjects. This view of international history deprives it of any such engaging interest and emancipatory power.

The question of whether the history of international politics goes somewhere even reaches beyond the professional concerns of a historians to wider ones for individuals and society as a whole. It has become a truism, even a cliché, to say that the survival of the world and its civilization depends upon bringing international politics and the international system under some better, more durable kind of rational control than in the past. Pares, speaking at the height of the cold war, claimed that this could not be done. Rationality in international politics could be achieved only by its abolition through world government. Many others especially in his generation reached the same conclusion. Someone who (like me) considers world government not an answer to this question but an impossible and horrible dream, yet who also does not believe that the indefinite continuation of "realist" power politics in the nuclear age is rational or tolerable, has a deeper reason to ask, "Does the history of international politics go anywhere?"

As a historian, I answer this question with an unequivocal "Yes." International politics has always gone somewhere in the past; its whole history is fundamentally one of systemic change. The structure of international politics, that is, its rules, practices, norms, aims, and constitutive procedures, are at once products of historical change and themselves produce change. Once we see where international politics has gone in the past, we can get some better idea of where it is going now and likely to go in the future. This gives us a certain amount of rational hope and emancipatory power in facing the future in international politics.

This chapter cannot prove this thesis, of course, or even make it plausible. The best it can do is to put down some earnest money for the undertaking, in the form of three propositions. They are, first, that the opposite view, that international politics has an unchanging power-political structure and core, is historically so inherently implausible, so out of line with our general knowledge of history, including international history, that it would require overwhelming proof to accept it, and this is not forthcoming. The second proposition is that besides detecting considerable gradual evolution and development in the nature and structure of international politics, we can show that at least one fundamental historic transformation occurred in this arena almost two centuries ago. The third proposition is that today we are experiencing an even more rapid and irreversible transformation of international politics.

To start with the first proposition: Of course there is continuity in the history of international politics, as everywhere in history. No good historian, however, lets continuity blind him/her to the reality of change. The fact that Britain has had a representative parliament since the thirteenth century, or that capitalism in some clearly identifiable form has existed since the Medicis and Fuggers, or democracy since the ancient Greeks, does not lead one to deny the ongoing, irreversible, directional change and development in the history of parliamentary government, capitalism, or democratic government.

Why should one assume otherwise of international politics? Certainly some aspects of it—war, diplomacy, struggles for power and resources, conflict between governments and peoples—are as old as human society itself. But international politics, defined as an enduring system of political relations and transactions between more or less fixed, permanent, independent states in regular, more or less inescapable contact and communication with each other, is a fairly recent development in human history. Before about 1500 there was no international politics in Europe as a whole, only at most among the city-states of Italy, and for a long time thereafter the practice of international politics even among the more developed states of Europe was episodic and rudimentary. Before 1648 there was no system of international politics in the sense of international relations conducted between juridically independent and supposedly equal states on the basis of accepted rules and treaties. Before the late-seventeenth and early-eighteenth centuries there was no working balance of power or even any clear concept of one, nor was there any considerable body of international law. Only in 1815 did a working Concert of Europe emerge, though the idea was much older. It was not until the late-nineteenth century that most of the world was included in a single international system. Before 1918 there was no global international organization. Only in recent decades since World War II has the entire world been organized in a system of formally recognized, juridically independent states. It is hard to see how even the most superficial glance at the history of international politics could support the notion of its having an unchanging, repetitive, power-political essence and character.

The second point: Besides all this evolution and development (uneven, spiral development, of course, marked by frequent breakdown and reverses—but what great developments are not?), there has been at least one unmistakable revolution in international politics, occurring in 1813–1815. Having published a good deal on this theme, I will say only enough here to make the claim of revolutionary change plausible, by comparing the historic eighteenth century (1700–1789) and the historic nineteenth century (1815–1914). (The great world wars just before and after each of these dates are omitted, though including them would actually support the picture of drastic change.)

Compare them first on the incidence of general systemic wars and major wars (a general systemic war being defined as one involving all or most great powers, thereby constituting a systemic crisis or breakdown, and a major war as one involving at least two great powers, but not all or virtually all, and therefore not automatically threatening the system as a whole). By these definitions, admittedly debatable but not, I think, unreasonable, I count three general systemic wars during the eighteenth century, and seven additional major wars. In the nineteenth century, there were no general systemic wars and only four major European wars.

A similar comparison holds on the score of battlefield deaths. My calculation, again challengeable in detail but not in terms of the broad picture, is that in relation to the population of Europe, the number of eighteenth-century battlefield deaths in European wars exceeds that of the nineteenth century by a ratio of 7 or 8 to 1.

Even more striking than the death rate on the battlefield was the death or murder rate among states. During the eighteenth century almost every European state, large and small alike, was the target at one time or another of planned partitions—"murders of states," one might call them. Some such murders were successful. Among states targeted for partition were: Spain, Russia, Sweden, Denmark, Poland, Prussia, the Ottoman Empire, Austria, Venetia, the Low Countries, and various smaller German and Italian states. During the nineteenth century, no great power planned or executed the partition of another state (though Prussia did swallow a number of German states and Sardinia-Piedmont a number of Italian ones in the process of so-called German and Italian unification, and a number of small powers plotted the partition of the Ottoman and Austrian Empires), and in a number of instances the powers cooperated to keep weak, threatened states like the Ottoman Empire or the Papal State in existence.

Equally impressive, especially in the first half of the nineteenth century, is the virtual absence of arms races. There were ideas for arms control in the eighteenth century, and a few half-hearted attempts at curbing arms races, but none ever worked effectively or for long. Even major wars usually were followed fairly quickly by another arms race. The very exhausting Seven Years' War (1756–1763), for example, brought only a temporary pause in Anglo-French rivalry at sea and Austro-Prussian or Russo-Turkish rivalry on land. The long peace from 1815 to 1854 was not only marked by no major wars, but also by no arms race at all. The fears that sometimes arose over one state's military might or dangerously aggressive intentions (fears, for example, of Russia's large army and military colonies after 1815, or of the French army in 1823 and in 1840) all proved baseless. One could almost argue that disarmament in the Vienna era went too far. When certain war dangers arose, as they did in 1830–1832, 1840, and 1848–1849, the states most threatened (usually the Low Countries, Germany, Prussia, Austria, and northern Italy) were clearly unprepared militarily to meet them. The German Confederation, despite experiencing several such crises and developing a number of major proposals and initiatives, never succeeded in carrying through serious military reform providing it the defensive capacity intended and needed. This condition of relative disarmament continued even after the European Concert broke down following the revolutions of 1848. The generally poor military performance of all the belligerent powers in both the Crimean War and the Italian war of 1859 demonstrates, among other things, the long neglect of military preparedness.

The general disarmament went beyond military unpreparedness and included a widespread moral, psychological, and political reluctance to use force. A major reason why so many revolutions brought down established regimes in the post-1815 era, often with considerable ease (the Spanish and Italian revolutions of 1810–1821, the revolutions in France, Belgium, the Papal State, and Poland in 1830–1831, and those in France, Germany, Prussia, Austria, and Italy in 1848) is that the armed forces in all these countries were generally weak and unprepared for action, and that rulers were reluctant to use the armed force they had against their own people or other states. It is remarkable how the standard historical treatments of this era constantly turn things upside down—emphasize, that is, how the Holy Alliance powers or others intervened to crush revolutions, but never discuss what is far more prominent and needs more explanation, namely, why both conservative powers and others let revolutionary tinder pile up and be ignited before they resorted to force—why in a real sense they allowed revolutions to happen. Nor were the repressive measures the conservative powers took, even in 1848–1849, nearly as harsh as those used in the age of liberalism and nationalism. Then Europe would witness the June Days, the Paris Commune, the crushing of south Italian resistance to unification, Bloody Sunday, the Easter Rising.

Along with a changed spirit in the international game in 1813–1815 came changes in its fundamental rules. The seventeenth and eighteenth centuries were the classic ages of wars of succession; dynastic succession supplied both the main basis for the creation and preservation of states, and the primary structural cause of wars. The nineteenth century, at least in its first half, was just as monarchic in spirit as the eighteenth; kings and princes were still vitally concerned with succession and dynastic issues, and plenty of such questions arose, new and old, especially as revolution and nationalism eliminated some independent states and created others—in Bavaria and Baden, Greece, Belgium, France (Napoleon III in 1851, the Bourbons after 1870), Rumania, Serbia, Bulgaria, Spain, Schleswig-Holstein, Albania. Yet not one war of succession ever occurred. Succession questions could still cause trouble and even be exploited to create a crisis (e.g., Spain in 1870 and Schleswig-Holstein in 1863). They were never themselves the cause of war.

Or look at the nature and purpose of alliances. Virtually every eighteenth-century alliance was overwhelmingly, almost exclusively, an instrument for power politics, designed and used for capability aggregation and territorial aggrandizement. Virtually every nineteenth-century alliance for the first forty years after 1815 was a restraining alliance used more to control one's allies and to preserve peace and manage international crises than to increase one's own capability, and all alliances specifically ruled out territorial aggrandizement.

Consider the causes and purposes of war. Every great European war in the later seventeenth and eighteenth centuries was also a world war, fought over extra-European, imperial rivalries and prizes as well as European issues. From the mid-seventeenth to the mid-eighteenth centuries war, both formal and informal, was one of the main ways of promoting a state's commerce, perhaps the main one. Frequently the destruction of the enemy's trade and the creation of a monopoly for one's own commerce was the avowed purpose of the war, sometimes the only one, and even where other causes predominated this one was seldom absent. The British, the French, the Dutch, the Spanish, and the Portuguese fought over prizes overseas; Swedes, Danes, Dutch, Russians, Poles, Prussians, and other Germans contended for the *dominium maris Baltici*. Commerce and revenue even played important roles in power struggles in the heart of the continent. Louis XIV coveted the Spanish inheritance partly for commercial reasons; Frederick the Great boasted that Silesia, which he stole from Austria by war, had brought him more treasure than all the silver mines of Peru.

As we know, 1815 did not bring an end to European colonial expansion. At most it slowed down a bit in the first half of the nineteenth century and then accelerated to its apogee in the latter half. Economic competition between European states was at least as important in nineteenth-century international politics as in the eighteenth century. Yet there was never a trade war or anything that could plausibly be called one, and from 1815 to 1898, never a war or major threat of war over an extra-European, colonial issue.[5] Even after the Fashoda crisis of 1898 broke down the fence erected in 1815 to separate European and extra-European politics, colonial imperialism still involved as much cooperation as rivalry between the powers, and was not per se a major cause of war in 1914.

Many more fundamental changes in rules, norms, expectations, and collective assumptions could be added to this list of startling contrasts between eighteenth- and nineteenth-century international politics. These, however, ought to suffice to make the point. Historians have no trouble detecting many other revolutions in eighteenth- and nineteenth-century Europe—in Great Britain in 1688 and 1832, in 1830 and 1848 over most of Europe, and of course in 1789 in France. Yet not one of these revolutions, including the French, can be shown to have produced durable changes in fundamental relationships and patterns of conduct in domestic politics and society comparable to those that differentiated international politics after 1815 from that which went before. Yet when historians discuss the Vienna System and the post-Vienna era, they speak of a restoration, a return to stability, a reestablishment of the balance of power, and even an age of reaction and the repression of revolution and change. This simply will not do. If any of the changes in this era deserve to be labelled "revolutionary," it is those of 1815 in international politics. Leaving aside the question of whether 1815 does not deserve more than 1789 to be called the birthdate of the modern world,[6] one can confidently claim that the one "revolution" of the period whose results were quickly apparent, effective, and in terms of international relations and peace clearly benign was the transformation of international politics.

This brings me to the third point: The Vienna era pointed toward a future now being realized. We are presently living in an era of international politics dimly foreshadowed by it; experiencing fundamental changes in the international system, the seeds of which were sown and began to ripen then. Three major changes, products of a long historic evolution coming to fruition in our time, can be identified. Once again they must be simply stated with little explanation and no proof, but the prima facie evidence pointing to them lies all around.

They are, first, the rise of the trading state. This refers not merely to the increasing importance of economic factors in international politics, but to a change in the main requirement for the survival and long-term prosperity of states. In the seventeenth and eighteenth centuries, the prime requirement, almost the only one, was success at war. Commercial prosperity was important for supplying the resources vital for military establishments and war, but commercial prosperity not wedded to military power and success never insured a state's survival and security and often increased the danger from enemies. The fate of trading republics—the United Provinces, Venice, Genoa, Ragusa, and others—is eloquent witness to this. By the nineteenth and early-twentieth centuries and the development of the international system, it had become possible for some states to survive and succeed relatively well without great military power by taking refuge in neutrality—Switzerland, Scandinavia, the Low Countries. In great crises, however, the hiding places tended to break down, and for most actors success at war remained the key to survival and prosperity. Now, in the late-twentieth century, the main key to a state's success, both domestically and in the international arena, is increasingly success at trade, the ability to compete in the international economic sphere and thereby to provide for the welfare of its citizens. A wide array of states has arisen both in the developed and the developing worlds which either have no significant military power or power far short of their economic strength and their defense requirements—Canada, Austria, Belgium, the Netherlands, Denmark, Norway, Sweden, Finland, Switzerland, Italy, Germany, Japan, Taiwan, South Korea, Singapore—which nonetheless are successful because of their skill at commerce. In contrast, the USSR, the real military victor of World War II, a superpower which, unlike the United States and other major powers, successfully maintained its empire against every military challenge from within and without for forty years thereafter, stands revealed today as a colossal failure, simply because it failed as a trading state. The United States, equal or superior in military power, now recognizes that without success as a trading state, all its military power will only temporarily mask its decline. This insight, a cliché in current political discussion, marks a breakthrough in the long historic development of international politics.

A second change, closely associated with the first, is the declining utility of military power and military victory. War was once not only unavoidable in international politics, but also often necessary, useful, and even beneficial as a way of settling international disputes and achieving fundamental national aims. It is steadily becoming less so and being seen to be so. Military power per se has not become obsolescent or dispensable; but the range of tasks it can be expected to do in international politics, though still important, is clearly shrinking in relation to the ever-widening range of problems that need to be managed or solved in the international arena. Even where and when it must be used military power serves best to check threats, not solve fundamental problems. The costs of its use, political and economic as well as military, are rising in comparison to its benefits; and for solving many urgent problems and advancing many interests it has no utility at all.

The third change, though harder to define, may be the most important. It is the rise of international integration and community, the growth of a consensus among governments and peoples on certain norms for conduct, both internal and international, which governments must meet to enjoy legitimacy, and a growing willingness among nations to cooperate to defend these norms and to promote conformity to minimal standards and bounds of law in international politics.

All these changes have deep historic roots. In terms of actions and institutions, we can see certain forerunners of them in the Vienna System and era; as ideas, many of the peace plans proposed by statesmen and writers since the late Middle Ages foreshadow them. Their role after World War II in the recovery, pacification, and economic and political integration of Western Europe is now clear. The process of decolonization and disimperialism among the former great colonial powers, mainly voluntary and peaceful, also shows them at work; so does the admission of an astonishing number of new nations into the world community with at least juridical equality, and the gradual growth of the effectiveness and reach of the United Nations and other transnational bodies. The progress seems discouragingly slow and dangerously precarious—until we see in historical perspective how impossible all these accomplishments would have been in any earlier era.

Until a few years ago, it is true, one could not speak of a breakthrough. These trends were clearly detectable, but not clearly winning out in world politics as a whole; the possibility remained that all the progress could be wiped out in some international disaster. The events of 1985–1990, in the Soviet Union, Eastern Europe, and South Africa, coming on top of what has been happening over recent decades in East Asia, the Pacific Rim, much of Central and South America, and the Mediterranean basin have surely done much to show what trends and principles are winning. One authoritarian, repressive regime after another came to terms with the primacy of economics over power politics; faced up to the declining utility of the military force still at their command, as a means either of solving their internal problems, securing their position in the world, or enforcing the old policies at home; and reacted to economic, political, and moral pressure from their own peoples and the outside world by changing their policies and even surrendering power. Here was the most dramatic proof possible that old patterns and rules in international politics no longer held; that international politics was going somewhere.

If I may be pardoned a personal reference to show how startling a historic development this was, in early 1985 I published a brief essay entitled, "Does Murphy's Law Apply to History?"[7] arguing that Murphy's Law ("whatever can go wrong, will") need not apply to history, and that in particular the existence of great stocks of nuclear weapons did not mean that nuclear war was inevitable sooner or later. There had already been great progress toward durable peace in international politics, and more was possible. In another previous essay I speculated tentatively about the possibility that the Soviet Union might someday recognize the futility of maintaining its current rigid system and might relax its grip on its own people and its East European empire.[8] This is not a claim to have been a prophet—rather the reverse. Though I was already convinced by that time that the international system was changing and that change within the Soviet empire was possible, every concrete prediction I would make to students and colleagues (fortunately not in print) about Soviet policy after 1985 was dead wrong. All my arguments, based on strong historical precedent, that the Soviet Union would not get out of Afghanistan, or allow its East European empire to disintegrate, or permit the reunification of Germany, or let a reunified Germany remain in NATO while the Warsaw Pact collapsed, or give up the Baltic states, or repudiate communism, or let the Soviet Union itself collapse, proved false. In other words, even while knowing that international politics was changing, going somewhere, I was too much caught in history to realize how far and how fast it would go, unprepared for revolutionary changes in international politics, changes with which scholars are still desperately trying to come to terms.[9]

There is, of course, an answer to the claim that in the last decade international politics has moved away from the old power politics and toward a new world order characterized by the primacy of commerce, the declining utility of military force as a solution to problems, and the rise of international consensus and cooperation. First of all, a critic might say, the aftermath of revolutions in the Soviet Union, Eastern Europe, and elsewhere gives us no good reason to believe that the next ten or twenty years will bring these areas a net increase of democracy, liberty, prosperity, integration into wider European and world communities, and general peace and cooperation. Many signs point to just the opposite—the breakdown of unstable regimes, economic decline, political instability, an explosive rise in political and economic nationalism and in ethnic, religious, and national conflict, serious new conflicts over borders, and in general far more danger of war and international instability than before.

Second, even if somehow these current and deepening problems in Eastern Europe, the former Soviet Union, the Middle East, and Africa are solved or managed without disaster, we have already had clear evidence that the basic power-political character of international politics has not changed, and that military power is still absolutely necessary both for deterrence and compellence to maintain any kind of tolerable world order, new or old. One dangerous dictator, Saddam Hussein, has already shown his view of the preeminence of economics, the declining utility of military power and victory, and the importance of international consensus and legitimacy. Only massive military force stopped his aggression and reversed his gains, and even this still has not changed his mind or felled his regime. In the former Yugoslavia the Serbian government, its army, its militias, and apparently a majority of Serbs have demonstrated their belief in armed force to achieve their ends, and demonstrated it by horrors reminiscent of some aspects of World War II. The Croats are not much different or better. Similar terrible conflicts are possible or likely in many other areas; in some, like Tajikistan and Armenia and Georgia, they are already going on. Organized terrorism belongs as much to the new world order as cooperation. Nothing therefore is more naive than supposing that the new world order, whatever it is, means less conflict, danger, and the need for vigilance, military power, and the willingness to use these elements if necessary.

Much of this argument is obviously true—that the road to liberal democracy, economic prosperity under a free market system, integration with the West, and stable constitutional government in Eastern Europe and the former Soviet Union will certainly be long and rocky, and some failures and disasters likely; that the same holds for South Africa, much of South and Central America, North Africa and the Middle East, and parts of Asia; and that the revolutionary developments of recent years have made more regional conflict, ethnic struggles, territorial disputes, civil war and struggles for power, and plain interstate war likely in the next decade or two. All this could well mean that some forms and uses of military power will become more necessary and frequent in coming decades rather than less.

Yet these facts and probabilities, far from proving that the international system is still essentially the same, show just the opposite. They prove that it has changed in the most basic sense: It no longer operates primarily on the basis of power politics or by the methods of a balance of power. The situation is parallel to that of the postrevolutionary and Napoleonic era. Just as in 1789–1815, the ultimate political, social, and economic results of the revolutions of the 1980s are not yet clear; what is clear is that the international system has been transformed.

To see this, one need only compare the international reaction today to developments in three prime trouble spots (the former Soviet Union, especially Russia; the rest of Eastern Europe; and the Balkans, especially former Yugoslavia) with the reactions of the international community in previous analogous eras. The year 1989 was not the first time that Russians have made a revolutionary bid for liberal democracy. In 1905 liberal and democratic forces (the so-called Octobrist and Kadet parties) led the movement for constitutional democratic government. When the tsarist regime was overthrown in March 1917, these same parties, though never in control of the revolution, headed the Provisional Government for a time, and until the Bolshevik takeover in November various socialist parties tried to keep the revolution on a democratic path, if not a liberal or capitalist one. Both bids for constitutional democracy were defeated, the first by tsarist repression, the second by the war, Russia's collapse, and Lenin's strategy. The current third bid could also fail. The question here, however, concerns international reaction. How did the other great powers react to these Russian bids for democracy then, and how are they reacting now?

The answer is well known. Whatever other governments felt about the revolutions and democratic movements in 1905 and 1917 per se, whether they inspired mainly fear and dislike as in Germany and Austria-Hungary or approval and sympathy as in France and Great Britain, concern for the fate of the revolution and the democratic movement made almost no difference for their foreign policies. What counted was power politics, the balance of power. In 1905 Germany (or at least Kaiser Wilhelm II) tried to use the revolution to draw Tsar Nicholas and Russia away from France and over to Germany's side; Austria hoped the revolution would frighten the tsar into renewing the old Three Emperors' Alliance; while Britain and France, in order to prevent this, worked directly against the democratic revolution, helping the tsarist government through large loans to govern without and against the Russian parliament (the Duma) and to use its police and army to restore semiautocratic rule. In 1917, the primacy of power politics over the struggle for democracy in Russia was even more clear. Germany, then under the military dictatorship of a right-radical general, Erich von Ludendorff, deliberately promoted a Bolshevik revolution in Russia to overthrow the Provisional Government and the democratic socialists, in order to draw Russia out of the war. Meanwhile the Western powers persistently rejected the Provisional Government's pleas for a peace conference and frustrated its efforts at a negotiated peace, thereby destroying that government's only chance for survival, because all that counted for them was to keep Russia in the war.

There is nothing whatever to be surprised at in these policies. The rules and stakes of the game of international politics as it was then played demanded that the liberal democratic cause in Russia and the chance to integrate Russia more closely into a peaceful Europe be sacrificed to the demands of balance of power politics, even by the Western democracies.

The current internal situation in Russia is disturbingly analogous in some ways to those of 1906 or 1917–1918. The decisive difference lies in international politics. Once again the fate of Russia's liberal democratic revolution hangs in the balance, but the one thing missing from the picture is the factor that used to dominate it: power politics. Amid all the uncertainty and controversy in the West over how to aid the democratic forces in Russia, and the criticism of Western governments, especially the United States, for doing too little too late, no one has any doubt what the prime goal of American and other Western policy toward Russia should be—to help the experiment in liberal democracy and a market economy to succeed. This goal, moreover, is not seen as important for power-political or economic reasons (for example, to gain Russia as a useful ally against some other enemy, or to prevent an undemocratic Russia from forming a hostile alliance with some other power or powers against the United States and its allies). One can still find such notions, of course; the old atavistic power-political thinking still survives in certain quarters. But surely today, sensible persons can see that the overriding reasons for wanting to see Russia free, democratic, and prosperous are intrinsic and systemic, not power-political. Russia is critically important not for its possible role in the balance of power but for its inescapable weight and influence in the whole emerging world order. A stable, free, and prosperous Russia will promote it; an unstable, unfree, and impoverished Russia will inevitably destabilize and endanger it.

The same point holds for East Central Europe. Here also internal developments may remind one ominously of what happened in the 1920s—how the initial gains after World War I in democracy and self-determination were quickly blighted by economic troubles, ethnic battles, political instability and immaturity, and territorial conflicts. Much of this scenario could easily be repeated now. What is not recurring, and will not, is the international politics of the 1920s and 1930s, with the new smaller states seeking security through military power and rival alliances, and the great powers seriously interested in them only for their role in the balance of power. Instead, the most astonishing series of changes in the potential power balance of this region—the disappearance of East Germany, the independence of the Baltic states, Poland, Belarus, and Ukraine, the peaceful dissolution of Czechoslovakia, the unification of Germany, and the withdrawal of Russia, leaving behind a territorial enclave on the Baltic—has occurred not only without major fighting, but, so far at least, without any serious power-political crises or repercussions. What better proof can there be that the old power politics no longer rules?

One area, the Balkans, especially former Yugoslavia, seems at first glance to belie this, and to prove that the old power politics is still alive and well. A closer look, however, reveals the same pattern of similarity in internal developments and drastic change on the international front. True, the current struggles in Bosnia and those that threaten to erupt in Kosovo and Macedonia display historical continuities both striking and frightening. Once again a sense of historical *déjà vu* threatens to overwhelm us; a common argument for intervening to stop the fighting in Bosnia is the reminder that World War I broke out precisely in this corner of the world— touched off by Great Serb nationalism and terrorism. But once again we need sound history to free us from the tyranny of a false historical analogy. Serb and Croat nationalism, South Slav and Balkan politics, have not changed much; the international system has. In every previous Near Eastern crisis or internecine Balkan conflict since the eighteenth century, no matter which side or faction the various great powers might favor or what they might try to do about the conflict itself, their policies always rested primarily on balance of power considerations. Today no major power cares much about its strategic position in the peninsula, the preservation of its alliances, the enhancement of its great-power influence there. Not even nationalist Russians think Serbia is vital as a power-political ally against some other state. They sympathize with the Serbs, or claim to, for reasons of historic tradition, religious and ethnic kinship, and Russian domestic politics and prestige. The very criticisms of West European states made by Americans and others for failing to get involved in Bosnia or to stop Serb aggression, even if they may be justified from the standpoint of crisis management or humanitarianism, prove the point that the international system is new. Imagine, if you will, Americans or Englishmen urging Germans or Austrians or Italians in 1914 or 1941 to get involved in the Balkans. Intervention today under the UN, whether or not it is effective, rests on a different set of motives than in the past, motives commercial, humanitarian, and above all general systemic. Intervention involves the recognition that territorial expansion and atrocities of the sort occurring in Bosnia are intrinsically dangerous and tend to undermine and destabilize the new international system, even when, as here, they have no important power-political effects.

In short, it is time for historians, especially international historians, to recognize that the age of classic international politics, governed by the structural determinants of anarchy, self-help, and balance of power, is over— even if some leaders and states in some corners of the world do not yet recognize it, and even if the exact dimensions and contours of the new system are not fully clear. What is clear is the duty and opportunity of international historians to join in the investigation, to help show how this decisive change came about, to uncover its deeper roots—in short, to write the history of international politics as it is, the story of long-term structural change.

I must not leave the impression, however, that this is a new idea I have discovered or new approach I have devised. Good diplomatic historians have been doing this, at least implicitly, for a long time. In one country, moreover, this approach to the history of international politics is already more or less standard—Germany. This is not the place for a bibliographic essay, but one cannot read much German international history today without repeatedly encountering terms like "structural change" and "systemic development," and still more important, seeing the history of international politics increasingly conceived and written as the story of long-term structural change. The explanations and schemata vary considerably, of course, but the goal is basically the same. This purpose shows up clearly in the work (to name just a few examples) of Konrad Repgen, Fritz Dickmann, Wolfgang-Uwe Friedrich, and Klaus Malettke in the seventeenth century; Klaus Zernack, Johannes Kunisch, Heinz Duchhardt, and Michael G. Müller in the eighteenth; Wolf Gruner and Anselm Doering-Manteuffel in the nineteenth; Klaus Hildebrand and Peter Krüger in the earlier twentieth; and too many historians to mention in the period since 1945. An *Arbeitsgruppe* of historians and other scholars at the University of Marburg has as its program the history of international politics as an evolving system and has published a book of essays discussing and illustrating how it can be done.[10] It seems fitting to me that in a country where historians once almost unanimously promoted a view of international politics as an endless struggle for power, and where power was pursued to its most extreme and destructive ends, historians should now take the lead in a different approach.

NOTES

This essay is a revised version of a Jubilee Lecture, College of Liberal Arts and Sciences, University of Illinois, 18 April 1994.

1. Charles S. Maier, "Marking Time: The Historiography of International Relations," in *The Past Before Us*, ed. Michael G. Kammen (Ithaca, 1980), 355–87.

2. For example, by Gordon A. Craig, in his AHA presidential address, "The Historian and the Study of International Relations," *American Historical Review* 88 (1983): 1–11.

3. Richard Pares, "Human Nature in Politics," in *The Historian's Business and Other Essays*, ed. R. A. Humphreys and E. Humphreys (Oxford, 1961), 37–39.

4. Kenneth Waltz, *Theory of International Politics* (New York, 1979).

5. This could be disputed in regard to Anglo-Russian rivalry over central Asia and the approaches to India (usually called "the Great Game in Asia"). My view is that the crises (Merv, Penjdeh, etc.) were mainly local, generated by men on the spot, the rivalry and threat exaggerated, especially on the British side, and the danger that the two countries would go to war never very great.

6. This is the case argued by Paul Johnson, *The Birth of the Modern World, 1815–1830* (New York, 1991).

7. Paul W. Schroeder, "Does Murphy's Law Apply to History?" *The Wilson Quarterly* (New Year's, 1985): 84–93.

8. Paul W. Schroeder, "Containment Nineteenth Century Style: How Russia Was Restrained," *South Atlantic Quarterly* 82 (1983): 1–18.

9. A few examples of recent attempts to do so: Richard Rosecrance, *The Rise of the Trading State* (New York, 1987); John Lewis Gaddis, *The Long Peace* (New York, 1987); John E. Mueller, *Retreat from Doomsday* (New York, 1989). For an excellent discussion of the impact of these developments on international relations see Gaddis, "International Relations Theory and the End of the Cold War," *International Security* 17, 3 (1992–1993): 5–58.

10. Peter Krüger, ed., *Kontinuität und Wandel in der Staatenordnung der Neuzeit* (Marburg, 1991); see also his edited work, *Das europäische Staatensystem im Wandel* (Munich, 1996).

2 The Diplomatic Revolution of Our Time

Paul Gordon Lauren

Diplomacy, like other human activities, must constantly adapt in a dynamic process of changing circumstances and conditions. The evolution of diplomatic practices, institutions, and norms thus has occurred for several centuries of time. No period, however, has presented more dramatic changes and challenges to diplomacy than our own time.[1] At the beginning of the twentieth century, diplomats still basked in the glow of a slow-paced, relatively easily managed and peaceful, classical diplomatic system that they had inherited and described as the *"gute alte Zeit"* and the "golden age" of diplomacy.[2] Yet, within less than two decades, political leaders vehemently denounced this system as old and corrupt, declaring that they would create a more open "new diplomacy."[3] Shortly thereafter emerged an ominous "totalitarian diplomacy" and an unsettling "democratic diplomacy."[4] After yet another world war and still further crises and diplomatic problems, these expressions were followed by those noting the rise of "atomic diplomacy," "petroleum diplomacy," and "ozone diplomacy."[5] By the last decade of the twentieth century, some even speculated that the world had reached "the twilight of diplomacy,"[6] describing international milieu as "a jungle filled with a bewildering variety of poisonous snakes."[7] These changes in expression, attitude, substance, and practice all have marked nothing short of a diplomatic revolution in our time.

EXPANSION OF THE INTERNATIONAL COMMUNITY

Only six actors at most played significant roles on the stage of international diplomacy when the twentieth century began. These were the mighty and self-confident Great Powers of Europe: Britain, France, Germany, Austria-Hungary, Russia, and to a lesser extent Italy, who through their sheer relative strength controlled the fate of much of the rest of the world. The only other states that showed any serious or sustained interest in international relations at the time also tended to be European. Two others, the United States and Japan, slowly emerging from their long isolation, still stood in the wings. All the rest were smaller or weaker states who lived as victims, subjects, or pawns at the hands of the elite Great Powers of Europe who made and enforced the rules of international behavior.

This small, well-defined, Eurocentric, relatively easily managed, and homogeneous system of diplomacy by and for the Great Powers began to change in the first decade of the twentieth century. The initial shock came from Asia, for in 1905 Japan stunned the world by defeating Russia in war. Alfred Zimmern, then a young lecturer at Oxford, was so struck by this event that he walked into his class announcing that he would put aside Greek history "because I feel I must speak to you about the most important historical event which has happened, or is likely to happen, in our lifetime: the victory of a non-white people over a white people."[8] As if the victory of an Asiatic power over a European power was not sufficiently shocking, an offer to mediate between the belligerents came not from the chancelleries of Europe, but from President Theodore Roosevelt of the United States. This so unnerved one French diplomat that he entered into his diary: "Something new and unexpected has happened—something which seems to presage important developments in world politics. For the first time in its history, the United States of America is intervening in the affairs of Europe."[9]

The process of expanding the number of actors in the international community greatly accelerated during and after the First World War of 1914–1918. The unparalleled devastation, the destruction of three monarchies, and the loosening of the ties of colonial empires abroad resulting from this conflict of arms, as well as the substantial intervention of the United States and Japan into the war, simultaneously destroyed any notion that a small number of European states alone could continue to be the lever that moved the world. Not only did the peace makers who assembled at Paris in 1919 specifically create new states in eastern and southeastern Europe, the Baltic, and the Middle East, they invited others heretofore excluded from diplomacy to either attend or observe as well. For this reason, W.E.B. Du Bois, the black leader from the United States, enthusiastically described the gathering as "THIRTY-TWO NATIONS, PEOPLES, AND RACES. . . . Not simply England, Italy, and the Great Powers are there, but all the little nations. . . . Not only groups, but races have come—Jews, Indians, Arabs, and All-Asia."[10] Yet another contemporary observer looked around this diplomatic conference and described it in the following words: "Chinamen, Japanese, Koreans, Hindus, Kirghizes, Lesghiens, Circassians, Mingrelians, Buryats, Malays, and Negroes and Negroids from Africa and America were among the tribes and tongues forgathered in Paris to watch the rebuilding of the political world system and to see where they 'came in.' "[11]

Precisely where and when these new actors "came in" and what role they would play in diplomacy would be sharply debated and strongly contested over the following years. The war, the rhetoric of a "new diplomacy," and the Paris Peace Conference certainly aroused the desire for sovereignty and independence in foreign affairs among the colonial dependencies, protectorates, and possessions of the Great Powers, particularly those in Africa and Asia. For most, their dreams of freedom would not be realized for decades. But for a few, their voices could be heard in the League of Nations, a new form of diplomatic organization created in part as a means of responding to these changes of an expanding international community. Australia, Canada, China, Haiti, India, Japan, the Latin American states, Liberia, New Zealand, Persia, Siam, and South Africa, among others, all joined with the victorious European powers and successor states to form the original forty-two members of the League. Through time, others joined as well, but not the United States. Representatives from most of these states greatly appreciated their membership in the League of Nations, for they came from countries that heretofore always had been excluded from participation in international diplomacy.[12]

The massive upheavals of the Second World War of 1939–1945 greatly accelerated this process and set into motion powerful and revolutionary forces of change. They smashed whatever was left of European dominance in diplomacy and simultaneously destroyed the ability of those with colonial possessions to resist the demands of their subject peoples for independence.[13] The war irrevocably destroyed the myth of Western superiority and invincibility and, in the words of one Afro-Asian nationalist leader, ironically "taught the subjugated peoples to fight and die for freedom rather than live and be subjugated" and encouraged them to look toward the new United Nations as a focal point for their efforts at independence.[14]

Initially, when the United Nations was created in 1945 as an international organization to maintain the peace and promote "the principle of equal rights and self-determination of peoples,"[15] fifty-one states joined as original members. Among these, three came from Africa (Ethiopia, Liberia, and South Africa), and among the three from Asia, only China was independent of colonial rule. Seven belonged to the Middle East. All the rest of the member states belonged to Europe (including the Soviet Union), the Americas, and the white Commonwealth countries.[16] Many thus assumed that this dominance by the Western, white world would continue in the future as it had for several centuries in the past. They were wrong, for in the simple words of one observer of diplomacy, "time had run out."[17]

The vast and profound process of decolonization expanded the number of states in the international system as never before. Within the single decade following the creation of the United Nations, twenty-five new states had joined in membership. By the end of 1965, forty-one more had been added from the ranks of former colonies, swelling the number and dramatically altering the composition of United Nations itself. This marked one of the greatest political changes in human history, creating new countries and transferring power from whites to nonwhites and liberating perhaps one billion people from colonial rule in Asia and Africa.[18]

New states and expanding membership in the United Nations continued unabated into the last decade of the twentieth century. In 1990 Namibia and Lichtenstein joined the organization, and the following year witnessed the admission of North and South Korea, Estonia, Latvia, Lithuania, Micronesia, and the Marshall Islands. Twenty new states became members in the single year of 1992. Today, membership is virtually universal. A walk along First Avenue in New York City in front of the United Nations Headquarters, for example, reveals the display of national flags of 185 members. This represents more than a tripling of independent states just since the end of the Second World War and truly marks a veritable revolution in the number of actors in international diplomacy. A recent book by Daniel Patrick Moynihan entitled *Pandaemonium* predicts that this trend will continue for the foreseeable future.[19]

The phenomenal number of sovereign nation-states in the world today, however, is only one dimension of the massive expansion of actors in the international community. Others also have emerged in the twentieth century with claims to participate in diplomacy. These include the international governmental organization of the United Nations and its many related specialized agencies such as the International Atomic Energy Agency, International Labor Organization, International Monetary Fund, and World Health Organization, among many others. They also include supranational or regional organizations such as the European Economic Community, Council of Europe, North Atlantic Treaty Organization, Organization of American States, The Arab League, Organization of African Unity, and the Association of Southeast Asian Nations. Still other actors include commodity cartels like the Organization of Petroleum Exporting Countries. Although composed of member nation-states, each of these organizations often can become much more than the mere sum of its parts, participating vigorously in diplomatic affairs and often challenging the traditional attributes of national sovereignty itself.

Other international actors today do not represent governments at all. Among the most striking of these are global, or transnational business corporations like International Telephone and Telegraph, Exxon, Mitsubishi, Gulf Oil, Nestlé, and Siemens, among others. In many cases, they are beyond the control of nations or international organizations. Their size and sophisticated ability to move goods, services, and capital worldwide often gives them significant global influence. Joseph Nye, Jr. in *Bound to Lead* observes, "In the traditional realist view, states were the only significant actors in world politics and only a few large states really mattered"; but notes the dramatic shift toward transnational corporations possessing enormous economic power. "Twenty corporations today have annual sales greater than the Gross National Products of eighty states," he estimates, thereby giving them a role around the globe that often exceeds that of many nations.[20]

Still other actors are groups of private citizens seeking to influence world politics through international nongovernmental organizations, or NGOs. Several hundred of these nonprofit groups operated during the period of the League of Nations, seeking to move policy in particular directions and to extend citizen participation in the conduct of diplomacy. Today, the Economic and Social Council of the United Nations grants official consultative status to more than 930 separate NGOs, and the United Nations Department of Public Information maintains contact with more than 1,400 associated organizations.[21] In recent years the number of these groups has expanded as never before in history. Indeed, the authoritative Union of International Associations estimates that the total of recognized international NGOs in the world now exceeds 21,000.[22] Such numbers—along with their inherent diversity of interests—would have been completely unimaginable to those diplomats who practiced their craft with only each other and with common values in a rarified world at the beginning of the century.

FROM UNITY TO DIVERSITY IN PRACTICES AND VALUES

With these dramatic quantitative changes came drastic qualitative transformations in diplomacy as well. The small number of actors in the international community with which the century began greatly facilitated a relatively simple and manageable system of diplomacy among those who participated. Few needed to be consulted or involved, for example, when crises occurred or threats to the system appeared; for, in the words of one contemporary, the conduct of diplomacy represented "holy ground, unapproachable for the profane world, and only accessible to the Levites and priests."[23] Those who managed diplomatic affairs, although certainly acknowledging their international disputes and disagreements, regarded themselves as members of an elite and culturally homogeneous *famille diplomatique*, bound together by common ties of cultural and historical tradition, language, religion, social status, and race. They defended common political and economic institutions as well as a Eurocentric perspective on the world. Moreover, they shared a remarkable level of consensus upon the nature and purposes of diplomacy, the appropriate role of diplomats, the need to establish certain normative rules and procedures to manage diplomatic behavior, and a willingness both to make and enforce collective decisions that might maintain their international system. These statesmen understood that their own preservation could not be achieved unless they accepted the existence of the others and defined their own state interests in terms of the larger system, and this required the ability to strike a difficult balance between their desire to improve, secure, or retain the purely selfish objectives of their own states on the one hand and the need to maintain their system as a whole on the other by accepting certain self-imposed restraints.[24] They all participated as members of "the inner ring" and "players of the great game" of diplomacy, according to one contemporary, that "had rules of its own which were known to all initiates."[25] Looking back on this system of diplomacy prior to 1914, one recent observer describes the general agreement and shared values in the following words: "Their regimes drew on a generally common fund of history. The frame of discourse among them was unified to a degree permitting any government participating significantly in world affairs to be confident of having its utterances understood by others in the sense intended. None was a revolutionary power. Ideologies were 'a minor theme.' . . . The basis of the general order was not at issue. A common notion of legitimacy prevailed."[26]

This consensus on the norms of international behavior and internal homogeneity within the diplomatic system began to break down with the rise of individuals possessing little sense of responsibility to the system as a whole, new international actors, prewar alliances and arms races, and especially the convulsions and slaughter of the First World War. The insightful French Socialist leader, Jean Jaurès, had foreseen just such a development, for prior to his own assassination and the outbreak of war he predicted: "When typhus finishes the work begun by bullets, and as death and misery strike all, men will turn on their rulers, whether German, French, Russian, or Italian—and demand an explanation for all those corpses."[27] Accordingly, as many looked around at all the dead and maimed bodies before their eyes, they argued that a small number of scheming diplomats within the confines of "old diplomacy" had failed to keep the peace, aggravated prewar tensions, and thus bore primary responsibility for the devastation and destruction. "The art of secret diplomacy is the worst survival of past absolutism," proclaimed one critic,[28] while another stated bluntly: "The old ambassadorial system has failed and is discredited."[29] U.S. President Woodrow Wilson concluded that the diplomats of the old school had created nothing more than a "complicated network of intrigue and espionage,"[30] and, along with the Bolshevik leader V. I. Lenin and many others, vowed that a "new diplomacy" must differ in its origins, objectives, and methods from that of the past.[31] "Diplomats were invented simply to waste time," asserted the British Prime Minister David Lloyd George in expressing his contempt for the professionals, declaring simply: "I want no diplomats."[32] He and his fellow politicians Georges Clemenceau of France, Vittorio Orlando of Italy, and Wilson (described by one career diplomat as "The Dread Amateur")[33] put these sentiments into practice at the Paris Peace Conference when they often rejected the advice offered by their staff experts and relied more upon personal intuition to solve intricate international problems.

Such assaults upon the practices and values of diplomacy and the traditional diplomatic corps continued unabated after the First World War with the rise of revolutionary ideology and the emergence of national leaders holding completely different values that prevented them from reaching accommodation, striving for the same goals, or even talking to each other. Indeed, in one of his most insightful observations, Gordon A. Craig writes:

> In a sense, the whole period between the two world wars was a *dialogue des sourds* [a French expression meaning a conversation among deaf people] between those governments which were attempting to construct a genuine comity of nations on the ruins left by the war and were seeking new rules that would be accepted by all its members, and those revolutionary powers which preferred to recognize no rules at all or desired to retain the freedom to determine when they would obey rules and when they would break them.[34]

The Bolshevik regime certainly confirmed this transformation in diplomacy from its very beginning by announcing that it intended to withdraw from the Western diplomatic community, repudiate all legal commitments signed by the previous government, publish secret treaties, confiscate all foreign properties in Russia without compensation to the owners, and refuse to conform to the rules and procedures that heretofore had prevailed in international relations. When Leon Trotsky became the new Commissar for Foreign Affairs, he declared his intention to "issue a few revolutionary declarations to the peoples and then shut up the joint [the Foreign Ministry]."[35] Then, when leading a delegation to the Brest-Litovsk Conference of 1918 to make peace with the Germans, he flatly rejected observing any of the amenities of traditional diplomacy, insisting that his Bolshevik delegates dine alone, accept no invitations of any kind from their hosts, and refuse to use the word "friendship" in the preamble to the draft treaty. When Lenin founded the Comintern to encourage subversion against non-Communist governments, the situation became even worse, prompting U.S. Secretary of State Bainbridge Colby to write of this new regime: "There cannot be any common ground upon which [the United States] can stand with a Power whose conceptions of international relations are so entirely alien to its own, so utterly repugnant to its moral sense. There can be no mutual confidence or trust, no respect even.... We cannot recognize, hold official relations with, or give friendly reception to, the agents of a government which is determined and bound to conspire against our institutions."[36]

This growing realization of a dangerous decay in shared values received further confirmation with the rise of Benito Mussolini in Italy and Adolf Hitler in Germany. Time and time again, Mussolini conveyed his contempt for traditional diplomacy, conventional diplomats, and collaborative negotiations. Instead, he preferred what he called *tono fascista*, or an emphasis upon a "Fascist style" that demonstrated a proud and militant bearing, constant hectoring and inveighing against the international status quo, and a strong orientation toward ideological purity. For this reason, when accredited abroad, his ambassadors often conducted themselves not as members of a common diplomatic community, but rather as if they were in "an enemy camp."[37] Hitler, of course, saw enemies everywhere; and although he could play what was for him a game of diplomatic behavior with consummate skill, he rejected the norms of diplomacy when they stood in the way of his dream of conquest for *Lebensraum*, or living space. He distrusted professional diplomats, referred to the German Foreign Ministry as "the Idiot House" staffed by incompetent rejects from other walks of life, and actually removed his ambassadors when he thought that they might be interested in seeking mediation or a peace settlement when he desired war.[38] Hitler never regarded diplomacy as a means of resolving conflict and preserving peace, but rather as an instrument of preparing for expansion and war. As he wrote in *Mein Kampf*, "An alliance whose aim does not embrace a plan for war is senseless and worthless. Alliances are concluded only for struggle."[39]

With the end of the Second World War and then beginning of the intense political and ideological struggle of the Cold War between the United States and the Soviet Union, there appeared to be no semblance of any shared norms at all. The antagonists viewed each other as dangerously obstructionist, scheming, threatening, and bent upon global domination. When U.S. President Harry Truman enunciated the Truman Doctrine in 1947 as a guide for American diplomacy, for example, he declared that "at the present moment in world history, nearly every nation must choose between alternative ways of life"—either Western democracy characterized by free institutions and capitalism or Soviet totalitarianism based upon terror and political oppression.[40] The Soviets responded by describing this speech as "venomous slander," "aggressive," "hostile and bellicose," and one specially designed "to interfere in the affairs of other countries on the side of reaction and counter-revolution."[41] From this point, the confrontations and competition became even more intense, convincing each side that they faced not a partner with common problems, but rather a hostile and brutal opponent that would stop at nothing. If any questions still remained about shared values within a larger diplomatic community, then they surely were dispelled by a shocking and uncompromising expression in one U.S. government report that concluded: "It is now clear that we are facing an implacable enemy whose avowed objective is world domination by whatever means and whatever cost. *There are no rules in such a game. Hitherto acceptable norms of human conduct do not apply*. If the U.S. is to survive, long-standing American concepts of 'fair play' must be reconsidered. . . . We must learn to subvert, sabotage, and destroy our enemies by more clever, more sophisticated, and more effective methods that those used against us."[42] Many years and crises later, an American president could still describe the cold war contest as a "struggle between right and wrong and good and evil," and speak of his adversaries in the Soviet Union as "the focus of evil in the modern world."[43]

This degeneration of accepted standards of international behavior and the values with which diplomacy should be conducted was not confined solely to the Soviets and Western antagonists of the Cold War. Indeed, expressions of hated enemies and justifications for changing diplomatic practices and norms came from many nations. The People's Republic of China, for example, described the United States as a "paradise of gangsters, swindlers, rascals, special agents, fascist germs, speculators, debauchers and all the dregs of mankind. This is the world's manufactory and source of all such crimes as reaction, darkness, cruelty, decadence, corruption, debauchery, oppression of man by man, and cannibalism," announcing that it would use its diplomacy as a means of destroying this enemy and "exploiting the contradictions among imperialists" around the world.[44] Many newly created or recently liberated states participating in the larger international community for the first time, particularly those with strong resentments inherited from a colonial past, often rejected legal arrangements, traditional principles of diplomacy, or methods of procedure simply because they were Western in origin or character.[45] In seeking immediate redress or compensation for past injustices, some announced that they would not feel bound by normal practices and language, producing what Harold Nicolson in his analysis of diplomacy has called mere "exercises in forensic propaganda."[46] Mounting the podium of the United Nations General Assembly with a holster, seizing diplomats as hostages from "The Great Satan," or violating diplomatic immunity in order to seek out and punish "blasphemers" could hardly be expected to inspire confidence in the ability of the international community to develop consensus about appropriate language or behavior. These dramatic changes recall the observation made by one experienced diplomat looking back at a much calmer past "when politeness was a tradition and tradition counted," and declaring: "Diplomacy could flourish only so long as there was a loose, tacit, and general agreement to behave *more or less* like gentlemen."[47]

TECHNOLOGICAL TRANSFORMATIONS

When the twentieth century began, diplomacy proceeded at a relatively slow pace. The daily atmosphere in the French Ministry for Foreign Affairs, for example, was relaxed enough to still foster a tradition known as *le thé de cinq heures*.[48] Here, visiting members of French missions abroad and permanent officials of the central administration gathered at tea time to socialize and relax on a regular and daily basis. Diplomats in other European capitals record similar experiences, fondly recalling limited working hours and "comparatively idle days," porters still meeting horse-drawn carriages, despatches written by hand, time to read and reflect upon correspondence, and the use of firewood for heat that seemed to confirm all the more the close family atmosphere and the cozy nature of diplomacy.[49] "The air was strictly reserved for real birds," wrote intellectual Paul Valéry in capturing a mood that still existed. "Electricity had not yet lost its wires.... Newton and Galileo reigned in peace. Physics was happy and its references absolute. Time flowed by in quiet days: all hours were equal in the sight of the Universe. Space enjoyed being infinite, homogeneous, and perfectly indifferent to what went on in its august bosom."[50]

This pace and mood of diplomacy began to change rapidly as a result of technology. Explosive invention and the practical application of technological discovery could be seen in electricity, the internal combustion engine, automobiles, and even airplanes. These machines with their staggering power and speed began to transform the daily lives of millions of people, including diplomats. The foreign ministries in Europe began to replace their horse-drawn carriages with automobiles, their candles and gas lamps with electric lights, their elegant curving staircases with elevators, and their clerks skilled with pen and ink with typists who could do the work faster. Moreover, the growing use of wireless telegraph for overseas communications and Louis Blériot's sensational crossing of the English Channel by airplane in 1909 all suggested further nullifications of former limits heretofore imposed by distance, national boundaries, and—perhaps most critically—time. Increased speed of international communications and transportation led to shortened elapsed time between transmission and receipt of diplomatic despatches, greater impersonalization of transactions, exercise of more control of missions abroad by their centralized ministries and politicians, and reductions in the length of time available for making decisions. Diplomats increasingly found themselves, for example, being forced by technology to write reports, study memoranda, choose between alternatives, issue instructions, and assume responsibilities for crisis management without the relaxed luxury of contemplation and careful judgment enjoyed just a few years before.[51]

Technology not only began to transform the way that diplomats conducted their business, but also how they considered one of the most crucial dimensions of statecraft: warfare. Bursting scientific discovery and technological invention quickly found application in weapons of destruction. The launching of the massive battleship H.M.S. *Dreadnought* in 1905, for example, immediately rendered all previous vessels obsolete, intensified an existing arms race, and fed the fears that produced it. Further developments in long-range artillery pieces, smokeless powder, and rapid-firing machine guns made the situation even worse. All of this presented a mere prelude to the nature of international tensions in the twentieth century, however, for traditional notions about the limitations of diplomacy and war working together were shattered by the First World War.

In terms of technology, and as Hanson Baldwin describes, the First World War "provided a preview of the Pandora's box of evils that the linkage of science with industry in the service of war was to mean [for the twentieth century]."[52] The combination of scientific patterns of machine gun fire and barbed wire entanglements, artillery capable of firing exploding shells to targets several miles away, poison gas, land mines, torpedoes, submarines and battleships mobilized on a massive scale, aircraft for combat on the ground and in the sky, and armored tanks all brought unimagined horror and devastation. The century's new science and technology armed the belligerents for four years of slaughter, unleashing forces of unparalleled destruction, revolutionizing modern warfare, obliterating the old and important distinction between civilian and combatant, laying waste entire provinces, destroying empires, leaving little differences between the "victor" and "vanquished," and transforming diplomacy. Perhaps the most fateful change effected by technology in the service of war, according to Craig, was the relationship between civilian diplomats and soldiers. "Warfare was revolutionized," he writes, "in a way that made it increasingly difficult for civilian authorities to control. Simultaneously, the expanding violence of the conflict smashed the very framework of traditional diplomacy and released forces which, in the subsequent period, militated against the kind of consensus necessary to effective international collaboration, and undermined the authority and prestige of professional diplomats in their own countries."[53]

All these trends continued apace during the Second World War, whose global geographical scope and destructiveness dwarfed its predecessor. Direct "summit" conferences among national leaders like Winston Churchill, Joseph Stalin, and Franklin Roosevelt, made possible over vast distances by technological advances in transportation and communication, tended to marginalize the role of professional diplomats even further. The war's "Battle of the Drawing Boards" seeking new technological breakthroughs produced even more horrifying weapons, for never before in history had the resources of science been so completely engaged in devising new instruments of destruction. These included the Stuka dive bombers, the Zero and Spitfire fighters, the Superfortress strategic bombers, jet aircraft, liquid fuel rockets, aircraft carriers, amphibious assault vessels, radar, technically advanced submarines, heavily armored tanks, proximity fuses, magnetic mines, and, more dreadful than all, the atomic bomb. As a result of these technological tools of war, no conflict in human history has been so destructive to human life, with perhaps as many as 50 million people killed in one way or another.

Technological sophistication accelerated after the war in communications, increasing both the pace of diplomacy and the volume of its work. Diplomats familiar with telegraphic cables and international telephone lines soon discovered the application of new technologies often providing instantaneous transmission of information. A visit to the communications center of any major foreign ministry today, for example, reveals a staggering array of complex electronic encryption telephones, computers with elaborate data bases, modems using fiber optic cables, and facsimile machines, among other devices, for encoding and decoding classified messages, sending and receiving satellite transmissions, maintaining constant mobile communication with those traveling by automobiles, ships, or aircraft. It is possible for a secretary of state to transmit instructions and reports, communicate with the president, or even to receive maps and runway patterns of new locations necessitated by unscheduled stops or changing itineraries by fax all while in midair.[54] Technologies also make it possible for diplomats to receive nearly unimagined intelligence about others in world affairs and thereby participate in the "information revolution" of collection and analysis. The current capacity to collect data by means of technical intelligence systems and then provide analysis through sophisticated processing and imagery simply staggers the imagination. As one author describes the capabilities:

Cameras carried in the satellites [can] photograph missile bases, airfields, submarine pens, harbors, and other defense installations from a hundred miles or more in space with such clarity that they [can] pinpoint a single man walking alone on a vast desert. Sensors in the satellites [are] not blinded by the dark; radar eyes and heat-sensing infrared sensors penetrate clouds and dark skies and [make] photos almost as sharp as those made during a clear day by normal cameras.... [E]ach satellite carries a battery of antennae capable of sucking foreign microwave signals from out of space like a vacuum cleaner picking up specks of dusk from a carpet.[55]

This revolution in communication technology occurred in transportation as well, with the result being a capacity to land men on the moon and a "shrinking" of the globe. At the beginning of the century it took nearly two weeks to cross the Atlantic by ship. In 1927 Charles Lindbergh flew it in one and one-half days. Today the Concorde flying at supersonic speed covers the same distance in three hours. Jet aircraft allow diplomats to travel to nearly any location in the world and to return home for consultation when necessary with a minimum of effort. It is also possible for their political superiors to travel themselves, occasionally dropping in out of the clouds without warning, personally conducting their own diplomacy, and thereby reducing the role of resident ambassadors who complained with some exaggeration that they were becoming "no more than a clerk at the end of the telephone."[56] U.S. Secretary of State John Foster Dulles, to illustrate, is estimated to have traveled a distance equal to eleven times around the earth during a period of three and one-half years on sudden and not always welcomed lightning trips, often arousing dismay in friendly nations, anger among others, and great resentment among his own chiefs of mission abroad.[57] Similarly, U.S. Secretary of State Henry Kissinger's penchant for personal control, attention, and "shuttle diplomacy" by aircraft among various capitals extended this trend even further, as has the recent proclivity of heads of state and government to be "seen" at international conferences or other diplomatic gatherings.

Technology also transformed modern weaponry. Diplomacy today must contend with thousands of warheads of mass destruction far more powerful than the bombs dropped over Hiroshima and Nagasaki and with the technological capacity to extinguish life as we know it. "Throughout history," observes Kissinger,

> humanity has suffered from a shortage of power and has concentrated all its efforts on developing new sources and special applications of it. It would have seemed unbelievable even fifty years ago that there could ever be an excess of power.... Yet this is precisely the challenge of the nuclear age. Ever since the end of the Second World War brought us not the peace we sought so earnestly, but an uneasy armistice, we have responded by what can best be described as a flight into technology: by devising ever more fearful weapons.[58]

This flight has produced not only nuclear, chemical, and biological weapons with sophisticated delivery systems to launch them toward targets continents away, but also a vast array of space technologies of particle beams and kinetic energy weapons designed to extend the potential for war beyond earth's atmosphere and precision-guided munitions to fight on the land, at sea, and in the air. The Persian Gulf War of 1991, for example, utilized cruise missiles with radar systems capable of comparing landmarks with prerecorded maps to guide them to their targets, jet fighters with radar-evading Stealth technology based upon shape and materials, electronic jamming equipment, night-vision devices, and so-called "smart bombs" guided by lasers, infrared or television cameras.[59] Diplomats in an earlier part of the century, and schooled in a Clausewitzian doctrine of limited means for limited ends serving political purposes, could not have even imagined such a revolution in weapons technology during their worst nightmares.

BURGEONING INTERESTS AND ISSUES

Diplomats at the beginning of the twentieth century focused their attention largely upon what they called "high politics." By this they meant the geopolitical interests of their sovereign nation-state in important international matters relating to war and peace, political and military alliances, relations among the Great Powers, and the acquisition and retention of colonial possessions. Although commercial affairs were considered, diplomats traditionally held trade and economics in low esteem and regarded them as relatively unimportant and mundane when compared to the seeming omnipotence and excitement of global politics. "The great flaw in the system," wrote one diplomat in looking back at this period, "was that economics had no place in it; the subject slightly alarmed a world still struggling against a predominance of prose."[60] Those engaged in this diplomacy rarely bothered with other interests and issues, and, despite complaints to the contrary, their concern about "outsiders" and public opinion remained almost nonexistent.

This narrow and isolated approach was shattered by the bloodshed of the First World War. Four years of warfare brought rising and irresistible pressure from politicians, business interests, journalists, and vocal members of the public at large deploring this "secret diplomacy" and announcing their determination to end, in the words of the *Berliner Tageblatt*, "an aristocratic collegium unapproachable to the ordinary mortal, like the table of the Holy Grail."[61] For this reason, critics argued that they had remained silent and subservient long enough and began to insert themselves into diplomacy and to create permanent legislative committees to deal with foreign affairs, insisting that they possessed a legitimate interest to be informed and consulted about external relations. Diplomats thus found themselves forced to spend ever larger amounts of time and effort throughout the rest of the century providing legislative or congressional briefings, making appearances and answering questions, sharing heretofore confidential documents, complaining about "interference," and attempting to build domestic political coalitions in order to conduct policy.[62] This, in turn, led to the rise of a phenomenon known as "Congressional diplomacy"[63] and a setting characterized by one observer as full of "hordes of junketing politicians, consultants to international corporations, journalists, television teams, and peripatetic academicians that are a feature of modern life."[64] Others described it as "fish-bowl diplomacy."[65]

This growing public dimension of diplomacy found further expression in the advent of efforts designed to influence opinion both at home and abroad. The deliberate use of propaganda during two world wars, and then the Cold War, convinced many that the struggle for the "hearts and minds" of people would be waged around the globe and thus would become an integral part of diplomacy. Even prior to the Second World War, one astute observer of history and international relations declared that "propaganda seems likely for the future to be recognized as a regular instrument of foreign policy."[66] Consequently, foreign ministries which once had assiduously refrained from providing any information about their activities to outsiders, increasingly began to hold daily press conferences for foreign and domestic journalists, provide interviews and "photo opportunities," hire press attachés, publish collections of diplomatic documents, release public statements, and at times even stage "media events" in order to influence stories in the press or images broadcast over television, particularly those with international capabilities like CNN. Indeed, one insider has estimated that the staff of the U.S. Secretary of State spends 80 to 90 percent of its time thinking about the news media.[67] In a closely related development, they also became convinced of the importance of engaging in "cultural diplomacy" by sending books, magazines, films, videotapes, music, works of art, scientific displays, and other symbols of national achievement abroad. Consequently, diplomats in the later-twentieth century occasionally find themselves being joined overseas by visiting painters, professors, poets, scientists, astronauts, ballerinas, movie stars, and rock musicians conducting their own form of people-to-people diplomacy from national capital cities to tiny rural villages. The cumulative effect of all this, of course, heightened the influence that public opinion exercised upon the formulation and execution of foreign policy.[68] Indeed, one government commission recently declared that "public diplomacy is a strategic component of foreign policy" and "indispensable" to contemporary international politics.[69]

Revolutionary changes in public diplomacy were matched, if not exceeded, in commerce and economics. Business firms, bankers and financiers, manufacturers, shipping companies, chambers of commerce, and private investors argued that in the twentieth century they needed their diplomats to promote and protect them actively and aggressively in the global marketplace. At the same time, writes one author,

Governments increasingly recognized that the distribution of goods and capital abroad might be utilized as an instrument of diplomacy. Investment could buy friendships or build and solidify alliances, while monies withheld or economic reprisals could coerce opponents into making certain diplomatic concessions. Financial penetration could facilitate political hegemony in developing countries. Commercial advantages offered to foreign suppliers of strategic raw materials could strengthen security. Moreover, profits from overseas markets could contribute to national wealth and perhaps increase international prestige.[70]

The combination of these private and public interests consequently resulted in foreign ministries taking more determined action than in the past to promote and protect trade by recruiting economic specialists, employing commercial attachés, compiling vital import and export statistics for its nationals, publishing reports on foreign market conditions and tariff policies, utilizing successful businessmen as trade negotiators, and upgrading the quality and professionalism of consular services, among many other activities. Through time, these activities expanded to include a close cooperation between business and diplomacy in areas of investment, trade, technical assistance, and foreign aid. Said one high-ranking diplomat in a recent speech to his colleagues: "We are going to have to acknowledge that our economic health and our ability to trade competitively on the world market may be the single most important component of our national security. . . . We must also become more activist in promoting American exports and in serving U.S. business interests overseas."[71] His words are echoed by diplomats in national capitals throughout the world today seeking to respond to the "globalization" of the world economy.

Similarly, the vast technological transformations that dramatically influenced the pace and the practices of diplomacy also increasingly affected substance as well. Rapid changes in nuclear power, telecommunications, biotechnology, computers, and innumerable scientific discoveries all appeared to render the traditional borders of nation-states less meaningful, and thus began to influence entirely new areas of international security, competitiveness, global epidemics like the AIDS virus, technology transfer, and ecology. All this prompted a deep concern among the Carnegie Commission on Science, Technology, and Government which recently called upon diplomats to become "more technologically literate navigators" in order that they might "integrate science and technology into decisions about where and how to proceed with political relationships." The commission asserted: "Foreign policy in the future seems likely to turn on trends in the global economic system, on environmental change and the need to reverse environmental degradation, and on global systems in communications and transportation. These developments will shape the operating environment over the next few decades, not only for business but for statecraft and diplomacy."[72]

One of the other profound changes brought to diplomacy by new interests and issues in our time lies not in science and technology but in the area of human rights. For much of recorded history, for example, the overwhelming proportion of the non-white world lived subjected to some of the worst kinds of discrimination based upon race in slavery, imperialism, segregation, and various forms of exploitation, genocide, and exclusion. During all this time the practices, institutions, and laws of the international community remained deathly silent on the subject of equal treatment, and individuals possessed no recourse against the discriminatory abuses of a state. Indeed, as late as the first part of the twentieth century, even the expression "prejudice of race" was never allowed in diplomatic parlance. Yet, due to the persistent efforts of the Japanese after the First World War, the global revulsion to the horrors of the Nazi Holocaust during the Second World War, and the rise of new actors from Asia and Africa who themselves had suffered as victims of racial discrimination, members of the international community began to speak out and set new standards for human rights around the world.[73] Consequently, first in the Charter of the United Nations and Universal Declaration of Human Rights, then in a series of binding treaties like the International Covenant on Civil and Political Rights and the Convention on the Elimination of All Forms of Racial Discrimination, states began a process of taking the treatment of citizens out of the formerly exclusive confines of domestic jurisdiction of states claiming exclusive national sovereignty. Recent meetings like the 1993 World Conference on Human Rights convened in Vienna and the 1995 World Congress on Women held in Beijing attracted literally thousands of participants and attracted worldwide attention. Today no government or diplomat can legitimately claim that they are unaware of the place that racial and gender equality in particular and that human rights in general possess on the global agenda, and of the process in diplomacy whereby individuals are being transformed from mere objects of international sympathy into subjects of international law.[74]

Closely related to the issue of discrimination are those of decolonization and development. As the dozens of new states from Asia and Africa joined the international community, they came to hold a majority of votes in the General Assembly of the United Nations. Here, they began to change the composition, character, tone, language, and much of the agenda of the organization and quickly revealed that their interests in diplomacy were not always synonymous with those of the great or superpowers. In fact, they often directly challenged their former colonial masters and used their newfound influence to focus international attention not upon the politics of the Cold War, but rather upon accelerating the processes of decolonization and promoting a redistribution of wealth from the north to the south in sustained economic and social development. The Afro-Asian countries and their supporters in the Third World succeeded in passing the revolutionary Declaration on the Granting of Independence to Colonial Countries and Peoples in 1960 and the Declaration for the Establishment of a New International Economic Order in 1974 demanding far-reaching concessions from industrialized nations.[75] Both of these declarations, as well as the anger and hope that inspired them, profoundly influence contemporary diplomacy and the struggle for distribution of the world's wealth and resources.

Finally, the interests of many governments and of international nongovernmental organizations brought a whole variety of new issues to diplomacy dealing with Planet Earth. During the last three decades of the twentieth century, the world has witnessed a growing concern about Earth as a whole, the planet as a "global village," and the phenomenon described as "complex interdependence." The proliferation of weapons, radioactive waste, environmental degradation and pollution, exploding populations, global indebtedness, starvation and agricultural production, the distribution and destruction of natural resources, biodiversity, social justice, the fate of indigenous peoples, and human rights, among many other issues, are increasingly seen as interrelated to one another and as requiring international solutions.

The "Earth Summit" held under United Nations auspices and accompanying "Global Forum" in Rio de Janeiro during 1992 symbolized many of these revolutionary changes in diplomacy. The official guest list of actors included one hundred heads of state or government and their accompanying entourages, but more than thirty thousand other people also attended ranging from climatogists to philosophers, environmentalists to economists, biochemists to gurus, human rights activists to nuclear scientists, and businessmen to tribal chieftains representing indigenous peoples. They traveled by foot, bus, train, ship, automobile, and airplane, and their actions were covered by the media and instantaneously transmitted to the world. Their interests ranged from those of nation-states to NGOs and from pressure groups to transnational corporations. Moreover, the issues they discussed ranged from rain forests to biotechnology, poverty to rare fish, birth control to acid rain, children to pesticides, refugees to interest rates, nuclear weapons to ozone depletion, women to electronic financial transfers, and development to biodiversity. Such issues would have been completely unrecognizable to students and practitioners of diplomacy just a few years before.

These many global forces and dramatic changes have revolutionized diplomacy. The vastly expanded number of actors in the international community, greater diversity in practices and values, complex technological developments, and a burgeoning array of interests and issues all have made statecraft infinitely more challenging than ever before in history. Indeed, at times, the unparalleled pace and the quantitative and qualitative expansion of diplomacy appear nearly overwhelming to those responsible for its conduct. "History is accelerating. The pace is alarming. The direction is not entirely known," observed United Nations Secretary-General Boutros Boutros-Ghali, with deep concern.[76] One former U.S. secretary of state believes that the only way to respond to this is to find "a new generation of diplomats" capable of dealing with the end of the Cold War, complex interdependence, the possibilities of mass extermination, the violence within and between states, and "who understand the policy implications of science, oceanography and the environment, economics and economic statesmanship, who can and will think broadly about the impact of computers, agricultural technology and nuclear science in a changing world. At the same time, Foreign Service officers will continue to perform their traditional functions of political and economic reporting, administrative management, and providing consular services."[77] Whether this new generation will be able to respond adequately to all these requirements of diplomacy, and to combine both the traditional functions of the past with those many new demands of the future, will be determined in large part by their ability to understand the forces behind this diplomatic revolution of our time.

NOTES

1. The inspiration for this chapter comes from a course taught both individually and collectively by Gordon A. Craig, Alexander L. George, and myself at Stanford University entitled "The Diplomatic Revolution of Our Time."

2. Heinz Sasse, "Von Equipage und Automobilen des Auswärtigen Amts," *Nachrichtenblatt der Vereinigung Deutscher Auslandsbeamten*, Heft 10, 20. Jahrgang (October 1957), 145; Charles Burton Marshall, "The Golden Age in Perspective," *Journal of International Affairs* 17, 1 (1963): 9–17.

3. France, Archives diplomatiques du Ministère des Affaires étrangères/Sénat, Commission des Finances, Rapport No. 165 (1911), 36; Zara Steiner, *The Foreign Office and Foreign Policy, 1898–1914* (Cambridge, 1969), 164–71.

4. Gordon A. Craig and Alexander L. George, *Force and Statecraft: Diplomatic Problems of Our Time* (New York, 1995 ed.), 75–86; Harold Nicolson, *Diplomacy* (London, 1968 ed.), 41–54.

5. See the editorial, "Soviet Atomic Diplomacy," *New York Times*, 28 March 1957; Gar Alperowitz, *Atomic Diplomacy* (New York, 1965); Forest Grieves, *Conflict and Order: An Introduction to International Relations* (Boston, 1977), 337 ff.; Richard Benedick, *Ozone Diplomacy: New Directions in Safeguarding the Planet* (Cambridge, Mass., 1991).

6. John Stoessinger, *The Might of Nations: World Politics in Our Time* (New York, 1993 ed.), 248, although the tone in this edition is optimistic.

7. James R. Woolsey, in testimony before the U.S. Senate, as cited in *New York Times*, "Nominee," 3 February 1993.

8. Alfred Zimmern, *The Third British Empire* (London, 1926), 82. Also see Kazuo Ito, *Issei* (Seattle, 1973), 3, for a Japanese perspective reaching the same conclusion.

9. Maurice Paléologue, *Un grand tournant de la politique mondiale* (Paris, 1934), 364.

10. W.E.B. Du Bois, "Opinion," *Crisis* 18 (May 1919): 7.

11. E. J. Dillon, *The Inside Story of the Peace Conference* (New York, 1920), 5. For more discussion, see Paul Gordon Lauren, *Power and Prejudice: The Politics and Diplomacy of Racial Discrimination* (Boulder and London, 1988), 76 ff.

12. This is revealed clearly in the Archives de la Société des Nations, especially material in the General and the Mandates divisions. Photographs of the diplomats of the League on display in the museum of the Société des Nations at the Palais des Nations in Geneva nevertheless reveal that most still came from the West, and very few represented nonwhite nations.

13. See Britain, Public Record Office, Foreign Office, 371/78945, Circular Despatch No. 25102, "Secret," from A. Creech Jones (Colonial Office) to Governors of the Colonies, 28 March 1949; Gordon A. Craig, "The Diplomacy of New Nations," in *War, Politics, and Diplomacy* (New York, 1966), 248.

14. Nddabaningi Sithole, *African Nationalism* (London, 1959), 23.

15. United Nations, Charter, Article 55.

16. See H. Tinker, *Race, Conflict, and the International Order* (London, 1977), 61.

17. Christopher Thorne, "External Political Pressures," in *African Diplomacy*, Vernon McKay, ed. (New York, 1966), 145.

18. See Lauren, *Power and Prejudice*, 197 ff.

19. Daniel Patrick Moynihan, *Pandaemonium* (New York, 1993).

20. Joseph Nye Jr., *Bound to Lead* (New York, 1990), 178. Also see Richard Belous and Kelly McClenahan, eds., *Global Corporations and Nation States* (Washington, D.C., 1991).

21. Figures from personal conversations with UN staff members of the NGO Unit of the Department of Economic and Social Development and the Department of Public Information, 1993.

22. Union of International Associations, *Yearbook of International Organizations, 1995–96* (Munich, 1995), 1671. Interestingly enough, this figure represents an increase of six thousand over the previous three years. Also see Kjell Skyelsbaek, "The Growth of International Non-Governmental Organizations in the Twentieth

Century," *International Organization* 25 (Summer 1971): 420-42; Peter Willetts, *Pressure Groups in the International System* (New York, 1982).

23. Moritz Busch, as cited in Paul Gordon Lauren, *Diplomats and Bureaucrats: The First Institutional Responses to Twentieth-Century Diplomacy in France and Germany* (Stanford, 1976), 25.

24. For background discussion, see Paul Gordon Lauren, "Crisis Prevention in Nineteenth-Century Diplomacy," in *Managing U.S.–Soviet Rivalry: Problems of Crisis Prevention*, ed. Alexander L. George (Boulder and London, 1983), 31–64.

25. J. A. Spender, *The Public Life* (London, 1925), 2:40, 48. Also see Gabriel Hanotaux, "L'Europe qui naît," *La Revue hebdomadaire* 48 (30 November 1907): 563; Germany, Politisches Archiv des Auswärtiges Amt, Abteilung IA, Frankreich 105 Nr. 1, Band 26.

26. Marshall, "The Golden Age in Perspective," 11.

27. Jean Jaurès, 29 July 1914 speech in Brussels, as reproduced in *L'Humanité*, 30 July 1914.

28. "Krieg und Diplomatie," *Vorwärts*, 26 May 1915.

29. Trevelyan, 19 March 1918, in Britain, House of Commons, *The Parliamentary Debates*, 104 (London, 1918), 846.

30. Woodrow Wilson, as cited in Bernadotte Schmitt, *Triple Alliance and Triple Entente* (New York, 1934), 1.

31. See Lauren, *Diplomats and Bureaucrats*, 68–78; Parti Socialiste et Confédération Générale du Travail, *Le Memorandum des socialistes des pays alliés* (Paris, 1918); Angelica Balabanoff, *Die Zimmerwalder Bewegung* (Leipzig, 1928); Arno Mayer, *Wilson vs. Lenin: The Political Origins of the New Diplomacy* (New York, 1964).

32. David Lloyd George, as cited in A. L. Kennedy, *Old Diplomacy and New* (London, 1922), 364–65.

33. Lord Vansittart, *The Mist Procession* (London, 1958), 176.

34. Gordon A. Craig, "The Revolution in War and Diplomacy, 1914–39," in *War, Politics, and Diplomacy*, 203–4. Also see Georges Hoyau, *Die Kunst des Arrangierens oder Diplomaten-Brevier* (Vienna, 1973), 85–122.

35. Leon Trotsky, as cited in Craig and George, *Force and Statecraft*, 76.

36. Bainbridge Colby, as cited in ibid., 77.

37. The words are those of Craig, "Totalitarian Approaches to Diplomatic Negotiation," in *War, Politics, and Diplomacy*, 224.

38. See Gordon A. Craig, "The German Foreign Office from Neurath to Ribbentropp," in Gordon A. Craig and Felix Gilbert, eds., *The Diplomats, 1919–1939*, 2 vols. (New York, 1968 ed.), 2:406–36; Paul Seabury, *The Wilhelmstrasse* (Berkeley, Calif., 1954); Gerhard Weinberg, *The Foreign Policy of Hilter's Germany: Diplomatic Revolution in Europe* (Chicago, 1970).

39. Adolf Hitler, *Mein Kampf*, trans. R. Manheim (Boston, 1962 ed.), 660.

40. Harry Truman, as cited in the *New York Times*, 13 March 1947.

41. See B. Ponomaryov, A. Gromyko, and V. Khvostov, *History of Soviet Foreign Policy, 1945–1970* (Moscow, 1974), 158–59.

42. Conclusions of a 1954 report on covert action against the Soviets, as cited in U.S. Senate Select Committee to Study Government Operations with Respect to Intelligence Activities, *Foreign and Military Intelligence: Final Report*, 94th Cong., 2d sess., 1976, Book I, 50 [emphasis added]. For more discussion on this point, see

Paul Gordon Lauren, "Ethics and Intelligence," in Alfred C. Maurer et al. (eds.) *Intelligence: Policy and Process* (Boulder and London, 1985), 69–87.

43. Ronald Reagan, 8 March 1983, as cited in Don Oberdorfer, *The Turn* (New York, 1991), 24.

44. "Look, This Is the American Way of Life," supplement to *Nan Fung Jih Pao*, CCP official organ, December 1950, as cited in John Stoessinger, *Nations in Darkness* (New York, 1990 ed.), 50.

45. See Craig, *War, Politics, and Diplomacy*, 204, 248–61.

46. Harold Nicolson, *The Evolution of Diplomacy* (New York, 1966 ed.), 121.

47. Lord Vansittart, "The Decline of Diplomacy," *Foreign Affairs* 28, 2 (January 1950): 178, 185.

48. Personal descriptions of this teatime are provided in Comte de Saint-Aulaire, *Confession d'un vieux diplomate* (Paris, 1953), 31 ff.; Jules La Roche, *Au Quai d'Orsay* (Paris, 1957), 11 ff.; and F. Charles-Roux, *Souvenirs diplomatiques d'un âge révolutionaire* (Paris, 1956), 92.

49. See Sasse, "Von Equipage," 145–48; Joseph Maria von Radowitz, *Aufzeichnungen und Erinnerungen*, 2 vols. (Berlin, 1925), 1:260; Vansittart, *The Mist Procession*, 43; Joseph Grew, *Turbulent Era: A Diplomatic Record of Forty Years, 1904–1945*, 2 vols. (Boston, 1952), 2:41–42; among many others.

50. Paul Valéry, *The Outlook for Intelligence* (New York, 1963 ed.), 126.

51. See Lauren, *Diplomats and Bureaucrats*, 34–39; Walter Zechlin, *Diplomatie und Diplomaten* (Stuttgart, 1925), 17.

52. Hanson Baldwin, *World War I* (New York, 1962), 159.

53. Craig, "The Revolution in War and Diplomacy," 197.

54. See the account in "Battle Ready," *Newsweek*, 20 August 1990, 23.

55. Robert Lindsay, *The Falcon and the Snowman* (New York, 1980), 59–62. Also see Consortium for the Study of Intelligence, *The Future of U.S. Intelligence* (Washington, D.C., 1996), 11–19; James Bamford, *The Puzzle Palace: Inside the National Security Agency* (New York, 1983); U.S. Central Intelligence Agency, Directorate of Science and Technology, "Careers That Can Make a Difference in Our World" (Langley, n.d.).

56. The words are those of Harold Nicolson, *Diplomacy*, 38. Also see J. Robert Schaetzel, "Is the Ambassador an Endangered Species, or Merely Obsolete?" in U.S. Commission on the Organization of the Government for the Conduct of Foreign Policy, *Appendices*, 7 vols. (Washington, D.C., 1976), 6:325–33.

57. Craig, "Dulles and American Statecraft," in *War, Politics, and Diplomacy*, 272–79.

58. Henry Kissinger, *Nuclear Weapons and Foreign Policy* (New York, 1957), 3.

59. See "The Weapons: High-Tech Payoff," *Time*, 28 January 1991.

60. Vansittart, *The Mist Procession*, 40. Also see Germany, Politisches Archiv des Auswärtiges Amt, Politisches Archiv und Historisches Referat, Aktenzeichen 11, "Geschichte der Politischen Abteilung," and Aktenzeichen 13, "Geschichte der Handelspolitischen Abteilung."

61. Theodore Wolff, in *Berliner Tageblatt*, 6 October 1919.

62. See Lauren, *Diplomats and Bureaucrats*, 111–14, 148–51; S. R. Chow, *Le contrôle parlementaire de la politique étrangère en Angleterre, en France, et aux Etats-Unis* (Paris, 1920).

63. The extensive holdings of the Mike Mansfield Papers, University of Montana Archives, provides ample demonstration of legislative involvement.

64. Gordon A. Craig, "On the Nature of Diplomatic History," in *Diplomacy: New Approaches in History, Theory, and Policy*, ed. Paul Gordon Lauren (New York, 1979), 33–34.

65. "Editor's Foreword," *Journal of International Affairs*, 17, 1 (1963): vii.

66. E. H. Carr, *Propaganda in International Politics* (New York, 1939), 12.

67. See Simon Serfaty, ed., *The Media and Foreign Policy* (London, 1990), xiv; and the discussion in Ernest May, "The News Media and Diplomacy," in *The Diplomats, 1939–1979*, ed. Gordon A. Craig and Francis Loewenheim, 665–700.

68. For more discussion, see the chapter entitled "*Civilization* and *Kultur*," in Lauren, *Diplomats and Bureaucrats*, 178–207.

69. United States Advisory Commission on Public Diplomacy, *1991 Report: Public Diplomacy in the 1990s* (Washington, D.C., 1992), 13, 16. Also see Miroslav Nincic, "New Perspectives on Popular Opinion and Foreign Policy," *Journal of Conflict Resolution*, 36 (December 1992): 772–89.

70. Lauren, *Diplomats and Bureaucrats*, 157, in the chapter entitled "Diplomatic Pouches and Pocketbooks: New and Expanded Responsibilities for International Commerce."

71. Deputy Secretary of State Lawrence Eagleburger, "International Business: Foundation of National Strength," speech to the American Foreign Service Association, 30 November 1989.

72. Carnegie Commission on Science, Technology, and Government, "Carnegie Commission Proposes Scientific Revolution for U.S. Diplomacy," news release, 29 January 1992. Also see Kenneth H. Keller, "Science and Technology," *Foreign Affairs* 69, 4 (Fall 1990): 123–38.

73. See U.S., National Archives, State Department, RG 59, Records of Harley Notter, Box 75, Advisory Commission on Post-War Foreign Policy, "Bill of Rights," 31 July 1942; Britain, Public Record Office, Foreign Office, 371/40716, Telegram from Lord Halifax (Washington) to Foreign Office, 29 September 1944.

74. For more discussion of this subject and its related dimension of decolonization, see Lauren, *Power and Prejudice*.

75. The dynamics of this process are revealed in United Nations Archives, DAG-1, Papers of the Secretary-General. Also see Paul Gordon Lauren, "The Diplomats and Diplomacy of the United Nations," in Craig and Loewenheim, eds., *The Diplomats, 1939–1979* (Princeton, 1994), 459–95.

76. Boutros Boutros-Ghali, "An Agenda for Peace: One Year Later," *Orbis* 37 (Summer 1993): 332. Also see the discussion in Henry Kissinger, *Diplomacy* (New York, 1994), especially the chapter entitled "The New World Order Reconsidered," 804–36.

77. James Baker III, as cited in U.S. Department of State, Application for the Foreign Service Officer Program, 1991, "Statement of Interest."

3 Monarchy, Court, and Society in Constitutional Prussia
David E. Barclay

At eleven o'clock on the morning of 6 February 1850 the king of Prussia, Frederick William IV, appeared in the Knights' Hall of the Royal Palace in Berlin to take an oath to the country's new constitution. In contrast to other monarchs like Louis-Philippe in France, Austria's Emperor Ferdinand, or his Bavarian brother-in-law Ludwig I, he had managed to keep his throne. He had survived the upheavals of 1848; but that survival had been achieved at the price of Prussia's transformation into a parliamentary and constitutional state. For decades Frederick William had fought against the forces of "revolution." Since his accession to the throne in 1840 he had attempted to resuscitate supposedly "historical," organic, corporative-estatist institutions as an alternative to "French" parliamentarism. Now, however, all his efforts seemed to have been in vain. The German monarch who, more than any other of his generation, had devoted his entire life to an unremitting ideological struggle against the forces of "revolution" had now agreed, under considerable duress and political pressure, to take an oath to what he regarded as a "Godless," "mechanistic," "French-modern" abomination, the monstrous offspring of 1848. It had taken him more than a year to face up to this moment. At one point in the late autumn of 1848, when his conservative government had confronted him with the necessity of granting a constitution, he had even spoken melodramatically of suicide.[1] And for the rest of his life he looked back bitterly on the events of February 1850, complaining that "from his belly to his mouth it was getting more difficult as an honest man to maintain his oath, which seemed to him to be untenable and absolutely unbearable."[2]

Accordingly, Frederick William IV was constantly on the lookout after 1850 for ways to amend or alter the constitution to reflect his own notions of monarchical authority; but he enjoyed mixed success at best. Although he was rightly described by Joseph Maria von Radowitz as the very antithesis of a constitutional monarch, the King of Prussia felt morally bound by his constitutional oath, and at no time seriously considered repudiating it.[3] The constitution could only be changed or eliminated through the very constitutional and parliamentary means that the King so distrusted; as Frederick William once noted plaintively in a letter to his nephew, Francis Joseph of Austria, "as long as we are afflicted by the French constitution, and especially as we free ourselves from it, we still need [parliamentary] majorities!!"[4]

Frederick William's dilemma points to the central issue that these remarks will address: how monarchical authority and monarchical institutions were recast in postrevolutionary, constitutional Prussia. Historians have, of course, long been aware of the persistence and durability of monarchical institutions and practices in post-1848 Prussia. Moreover, in the wake of several important studies that have appeared in the last two decades, historians of nineteenth-century Europe have been increasingly inclined to "take monarchy seriously" as an object of study.[5] In the case of non-Habsburg Germany, much of this recent attention has been directed either toward the Vormärz period, toward the reign of William II, or toward the rulers of medium-sized states such as Bavaria, Saxony, and Württemberg.[6] Curiously, historians have so far paid relatively little attention to the monarchy in Prussia itself: that is, to the actual structure of monarchical institutions, the ways in which they were transformed, or the significance of these processes for our understanding of the distribution of political power in that state between 1848 and 1890.[7]

This chapter will attempt at least partially to redress this situation by focusing on three interrelated themes. First, it will briefly describe the structure and significance of the court from 1848 to 1888. It will then consider the reciprocal (and constantly changing) relationship between monarchical institutions and Prussian society during those years. Finally, it will draw some conclusions about the limits and extent of monarchical authority in Prussia by briefly describing the crown's relationship to other constitutive structures of the Prussian state.

At first glance, a study of the Prussian court during the four decades between the revolution and the accession of William II would not seem to offer edifying opportunities for the historian. Virtually all contemporary observers, from Austrian diplomats in the early 1850s to the French poet Jules Laforgue in the 1880s, agreed that the court was a dull and even stifling place that largely failed to function effectively either as an instrument of monarchical representation or as a showcase for Prussia's ruling elites.[8] At no time in those decades could it compare in splendor, visibility, or magnificence to other European courts, especially the glittering Second Empire court of Napoleon III and Eugénie. Such glamor as it had enjoyed had largely been confined to the eight years before the March revolution; thereafter it often seemed to be a rather claustrophobic and provincial preserve of aging and often bigoted aristocratic families, an institution remote from and apparently irrelevant to a rapidly transforming Prussian society beyond its narrow and exclusive boundaries.

But when one looks a bit closer at the court, the picture changes somewhat. In fact, an examination of the changing structure and function of the court will offer interesting insights into the actual forms of monarchical practice in constitutional Prussia, and so can help us understand a great deal about the continuing role of monarchy in that system. Under Frederick William IV and William I the court served three functions: It constituted at once an administrative institution, a political arena, and an instrument for the representation and diffusion of monarchical values. Although, in the final analysis, it may not have been very successful as far as the last of those functions is concerned, there can be little doubt that the first two remained exceptionally important, and it is to them that we shall now turn.

Thanks to the work of scholars like Günther Grünthal and Wolfram Siemann, we are at last beginning to understand that for Prussia the decade of reaction was in fact a time of quite complex change, readjustment, and reorientation.[9] As another historian, Dieter Langewiesche, has noted, a period of *reaction* is not necessarily a period of *restoration*, and Prussia's dominant elites could not simply turn the clock back to 1847 or 1840 or 1815, even if they had wished to do so.[10] The years between 1848 and 1858 witnessed the emergence of a new alignment of forces at the summit of the Prussian state: a new kind of relationship between monarchical structures, on the one hand, and cabinet, parliament, bureaucracy, and newly emergent forms of political organization and interest articulation on the other. What Hans-Ulrich Wehler has described as the older "monarchic-bureaucratic-aristocratic condominium" of the Vormärz years was being restructured in fundamental and important ways, and the court was not immune to those changes.[11]

Superficially, at least, the post-1848 court had to accommodate itself to a somewhat diminished status, which in turn represented the culmination of a process that had been going on for several decades: that is, an increasing "differentiation between crown and state."[12] As early as 1820, the old royal domains (*Domänen*) had come to be regarded as state property and not as crown property; moreover, according to the Law on State Debts (*Staatsschuldengesetz*) of that year, an annual subsidy of 2.5 million Taler, derived from the profits of the *Domänen*, was to be used as a "royal feoffment in trust" (*Kronfideikommiss*) to meet the public expenses of the court and the royal house.[13] The *Kronfideikommissfonds* was in some ways analogous to the "civil lists" that pay for royal expenses in constitutional monarchies, though in Prussia it was not subject to any kind of parliamentary control either before or after 1848. Moreover, even after the coming of constitutionalism to Prussia the royal house continued to draw upon substantial, purely private resources. The king's privy purse (*Schatulle*) was steadily augmented through the profits of the monarch's private estates in the Mark Brandenburg and Silesia, while Frederick William III's notorious miserliness had made it possible to create a substantial "Crown Reserve" (*Krontresor*) out of the unspent portions of *Kronfideikommiss* subsidies; those funds were to be available to members of the royal family in the event of financial emergency. There was also a *Hausfideikommiss*, which Frederick William I had set up for his younger sons and their descendants, and a similar *Königlich-Prinzliches Fideikommiss* for the younger sons of Frederick William III.[14]

Until 1848, the distinction between the king's functions as the embodiment of the Prussian state and as a quasi-private individual remained unclear. The Ministry of the Royal House, which had been established in 1819, was responsible both for managing the royal family's private affairs and for administering various matters of state. In 1848, however, the ministry (which since its inception had been occupied by the fearsome Prince Wittgenstein) was detached from the state; the House Minister was not regarded as a member of the cabinet, but as the king's private employee. He was not required to take an oath to the constitution, and all his expenses now had to be met entirely out of the annual 2.5 million Taler subsidy from state-owned *Domänen*. The crown budget was rather strained as a result; and after 1854 the new Minister of the Royal House, the highly skilled court bureaucrat Ludwig von Massow, and the Marshal of the Court, Count Alexander von Keller, complained constantly that it had gotten impossible to make ends meet.

In the long run, however, the "privatization" of the crown's budget helped to ensure the monarch's continued freedom from parliamentary control and accountability. Massow, Keller, and, of course, Frederick William IV himself were determined to avoid the introduction of any kind of parliamentary civil list. Accordingly, in 1856 Massow proposed that both the Debt Law of 1820 and Article 59 of the Constitution of 1850 (which had affirmed the continued independence of the crown) be amended to make it possible to extract more than 2.5 million Taler a year from the nationalized crown domains. Finally, in 1859, during the period of the so-called "New Era" regency, the cabinet and the parliament agreed to provide an annual supplement of five hundred thousand Taler from state funds, which, the cabinet argued, should help cover all the court's costs for years to come. After 1859, however, the income and the expenses of the court increased dramatically. The subvention of 1859 was doubled in 1868 and increased again in 1889 and 1910. Although the Prussian court thus continued to be the beneficiary of growing amounts of state money, those subsidies never served as a lever for increased parliamentary control over crown and court.[15]

Despite its continuing reputation for stodginess, then, the Prussian court got both larger and more expensive under the conditions of a constitutional order. In fact, the reaction decade witnessed the beginnings of what has been described as a steady "inflation" of court structures and institutions that continued throughout the latter half of the century.[16] Not only did the years after 1850 bring a proliferation of new court offices, titles, and positions, they also introduced a quite unprecedented elaboration of formal details concerning etiquette, rank, and admission to court functions. Except for one notable revision in 1817, the order of precedence at court (*Hofrangordnung*) had remained essentially unchanged since 1713; nor had any revised list been published since that date. Although Frederick William IV had decided in 1850 that the time had finally come to publish such a list, he was ultimately dissuaded from this course by the Minister of the Royal House, who argued that a printed order of precedence could lead to friction between officers, all of whom could be admitted to court, and those relatively few civilians who were deemed to be presentable at court (*hoffähig*).[17] Only with the establishment of the Reich in 1871 was the order of precedence again revised; and not until 1877, after a further revision, was it included in a published *Ceremonial-Buch für den Königlich Preussischen Hof*. The author of the latter was a man who hovered over the entire court for decades, enjoying the confidence of both Frederick William IV and William I and orchestrating grand court ceremonies and pageants for more than thirty years: the royal Master of Ceremonies, Baron Rudolph von Stillfried-Rattonitz (he later was elevated to the title of "Count Stillfried-Alcantara").[18] Although Stillfried was himself a stickler for the niceties of etiquette, until the reign of William II court life in Berlin remained significantly less grand and imposing than in other European capitals.[19]

The number of court officials, and especially of members of the royal retinue (*Hofstaat*), increased steadily, particularly during the reaction decade, which, of course, corresponded to the last decade of Frederick William IV's active rule. With his penchant for ceremony and for the "medieval" and the "historical," in 1853 Frederick William reorganized the retinue by resuscitating old and largely forgotten court titles. For example, the Lord Chamberlain or *Oberkammerherr* now became "Supreme Chamberlain" (*Oberstkämmerer*), while a "Supreme High Steward" (*Oberst-Truchsess*), a "Supreme Cupbearer" (*Oberst-Schenk*), and a "Grand Master of the Wardrobe" (*Grand-maître de la Garderobe*) were added to the *Hofstaat* for the first time. These reforms were generally greeted with public indifference or derision as yet another example of the king's determination to "revive historic, medieval reminiscences." They were not intended, however, to be merely decorative or ceremonial. In fact, they were part and parcel of a huge propaganda offensive by Frederick William to revise the constitution and transform the upper house, or First Chamber, of the Prussian parliament into a British-style House of Lords. In 1854 he essentially succeeded in this objective; and the reorganized court was supposed to reflect the new prestige of monarchical and aristocratic values. According to the Austrian minister in Berlin, Count Thun, the reorganized House of Lords was "clearly intended to increase the splendor of the court, and thus a splendid *Hofstaat* is also being created."[20] Despite William I's supposed modesty and simplicity, Frederick William's successor did not alter or simplify the structure of the court after his accession to the regency and, later, the throne itself.

The example of the court reorganization in 1853 brings us to the second dimension of the court after 1848, and that was, of course, its political function. Despite the steady growth of parliamentary and other centers of political power, during the 1850s the court nevertheless remained a critically important arena of political activity. The King himself still constituted the heart of the Prussian political system, and throughout the 1850s there was tremendous jockeying for advantage at court and for access to that impressionable monarch; in short, the court constituted a field of play upon which competing interests fought for the king's attention and sought to influence his policy choices. Frederick William himself turned out to be a remarkably skillful political player; especially notable was his ability to play various court factions off against each other to his own advantage. Moreover, as the example of the court reorganization suggests, it provided an instrument that he could use in his endless struggle to revise the constitution and neutralize the parliament. Accordingly, the highest reaches of Prussian politics often presented a scene that to outside observers bordered on anarchy. In the caustic words of one British emissary in 1854, "There is perhaps no Court in Europe at the present moment where such a maze of intrigue is being carried out as at Berlin."[21] As a result, no single group could claim to control the king or direct his policies, not even the group of ultraconservatives around the adjutant general, Leopold von Gerlach, and the king's private secretary, Marcus Niebuhr. The latter individuals formed the heart of what has usually been called the "Camarilla" or the "court party" during the 1850s, a supposed kitchen cabinet of Ultras linked to the well-known *Kreuzzeitung* party. Nevertheless, factional conflict remained immensely complex during that decade, while the king himself was so impervious to permanent outside influences that it is probably not very helpful even to speak of a Camarilla at all after the spring of 1849, or, at the very latest, after the Olmütz accords of November 1850.[22]

Moreover, Frederick William's court was not the only official royal establishment in the Prussia of the reaction decade. His designated successor, William, the Prince of Prussia, had become military governor of the Rhine province after the revolution; and in Koblenz he and especially his wife, the Anglo- and Francophile-Princess Augusta, established a kind of "countercourt" after 1850 in implicit opposition to the officials of Frederick William's own establishment. Vastly more glittering and brilliant than its counterpart in Berlin and Potsdam, the Koblenz counter-court became a refuge for the moderate conservative opposition to the so-called "high conservative" elites that so often seemed to have the upper hand in the capital itself. It also provided a kind of institutional focus for William's resistance to his older brother's policies, which reached a climax at the time of the Oriental crisis in 1853–1854.[23] Many of the individuals associated with the Koblenz court were linked to the *Wochenblatt* party of Moritz August von Bethmann-Hollweg, and quite a few of them in turn assumed ministerial and other positions in the "New Era" cabinets that were established after Frederick William's incapacitation and his brother's assumption of the regency in 1857–1858. In other words, the Koblenz court had served as a kind of training ground for New Era elites; but with the coming of the constitutional conflict they—and Queen Augusta, their sponsor—increasingly found themselves on the defensive.[24]

What, then, was the political significance of the court after 1861? Surprisingly, that question is not as easy to answer as it may seem; Günther Grünthal's forthcoming study of the New Era and the constitutional conflict will no doubt shed some new light on it. It is well known, of course, that the effective bases of monarchical power and authority had survived the trials of the years between 1848 and 1867, and that the most obvious manifestation of that continuing authority could be found in the royal *Kommandogewalt* over the military. One of the most interesting and heretofore insufficiently regarded aspects of Frederick William IV's reign was the ferocity with which he sustained royal control over the military during the constitutional debates after December 1848. Throughout the reaction decade the king remained adamant in his resistance to parliamentary or ministerial authority over the Prussian army. As he put it in an extremely important royal minute of 1 July 1849, "Every officer sees in the King his personal master, who promotes him, protects him, and represents him. The country owes the reliability and the devotion of the army to this intimate relationship between the army and its supreme warlord. . . . Only by unalterably maintaining the old—and uniquely intertwined—relationship between crown and army can the army remain what it is: the firm pillar upon which the monarchy leans."[25] In his defense of this ultimate royal prerogative Frederick William demonstrated none of the vacillation and uncertainty for which he was otherwise so notorious; the preservation of the royal *Kommandogewalt* that he so vigorously defended throughout his lifetime was finally assured after his death "by the victories and the Indemnity Bill of 1866."[26] Moreover, even under the unmartial Frederick William, the so-called *maison militaire*—especially the reporting adjutants general and the "aides-de-camp in service" to the monarch (*dienstthuende Flügeladjutanten*)—had been one of the foci of the court as a political structure; and obviously that remained the case after 1861, despite the increasingly important role of the General Staff and the Military Cabinet.[27]

Still, there can be little doubt that under William I the court lost some of its importance as a center of political action and intrigue. Bismarck himself liked to fulminate against what he called the *"junkerhaften Idiotentum abgelegter Hofschranzen,"* and often regarded the court as an instrument in the hands of his enemy, Queen (and later Empress) Augusta.[28] Certainly many of William I's court officials could be counted in the camp of Bismarck's opponents. Among them were the veteran Minister of the Royal House, Alexander von Schleinitz, who Philipp zu Eulenburg once described as "among the most hated personalities in the Bismarck family" and who was suspected by the chancellor of constantly conniving with Augusta through the vehicle of a court-based "kitchen cabinet" or *Gegenministerium*.[29] Still other court officials shared William's distaste for Bismarckian innovation, encouraging him, for example, in his resistance to accepting the Imperial title in 1870.[30] Accordingly, Bismarck seems to have devoted a great deal of attention to the Prussian court and to its political neutralization, especially before the early 1880s. Not surprisingly, he turned out to be exceptionally skillful as a court politician. He had himself once asserted that he was really destined to be a courtier, and not a politician or a diplomat; and he had a deserved reputation for his manners, his deference, and his faultless etiquette at grand court occasions.[31] More important, though, he was able to forge alliances with crucial court officials and members of William I's court entourage; these arrangements in turn enabled him to counter the supposed intrigues of rivals for the old emperor's attention and to influence administrative and military appointments. Among his allies were General Emil von Albedyll, head of the Military Cabinet; Count Heinrich August von Lehndorff, who as adjutant general occupied the same powerful position at court that Leopold von Gerlach had enjoyed under Frederick William IV; and Count Perponcher-Sedlnitzky, Supreme Marshal of the Court. In the words of one embittered enemy, "This ring disposes over effective instruments to encourage the vanity, greed, and ambition of the high and mighty. These gentlemen can arrange for the distribution of orders, ennoblements, the appearance of the emperor at balls and festivities, and a hundred other small but effective forms of preferment."[32]

This reference to ennoblements and awards leads to a second theme, and that is the changing nature of monarchical representation and monarchical symbolism between 1848 and 1890. Again, rather little work has been done in this area, despite the important contributions of such scholars as Werner K. Blessing, Elisabeth Fehrenbach, Manfred Hanisch, and Isabel V. Hull to our understanding of these problems, especially for the period after 1871 or 1890.[33] With a couple of important exceptions, the rituals and ceremonials of court life in constitutional Prussia did not serve as significant vehicles for what might be called "monarchical socialization," or for the encouragement of new forms of popular monarchy. To be sure, such occasions as the annual Opera Ball, to which members of the Berlin-Potsdam plutocracy could expect to be invited, were court-organized affairs that always attracted a certain amount of public attention; but, for the most part, after 1850 the annual court season between Christmas and Lent tended to be both dull and socially exclusive, as lists of invitees to court functions suggest.[34]

The most important exception to this rule was the Festival of the Coronation and Orders, or *Krönungs- und Ordensfest*, which took place every year on that Sunday closest to 18 January, the date on which the Prussian monarchy and the Prussian-dominated Reich had been established in 1701 and 1871 respectively. Perhaps the best example of an "invented" monarchical tradition in nineteenth-century Prussia, it had only been established in 1810, and by the time of Prussia's transition to constitutionalism in the 1850s and 1860s it had become a splendid showcase for monarchical values. The festival was a celebration of all those individuals who had received honors or decorations in the previous year, regardless of rank or status. It always took place in the presence of the king and queen, all the royal princes, high-ranking officers, and members of the various orders of the Prussian crown. The categories that were usually most heavily represented were the Fourth Class of the Order of the Red Eagle as well as the General Badge of Honor, both of which were frequently awarded to humble public servants and private citizens. The opportunity for otherwise obscure local notables to travel to the capital and be received by the king represented a highly effective form of monarchical socialization, and one which no doubt contributed to those individuals' prestige and to the popularization of monarchical values in their communities. During the festival itself the usual rules of court precedence were suspended, which further demonstrated the singularity and honor of the whole affair. The ceremony ended with a great banquet to which, by the late 1860s, more than a thousand guests were invited.[35]

Of the various forms of monarchical representation and socialization after 1848, the Coronation Festival was clearly the most court oriented. But there were plenty of additional opportunities, ceremonial and otherwise, for the king to make himself visible to his subjects in impressive ways. Even before 1848, Frederick William IV had shown himself to be an indefatigable traveler who loved to make public appearances; although William I was much less voluble and gregarious, and his annual travel routine (for example, to Bad Ems or to Baden-Baden) more predictable, he too managed to stay in the public eye rather constantly. So, for example, between 1842 and 1880 both monarchs journeyed frequently to Cologne to participate in widely advertised ceremonies associated with the completion of Cologne Cathedral as a symbol of German unity. And there were other activities besides, including the lavish coronation of William I in Königsberg in October 1861, the first ceremony of this sort in Prussia since Frederick I's coronation in 1701.[36] All of these activities have to be understood within the context of a continuing, and surprisingly successful, campaign to modernize and popularize the Prussian monarchy. This attempt to shape and mobilize public opinion was based upon an image of the king as the *real* binding force of state and society in Prussia, bound to his subjects both by the constitution and, more important, by ties of mutual affection and loyalty. Those ties were in turn to be sanctified and justified by the king's ordination "through the Grace of God," and sustained by his role as supreme *Feldherr* of the Prussian army. This kind of monarchical socialization—reinforced through the influences of the educational system, the military, the press, and the church—played no small part in encouraging the development of an increasingly modern and popular form of monarchism in Prussia that reflected those larger processes by which conservative elites adapted themselves, with varying degrees of success, to an altered institutional setting. (Grünthal has aptly described this process as the "pseudoconstitutionalization" of Prussia's elites.)[37]

This leads us to the third and final theme of this chapter: the relationship of the monarchy in postrevolutionary Prussia to other constitutive elements of the Prussian state. During the reaction decade Frederick William IV largely succeeded in his efforts to sustain the effective power and authority of monarchical institutions. Despite frequent opposition from his entourage and his own relatives, he was determined to persist in his project of monarchical restoration; and he was far more successful than many historians have realized. Despite his reputation for instability and unpredictability, he remained adamant in his conviction and tenacious in his efforts to ensure that the monarchy should continue at the heart of the Prussian state. He thus left a legacy of effective monarchical authority that William I—or, rather, Bismarck—was able to utilize after 1861. As Frederick William put it in a letter to his brother and heir in March 1852, "I will not give up, and I will come back again and again until I have won. And my victory is much less for me than for you and your son."[38]

Günther Grünthal has recently argued that the "Manteuffel system" of the 1850s anticipated Bismarck's own style of governance.[39] Similarly, it can be argued that Frederick William IV's reassertion of the prerogatives of the Prussian crown during the same period also contributed to Bismarck's later success; for crown and court continued to occupy the strategic and institutional center of the Prussian state, around which the other structures—the bureaucracy, the cabinet, the military, *and* the parliament—themselves continued to revolve. To be sure, it would be absurd and simplistic to attribute this development solely to Frederick William IV's own tenacity, determination, and individual effort. After all, he was the beneficiary of the so-called "*rettende Tat*" of the Camarilla and Count Brandenburg in November-December 1848 and of the decade of reaction that followed it. Nevertheless, his contribution to the preservation of monarchy in a constitutional age was vital, if not decisive. So too, as Dirk Blasius has recently observed, was his contribution to the increasing rigidity and narrowness of German public life thereafter.[40]

Still, it is important to emphasize that in constitutional Prussia the crown was neither absolutist nor all-powerful. It may have been the inescapable institutional focus of the Prussian state, but it also had to make important compromises with other structures and institutions. One revealing incident from the reaction decade illustrates the extent to which the crown had to confront the limits of its authority in a constitutional age. In the summer of 1852 Frederick William IV was taking his usual August vacation on the Baltic island of Rügen. He had never really accommodated himself to the loss of his closest political confidant, Joseph Maria von Radowitz, who had been forced out of office during the autumn crisis of 1850, that had ended with the Olmütz accords. Now, almost two years later, Frederick William decided on his own, and without consulting Minister President Manteuffel, to appoint Radowitz as head of the Prussian military education system. The king issued the order directly to War minister Eduard von Bonin and simply ignored the minister president. Frederick William insisted that as supreme commander of the Prussian army he was not obliged to inform anyone, especially civilians, about his military decisions. It was all too much for Radowitz's old rival Manteuffel, who journeyed to Rügen and threatened to resign. Frederick William immediately realized that he had committed a gaffe, effusively begged Manteuffel to stay, and on 8 September 1852 agreed to a cabinet order that systematized and dramatically increased the powers of the Minister President. That official now gained the right to proclaim the affairs of a single ministry to be a matter for general cabinet discussion. The order further stipulated that any minister who wished to report to the king should inform the minister president first, so that the latter could, if he wished, attend the meeting. Finally, in most cases the minister president would be the official who would pass cabinet reports on to the king. It had thus become much more difficult for the monarch to circumvent his chief minister.

Manteuffel had turned a serious personal and political embarrassment into a major political victory and one that represented a real barrier to monarchical absolutism.[41] Still, Manteuffel never managed either to gain full control over his cabinet or to assert the real autonomy of his own office. With Bismarck, of course, things were different, at least until 1890: For, as is well known, in March 1890 the same cabinet order, that had so strengthened Manteuffel's hand, now played a critical role in precipitating the Iron Chancellor's own fall from power. Ironically, in departing from office Bismarck tried to justify his support for the cabinet order by posing as a defender of constitutionalism and ministerial responsibility.[42] The young William II won his confrontation with Bismarck; but in the years that followed, he rapidly managed to deplete what Friedrich von Holstein called the "royalist capital" that his predecessors had so assiduously cultivated.[43] By 1918, sixty-eight years after Frederick William IV's oath in the Knights' Hall, there was no more room for monarchy in Germany, constitutional or otherwise.

NOTES

This chapter originated many years ago in one of Gordon Craig's unforgettable graduate seminars at Stanford. I am grateful to him for the advice and guidance that he has so generously provided to me for more than twenty-five years. I am also grateful to the Alexander von Humboldt Foundation, the National Endowment for the Humanities, and the Kalamazoo College faculty development program for their financial assistance.

1. David E. Barclay, *Frederick William IV and the Prussian Monarchy 1840–1861* (Oxford, 1995), 182–83.

2. Handwritten remarks of Crown Prince Frederick William (later Emperor Frederick III), "Friedrich Wilhelm IV. (Stellung zur Verfassung ab 1848)," undated, Geheimes Staatsarchiv Preussischer Kulturbesitz, ehemalige Merseburger Bestände (hereafter: GStA PK [M]), Brandenburg-Preussisches Hausarchiv (hereafter: BPH), Rep. 50 F 1 Nr. 7, Bl. 2. For a description of the king's oath-taking ceremony, see Barclay, *Frederick William IV*, 214–15.

3. Günther Grünthal, "Bemerkungen zur Kamarilla im nachmärzlichen Preussen," in *Friedrich Wilhelm IV. in seiner Zeit. Beiträge eines Colloquiums*, ed. Otto Büsch (Berlin, 1987), 46.

4. Frederick William IV to Francis Joseph I, 28–29 September 1853, GStA PK (M), BPH Rep. 50 J Nr. 939, Bl. 59^v–60.

5. Anthony Arblaster, "Taking Monarchy Seriously," *New Left Review* 174 (April 1989): 97–110. Among various titles, see David Cannadine, "The Context, Performance and Meaning of Ritual: The British Monarchy and the 'Invention of Tradition', c. 1820–1977," in *The Invention of Tradition*, eds. Eric Hobsbawm and Terence Ranger (Cambridge, 1983), 101–64; Karl Ferdinand Werner, ed., *Hof, Kultur und Politik im 19. Jahrhundert. Akten des 18. Deutsch-französischen Historikerkolloquiums Darmstadt vom 27.-30. September 1982* (Bonn, 1985); Philip Mansel, *The Eagle in Splendour: Napoleon I and His Court* (London, 1987); idem, *The Court of France 1789–1830* (Cambridge, 1988); Karl Möckl, ed., *Hof und Hofgesellschaft in den deutschen Staaten im 19. und beginnenden 20. Jahrhundert* (Boppard am Rhein, 1990); Richard Wortman, "Rule by Sentiment: Alexander II's Journeys through the Russian Empire," *American Historical Review* 95, 3 (June 1990): 745-71. Professor David Cannadine (Columbia University) is planning a major study of the British monarchy in the nineteenth and twentieth centuries. Recent years have also witnessed the appearance of a number of academically serious biographical studies of nineteenth-century European monarchs, including Ferdinand VII of Spain, Louis XVIII, Charles X, Victoria and Albert, Napoleon III, Leopold II of Belgium, Francis Joseph, and Nicholas II.

6. For the period before 1848, see the recent studies by Heinz Gollwitzer, *Ludwig I. von Bayern. Königtum im Vormärz. Eine politische Biographie* (Munich, 1986), and Thomas Stamm-Kuhlmann, *König in Preussens grosser Zeit. Friedrich Wilhelm III. Der Melancholiker auf dem Thron* (Berlin, 1992). On Frederick III, see Patricia Kollander, *Frederick III: Germany's Liberal Emperor* (Westport, Conn., 1995). For William II see the growing body of literature by Lamar Cecil, Willibald Gutsche, Isabel V. Hull, Thomas Kohut, and John C. G. Röhl. For examples of recent work on the rulers of medium-sized states, see Paul Sauer, *Der schwäbische Zar. Friedrich, Württembergs erster König* (Stuttgart, 1984); Max Brunner, *Die Hofgesellschaft. Die führende Gesellschaftsschicht Bayerns während der Regierungszeit König Maximilian II.*

(Munich, 1987); Haus der Bayerischen Geschichte, ed., *König Maximilian II. von Bayern 1848-1864* (Rosenheim, 1988); Walter Fellmann, *Sachsens letzter König. Friedrich August III.* (Berlin and Leipzig, 1992).

7. To be sure, the last few years have witnessed a spate of interest in Frederick William IV. For example, see the essays in Otto Büsch, ed., *Friedrich Wilhelm IV. in seiner Zeit*; Frank-Lothar Kroll, *Friedrich Wilhelm IV. und das Staatsdenken der deutschen Romantik* (Berlin, 1990); Walter Bussmann, *Zwischen Preussen und Deutschland. Friedrich Wilhelm IV. Eine Biographie* (Berlin, 1990); Dirk Blasius, *Friedrich Wilhelm IV. 1795-1861. Psychopathologie und Geschichte* (Göttingen, 1992); Barclay, *Frederick William IV*; and David E. Barclay, *Anarchie und guter Wille. Friedrich Wilhelm IV. und die preussische Monarchie* (Berlin, 1995).

8. For example, see Jules Laforgue, *Berlin, la cour et la ville* (Paris, 1922), 23–26, 52–71. Laforgue, a brilliant French poet, worked for a time in the 1880s as *Vorleser* for Empress Augusta; his panorama of court life during that decade remains an important source.

9. Günther Grünthal, *Parlamentarismus in Preussen 1848/49–1857/58. Preussischer Konstitutionalismus—Parlament und Regierung in der Reaktionsära* (Düsseldorf, 1982); Wolfram Siemann, *Gesellschaft im Aufbruch. Deutschland 1849–1871* (Frankfurt am Main, 1990).

10. Dieter Langewiesche, *Liberalismus in Deutschland* (Frankfurt am Main, 1988), 65.

11. Hans-Ulrich Wehler, *Deutsche Gesellschaftsgeschichte*, vol. 2, *Von der Reformära bis zur industriellen und politischen "Deutschen Doppelrevolution" 1815-1845/49* (Munich, 1987), 299.

12. Thomas Stamm-Kuhlmann, "Der Hof Friedrich Wilhelms III. von Preussen 1797 bis 1840," in *Hof und Hofgesellschaft*, ed. Möckl, 275.

13. For this translation of *Kronfideikommiss*, see Rudolf Braun, "Taxation, Sociopolitical Structure, and State-Building: Great Britain and Brandenburg-Prussia," in *The Formation of National States in Western Europe*, ed. Charles Tilly (Princeton, 1975), 277.

14. Hermann Schulze, *Die Hausgesetze der regierenden deutschen Fürstenhäuser*, 3 vols. (Jena, 1883), 3: sec. 2, 619–21; Herbert Obenaus, *Anfänge des Parlamentarismus in Preussen bis 1848* (Düsseldorf, 1984), 125–26; Stamm-Kuhlmann, "Hof," 278–80.

15. For details on the above paragraphs, see David E. Barclay, "Hof und Hofgesellschaft in Preussen in der Zeit Friedrich Wilhelms IV. (1840 bis 1857). Überlegungen und Fragen," in *Hof und Hofgesellschaft*, ed. Möckl, 333–44. Cf. John C. G. Röhl, "Hof und Hofgesellschaft unter Kaiser Wilhelm II.," in idem, *Kaiser, Hof und Staat. Wilhelm II. und die deutsche Politik* (Munich, 1987), 80–82.

16. Ibid., 111.

17. Count Anton zu Stolberg-Wernigerode to Frederick William IV, 26 January 1854, GStA PK (M), Geheimes Zivilkabinett, 2.2.1., Nr. 3291, Bl. 22^v-23.

18. Barclay, "Hof und Hofgesellschaft," 331–33.

19. Laforgue, *Berlin*, 23.

20. Count Friedrich von Thun-Hohenstein to Count Karl Ferdinand von Buol-Schauenstein, 23 April 1853, Österreichisches Staatsarchiv, Vienna: Haus-, Hof- und Staatsarchiv, P.A. III, Karton 48, VIII. Interna Preussens, fol. 2^r-3^r; Barclay, "Hof und Hofgesellschaft," 334–37.

21. Lord Bloomfield to Earl of Clarendon, 10 February 1854, Public Record Office, Kew, FO 64/368.

22. David E. Barclay, "The Court Camarilla and the Politics of Monarchical Restoration in Prussia, 1848–58," in *Between Reform, Reaction, and Resistance: Studies in the History of German Conservatism from 1789 to the Present*, ed. Larry Eugene Jones and James Retallack (New York and Oxford, 1993), 151–54.

23. On William's dispute with Frederick William, see above all Elisabeth Richert, "Die Stellung Wilhelms, des Prinzen von Preussen, zur preussischen Aussen- und Innenpolitik der Zeit von 1848 bis 1857" (Inaug.-Diss. Universität Berlin, 1948); Peter Rassow, *Der Konflikt König Friedrich Wilhelms IV. mit dem Prinzen von Preussen im Jahre 1854. Eine preussische Staatskrise* (Mainz, 1961).

24. Karl Heinz Börner, *Kaiser Wilhelm I. 1797 bis 1888. Deutscher Kaiser und König von Preussen. Eine Biographie* (Cologne, 1984), 109–14.

25. Text of the *Handbillett* of 1 July 1849 in "Unveröffentlichte Handbillette des Königs Friedrich Wilhelm IV.," *Deutsche Revue* 32, 4 (October–December 1907): 155–56. See also Rudolf Schmidt-Bückeburg, *Das Militärkabinett der preussischen Könige und deutschen Kaiser. Seine geschichtliche Entwicklung und staatsrechtliche Stellung 1787–1918* (Berlin, 1933), pp. 39–42; Manfred Messerschmidt, "Die politische Geschichte der preussisch-deutschen Armee," in *Handbuch zur deutschen Militärgeschichte*, vol. 2, part 4: *Militärgeschichte im 19. Jahrhundert 1814–1890*, ed. Militärgeschichtliches Forschungsamt (Munich, 1979), pt. 1, 166–68.

26. Michael Stürmer, *Das ruhelose Reich. Deutschland 1866–1918* (Berlin, 1983), 102.

27. David E. Barclay, "The Soldiers of an Unsoldierly King: The Military Advisers of Frederick William IV, 1840–1858," in *Geschichte als Aufgabe. Festschrift für Otto Büsch zu seinem 60. Geburtstag*, ed. Wilhelm Treue (Berlin, 1988), 247–66. For the rise of the General Staff and the Military Cabinet, see the masterful treatment in Gordon A. Craig, *The Politics of the Prussian Army 1640–1945*, 2d ed. (New York, 1964), 219–32.

28. Marie von Bunsen, *Kaiserin Augusta* (Berlin, 1940), 238.

29. Ernst Engelberg, *Bismarck. Das Reich in der Mitte Europas* (Berlin, 1990), 353; Otto Pflanze, *Bismarck and the Development of Germany*, vol. 2, *The Period of Consolidation, 1871–1880* (Princeton, 1990), 358.

30. Börner, *Wilhelm I.*, 210.

31. Bunsen, *Kaiserin Augusta*, 237.

32. Quoted in Börner, *Wilhelm I.*, 219–20.

33. Werner K. Blessing, *Staat und Kirche in der Gesellschaft. Institutionelle Autorität und mentaler Wandel in Bayern während des 19. Jahrhunderts* (Göttingen, 1982); Elisabeth Fehrenbach, *Wandlungen des deutschen Kaisergedankens 1871–1918* (Munich, 1969); Manfred Hanisch, *Für Fürst und Vaterland. Legitimitätsstiftung in Bayern zwischen Revolution 1848 und deutscher Einheit* (Munich, 1991); Isabel V. Hull, "Prussian Dynastic Ritual and the End of Monarchy," in *German Nationalism and the European Response, 1890–1945*, ed. Carole Fink, Isabel V. Hull, and MacGregor Knox (Norman, Okla., 1985), 13–41.

34. For example, see "Personenliste für den Karneval am Hoflager in Berlin 1854," GStA PK (M), Ministerium des Königlichen Hauses, 2.2.10., Nr. 514.

35. For further details, see David E. Barclay, "Ritual, Ceremonial, and the 'Invention' of a Monarchical Tradition in Nineteenth-Century Prussia," in *Euro-*

pean Monarchy: Its Evolution and Practice from Roman Antiquity to Modern Times, ed. Heinz Duchhardt, Richard A. Jackson, and David Sturdy (Stuttgart, 1992), 211–13.

36. Ibid., 217–18; Walter Bussmann, "Die Krönung Wilhelms I. am 18. Oktober 1861. Eine Demonstration des Gottesgnadentums im preussischen Verfassungsstaat," in *Politik und Konfession. Festschrift für Konrad Repgen zum 60. Geburtstag*, ed. Dieter Albrecht et al. (Berlin, 1983), 189–212.

37. Grünthal, "Bemerkungen," 46. The above paragraph largely follows the more extensive analysis in Barclay, "Ritual," 218–19.

38. Frederick William IV to Prince of Prussia, 4 March 1852, GStA PK (M), BPH Rep. 50 J Nr. 976, Bl. 4v.

39. Günther Grünthal, "Bismarck Anticipated? The Manteuffel 'System' and the Politics of Reaction in Postrevolutionary Prussia, 1848–58," paper presented at the American Historical Association, 107th Annual Meeting, Washington, D.C., 28 December 1992.

40. Blasius, *Friedrich Wilhelm IV.*, 245.

41. Leopold von Gerlach, diary (20 August 1852), Gerlach-Archiv am Institut für politische Wissenschaft, Friedrich-Alexander-Universität Erlangen-Nürnberg, "Abschriften des Nachlasses Leopold von Gerlachs," 9: 152, 153–54; Frederick William IV to Queen Elisabeth, 2 and 10 September 1852, GStA PK (M), BPH Rep. 50 J Nr. 995 Fasz. 23, Bl. 9–11v, 20–22v; Otto Freiherr von Manteuffel, *Unter Friedrich Wilhelm IV. Denkwürdigkeiten des Ministers Otto Freiherrn von Manteuffel*, ed. Heinrich von Poschinger, 3 vols. (Berlin, 1901), 2:242–51; Ernst Rudolf Huber, *Deutsche Verfassungsgeschichte seit 1789*, vol. 3, *Bismarck und das Reich*, 3d ed. (Stuttgart, 1988), 65; John R. Gillis, *The Prussian Bureaucracy in Crisis 1840–1860: Origins of an Administrative Ethos* (Stanford, 1971), 147.

42. See the recent description of Bismarck's clash with William II in Otto Pflanze, *Bismarck and the Development of Germany*, vol. 3, *The Period of Fortification, 1880–1898* (Princeton, 1990), 363–73.

43. Bernd Sösemann, "Der Verfall des Kaisergedankens im Ersten Weltkrieg," in *Der Ort Kaiser Wilhelms II. in der deutschen Geschichte*, ed. John C. G. Röhl (with Elisabeth Müller-Luckner) (Munich, 1991), p. 148; Barclay, *Frederick William IV*, 289.

4 Karl Lamprecht: A Historian's History
Roger Chickering

Karl Lamprecht died on 10 May 1915. Amidst the urgent news of the war, his death attracted little notice outside Leipzig. In this city, however, the historian had remained a leading figure both in the university and among the municipal elites long after his defeat in a spectacular controversy over historical method; and his passing was an important event. It was commemorated three days later at a service in the university chapel, where his colleagues and friends paid tribute to a remarkable career. One of these friends was Arthur Nikisch, whose tribute was to conduct the Gewandhaus orchestra in a performance of the funeral march from the *Eroica*.[1]

The musical tribute was of special significance. Before his death Lamprecht himself had arranged for its performance, and most of those who heard it in the university chapel could recognize it as a final reading by the historian on his own life. Several years earlier, in a passage in his magnum opus, Lamprecht had characterized Beethoven's symphony as a musical portrait of "the passage of genius through this world of imperfection—its heroic struggle to realize and exert its innermost essence, the moment of its apparent defeat, but then its joyful recovery and final victory in an ideal world."[2]

It was fitting that Lamprecht chose to bid farewell to his friends in this fashion, for his entire career was in a sense devoted to framing an appropriate reading of his own life—in other words, to writing his own history.[3] The immense corpus of his scholarship constituted a kind of autodiscourse, in which he framed representations of his own life and career. This feature of his work has significantly complicated the efforts of subsequent scholars to analyze the historian's history, for his autobiographical understanding intrudes insistently into his biography. It framed in his own mind the professional experiences that were central to his life; and in framing these experiences new, other scholars cannot ignore its powerful claims. Therein lies the challenge, the charm, and the exasperation of the historian's history.

The problem emerges in the central and most spectacular scenes in the biography. The first volume of Karl Lamprecht's *German History* was published in 1891. At the time it appeared, the author was being hailed as one of the rising stars in the German historical profession; and he had just accepted a chair at the University of Leipzig, which then ranked second in prestige only to the University of Berlin. He presented his grand project, of which this volume marked the beginning, as an exercise in "cultural history" (*Kulturgeschichte*)—a genre perhaps better described today as "total history." Lamprecht proposed to write the history of the German nation from the tribal era to his own day. But he would also, he announced, write the history of every phase of the nation's experience—not merely the history of politics, work, and social structure, but of ideas, morals, and manners. He proposed to bring unity to the vast diversity of the nation's past by means of an elaborate scheme of historical periods. A succession of epochs, he wrote, not only bounded the essential chronological units that lent meaning and pattern to historical development; these periods, which he called *Kulturzeitalter*, also defined the essential commonalties that stretched across and unified all dimensions of the nation's existence—material and ideal—at any moment of that development.

Lamprecht identified five such epochs and argued that developmental laws prescribed the nation's procession through them: they were the "Symbolic" period (from prehistory to about A.D. 350), the "Typical" (350–1050), the "Conventional" (1050–1450), the "Individualistic" (1450–1750), and the "Subjectivistic" (from 1750 to his own day). Several features of this schema are critical to an understanding of what then happened. In the first place, the historian insisted that each epoch imposed norms and conventions that conditioned collective behavior, which he also insisted was the proper object of historical scholarship—the only kind of human behavior accessible to scientific study and empirical investigation. In the second place, the historian appeared to accord to the material realm a privileged place in his analysis and to argue that economic and social change provided the motor of transformations in politics and the realm of ideal culture. He argued, for example, that the evolution of forms of bondage and dependence in medieval society and politics conditioned prevailing ideas of collective identity and obligation, until the loosening of the bonds of feudalism led to a more profound kind of moral consciousness, which was based upon a growing awareness of individual identity. Finally, the historian argued that the nation was a cultural, not a political phenomenon and that the state, no less than moral precepts and forms of aesthetic expression, derived from anterior forces of social and economic development.

It is difficult not to marvel at the majestic vision, ingenuity, scope, and ambition of Lamprecht's project. The volumes that now began to appear touched on the history of lifestyles, diet, manners, tastes in clothing, the family, sexuality, education, popular religion, and a host of other topics that have since occupied social and cultural historians. In Lamprecht's volumes one found things that could be found nowhere else. Yet these volumes also harbored grave problems; and their broad vision and methodological audacity made them as vulnerable as they were marvelous.

In its emphasis on lawful development, collective behavior, and the epiphenomenal status of the political and ideal, Lamprecht's *Kulturgeschichte* seemed calculated to challenge the methodological consensus that then reigned in the German historical profession.[4] Those who participated in this consensus—and it comprised virtually every academic historian in Germany, save one—emphasized the singularity and diversity of all historical events. These scholars rejected abstract systems of laws, norms, or other concepts that implied the limitation of historical actors' freedom to make moral decisions. The office of the historian was to reexperience this freedom by means of a process of sympathetic intuition. The historians who subscribed to this view insisted furthermore that the motive forces in history were the ideas that informed the purposive behavior of all historical actors, be they individual human beings or human communities. The highest of these communities was the state, whose development accordingly constituted both the essential theme of history and the proper focus of historical study.

As installments of Lamprecht's breathtaking project poured out at a rapid rate in the early 1890s, the profession's leadership mobilized to beat back the challenge. Headquarters for the campaign were the bastions of the profession in the capital. At the University of Berlin, Hans Delbrück, Max Lenz, and their students began to examine Lamprecht's claims and to scrutinize his scholarship; several blocks away, in the editorial offices of the *Historische Zeitschrift*, Heinrich von Sybel, Max Lehmann, and a young editorial assistant, Friedrich Meinecke, did the same.[5]

The battle began in earnest in 1895, by which time Lamprecht had carried his survey, in six volumes, to the Peace of Westphalia. The controversy, which raged over the next four years and quickly became known as the *Methodenstreit*, was one of the most remarkable spectacles in the history of any country's historiography; and it compelled the contending historians, most of whom, like Lamprecht, were young men (in their thirties), to examine a range of methodological issues that they had hitherto taken for granted.[6] What was the proper object of historical study? Was it individual or collective action, state or society? What was the source of historical knowledge? Could the historian seek, like the natural scientist, to explain events by means of induction, statistics, and causal analysis? If so, what were the attending implications for free will and moral autonomy? Could the historian dispense with theory? What was the role of hypothesis, comparison, and generalization in historical scholarship?

The mountains of polemical literature that addressed these questions revealed an uncommon amount of confusion, self-deception, obfuscation, and posturing on both sides. Lamprecht moved into ever more radical statements of his position, for he was determined to turn the debate into what might later (with qualification) be called a paradigm conflict, which pitted the "old direction" of German historiography, whose symbol was Leopold von Ranke, with the "new direction," whose symbol was Lamprecht himself. The controversy pivoted on charges raised against Lamprecht in two devastating reviews of his work. Paradoxically, the first was positive. It came, however, from the pen of Franz Mehring, the country's leading Social Democratic cultural critic; and it confirmed the worst suspicions of the profession's leaders, who had argued that Lamprecht's position was implicated ideologically in historical materialism.[7] Lamprecht himself was enough shaken by this charge that he abruptly changed his position in the middle of the debate, so that Marx and Engels, whose influence was transparent in the first volumes of his survey, retreated before Leibniz, Herder, and Hegel, who inspired the transformation of Lamprecht's five developmental epochs into spiritual entities which, but for the terminology, looked a lot like Ranke's ideas with an admixture of Comte, Buckle, and Darwin.[8]

Lamprecht scored telling points in his counterattacks, but in the end his failings were more critical and of a different order than those of his adversaries. These failings were the subject of the second devastating review, which Hermann Oncken, then a student of Max Lenz in Berlin, published in late 1897 in Delbrück's journal, the *Preussische Jahrbücher*.[9] Oncken subjected one of Lamprecht's volumes, the one that dealt with political developments in the late sixteenth and early seventeenth centuries, to line-by-line, word-by-word scrutiny. He revealed how Lamprecht had been able to produce his volumes so rapidly. The review disclosed scores of careless errors (sixteen wrong dates in a passage of one hundred pages), factual mistakes, garbled sequences of events, misidentified characters, and manifold inconsistencies and contradictions. Worse, by means of parallel analyses of texts, Oncken revealed that Lamprecht had lifted major portions of his volume almost verbatim and without attribution, from standard monographs and schoolbook surveys of the era in question.

Oncken's astonishing revelations destroyed Lamprecht. The reviewer's charges addressed a dimension of scholarship that was at once technical and ethical. In his carelessness and haste, Lamprecht stood accused of violating the profession's most basic standards of integrity. By impugning his scholarship, Oncken destroyed the credibility of Lamprecht's methodological position. The profession's leadership thus escaped from the controversy with the fundamentals of his own position intact, in fact fortified. The primacy of political history and a hermeneutic of sympathetic intuition survived to inform the writing of academic history in Germany for the next half-century—along with an animus against theory, comparison, and social history, which henceforth became the preserves of economists, sociologists, ethnographers, and geographers in the German academy.

The outcome of the *Methodenstreit* suggests an interpretive framework for Lamprecht's biography. The historian's history displays the classic features of tragic heroism. His hubris provoked the wrath of the profession's elders. These men thereupon summoned their young followers to seek out the hero's flaw and defeat him in battle. The triumphant contenders were rewarded in the end with distinctions, the vanquished apostate banished. In no sense does this schema exaggerate the outcome of the methodological controversy. Without exception, the young scholars who took the field against Lamprecht were rewarded with professorial chairs—Meinecke, for example, in Freiburg in 1901, Oncken in Giessen in 1906. The banishment of Lamprecht was as complete as could be imposed, within the German tradition of academic freedom, on a scholar with lifetime tenure at a university. His colleagues shunned him. The professional journals neither published nor reviewed his subsequent scholarship. His broad conception of history was declared anathema, along with his views on methodology. His students could not find positions in the German academy, for association with Lamprecht was a stigma that practically assured professional failure.

The historian as tragic hero? Judgment is best withheld for the moment, for there are some additional scenes. The historian's behavior during the *Methodenstreit* makes another biographical problem acute. Why did he act as he did? What accounts for his eccentricity? Why did he become the great renegade, who single-handedly challenged his own profession's most basic creeds? The contours of Lamprecht's early career provide no help whatsoever, for they conform so faithfully to typical patterns of background and training among German historians (and the German professoriate in general) that one might almost speak of Lamprecht as a "modal figure."[10] He was born in 1856 in provincial Saxony. His father was a Lutheran pastor; the boy grew up in the pious ambiance of the Pfarrhaus, that great locus of German culture and cultivation—the origination point of a parade of genius that includes Lessing, the Schlegels, Droysen, Theodor Mommsen, Burckhardt, Schelling, Schleiermacher, and Dilthey. Lamprecht's education and professional training likewise typified in its contours the experience of the German academic middle class. After attending *Schulpforta*, perhaps the most famous boarding school in Germany (whose alumni included Klopstock, Fichte, Ranke, and Nietzsche—the last also the son of a pastor), Lamprecht studied at the universities in Göttingen, Munich, and Leipzig, where he took his doctorate. He then habilitated in Bonn, where he served several years as *Privatdozent* and extraordinary professor before he arrived among the elite of university chairholders in 1890.

Upon closer scrutiny, however, the historian's early experiences prove to be not so typical. His relationship to his father was difficult, owing to his father's bereavement over an older son (also named Karl Lamprecht), who had died two years before the historian was born.[11] The father idealized the dead child and regularly invoked his presence in front of the other boy of the same name. The evidence that survives, principally in a memoir and in the correspondence between father and son, allows only the most tentative reconstruction of the psychological problems that this extraordinary situation created, as the young Karl Lamprecht found himself in constant competition for the attention, affection, and approval of his father—in circumstances all the more bewildering for the physical absence of his competitor. Several motifs surfaced in the boy's behavior at play that suggested an effort to repair what would today be called in another idiom his "narcissistic injury"—to establish an acceptable sense of himself in his own eyes (and his father's) as a being separate from his dead brother. These motifs included a passion for collecting and a proclivity for solitary ventures beyond the grain fields that established the bounds of home and village, despite (or more probably, because of) the risk of his father's wrath, which represented a form of recognition of the child. Other traits in the boy indicated, however, that the problems of identity were not entirely resolved, that he was growing up unsettled—hurried, restless, impatient, and careless. In addition, fantasies of his own immortality suggested that he was nurturing aspirations that knew no bounds.

During his university studies, Lamprecht was exposed to the conventions and values that already reigned in the German historical profession and identified the state as the proper object of study. The student soon became uncomfortable within the bounds that these conventions prescribed, and he ventured out. He became interested in the force of social and economic circumstance (*Zustände*) which, he was convinced, intruded into and conditioned the history of the state. His studies became unconventional. He read in the wider fields of philosophy, psychology, economics, and social theory, where he encountered not only Comte, but Marx and Engels. During a semester of study in Munich he also became fascinated with art history after an encounter with the work of Jacob Burckhardt. By the time he habilitated in Bonn, the outlines of the great project had begun to take shape in his mind. His goal was—to extend the metaphors in which it was originally framed—to venture into the broadest fields imaginable, to collect the particulars of the past, and to synthesize them all into a total history of the nation's development. His success, he concluded, would make him the legitimate heir to Ranke, the nation's greatest historian. In the 1890s, then, he began to carry out the project with a fury that suggested not only the survival of boyhood traits in the adult historian, but the emotional significance that the project had acquired.

The product of his furious labors contained additional evidence of the project's emotional significance. An extended discussion of the early volumes of the *German History* is out of place here. It suffices to emphasize several themes in order to suggest that what purported to be the history of the German nation was in fact the history of something else. A close reading of the work reveals several subtexts. The central theme of the work was the interaction of material and ideal culture, but the key to the whole project lay in the development of ideal culture. This story comprised several interrelated plots, each of which moved toward its own telos. As the core of ideal culture, the historian traced the evolution of German national consciousness, the growth of a sense of collective identity. The specific contours of this development, however, betrayed the fact that it was a metaphor for other kinds of growth.

Lamprecht's *German History* was, on the one hand, the story of the growth and maturation of German culture and of the educated or cultivated middle class, whose destiny in his schema, particularly with the onset of the period of Individualism, was to serve as the custodian of this culture. Here the historian was recounting the history of his own class and registering its claims to exercise spiritual leadership in the new state that had emerged from the great upheavals of the mid-nineteenth century to bring fulfillment to the development of national identity.

Another subplot was even more revealing. Lamprecht's *German History* was in the last analysis an essay on personal experience. The subject of this subplot was the historian himself. The text was a chronicle of cumulative personal growth, in which the primary motif was the progressive emergence of a sense of individual identity, which Lamprecht understood as self-knowledge through knowledge of the world. In his account, personal growth had both an inward and an outward aspect—a social and a psychological dimension. The loosening of outer, institutional constraints at the end of the German Middle Ages corresponded to both the increasing subjection of the individual will to the intellect and to the growing weight of the intellect in the makeup of German culture.

In Lamprecht's schema, the onset of the modern era (which he dated from the beginning of the Individualistic epoch in the mid-fifteenth century) directed personal growth into *Bildung*, the cultivation of the intellect, a process that he defined as intellectual transcendence to progressively higher and more comprehensive levels of understanding. The first stage was the self-transcendence required to understand the individual as a discrete and autonomous being. The next was the intellectual comprehension of collective identity, the transformation of national feelings into the "clearly understood, outwardly manifested consciousness" of nationality.[12] Luther's achievement in the period of Individualism was to broaden intellectual autonomy to the bounds of personal faith in God; and Kant's achievement, at the onset of the Subjectivistic period, was to eliminate even this constraint by bringing ethics within the domain of understanding. Personal growth thereafter meant the unfettered pursuit of *Wissenschaft*, broadening the range of human understanding, and the synthesis of all knowledge.

The *Methodenstreit* interrupted the historian before he could bring this theme to its conclusion, but the logic of his argument pointed toward the framing of a vast intellectual panorama, a *Weltbild* analogous to the perfected landscape whose artistic reproduction required, as he observed in the fifth volume of his survey, the ultimate venturing out—the transcendence of nature, a condition in which one "is able to remove oneself entirely from nature."[13] The fulfillment of personal growth was to come in self-knowledge, in the individual's transcending the final constraints to an objective understanding of the full panorama of existence, which meant historical understanding, or more accurately, the understanding uniquely afforded by *Kulturgeschichte*.

Lamprecht's *German History* was his account of his own personal growth. The progress of the German nation through the successive periods of its history was a metaphor for his own emancipation by stages from the constraints on his intellectual development. These constraints were symbolized by his father and Ranke. The first were the external constraints imposed on the boy by home and village. The next were the constraints imposed by the historiographical conventions of the profession that he intended to join. The last—and these were symbolized by both Ranke and his father—were the moral and intellectual constraints of Lutheran Christianity, which enjoined as sacrilegious the drive to grasp final truths. Lamprecht's ambition far exceeded Ranke's hope of glimpsing the "finger of God" in history. The goal of Lamprecht's *Bildung* was to understand the entire past, to frame the ultimate intellectual landscape. The success of the project would bring the fulfillment of both German history and its historian. Lamprecht's volumes broke off in the mid-1890s after recounting Luther's achievement and in anticipation of Kant's. After Kant's there could be only Lamprecht's.

This was no tragedy. The *German History* was instead a story of growth, fulfillment, and triumph. Northrup Frye and Hayden White would probably classify its plot-structure as comic, or perhaps romantic.[14] At all events, it framed the historian's autobiography and, in his own eyes at least, it gave the *Methodenstreit* a meaning altogether different from tragic heroism. In this light the controversy represented no more than a temporary setback—the fleeting advantage to his adversaries in the profession, but also the prelude to his vindication. The belief in his own ultimate fulfillment was a source of extraordinary emotional strength for the historian, who arguably might not otherwise have survived the massive blows dealt to his self-esteem during the controversy. However, the radical incongruity between the outcome of the dispute and his own construction of its significance recommends still another framework for the historian's history. This central moment in it now seems better framed in terms of dramatic miscommunication, self-deception, and misunderstanding; and these are the ingredients of low comedy or farce. In this frame the moments of grim humor in the dispute are not inadvertent. Lamprecht exclaims, "exactly my opinion," when he reads an opponent's text too quickly to recognize a paraphrase of his own opinion.[15] The historian constructs an argument whose circularity invokes the image of Baron von Münchhausen as he lifts himself out of the swamp by his own pigtail.[16] The fool was also the role cast for Lamprecht by Max Weber, who, in perhaps the most penetrating critique of both sides in the historians' controversy, made the epithet "dilettante" a synonym for him.[17]

It is best to withhold judgment a little longer, for there is still another act. The hero (or the fool) refuses to retire from the scene in the aftermath of his defeat. In 1909 Lamprecht finished the final chapter in what had become a nineteen-volume autobiography called *German History*. The later volumes, which carried the story to his own day, made the autobiographical dimension of the work even more transparent, as they documented the halting progress of all German scholarship, that crown of German culture, toward its telos, the grand synthesis of all its elements in Lamprecht's own vision of history. By the time he completed his magnum opus, Lamprecht was the most famous and popular academic historian in Germany. Close to a hundred thousand copies of his volumes were in circulation. He was also the most renowned German historian outside his own country. In the United States he was known as the comrade-in-arms of the advocates of the "New History," and at Columbia he enjoyed a triumphal moment in the fall of 1904, when he presented a cycle of lectures before an audience that included James Harvey Robinson, Carl Becker, and Charles A. Beard. The historian returned home with an honorary doctorate of laws from Columbia and an honorary life-membership in the American Historical Association.

He also returned home to the greatest triumph of his life. In an astounding feat of academic entrepreneurship, he raised a fortune in contributions from business and civic leaders, who evidently cared nothing about winners and losers in methodological disputes among academic historians. With this money he founded, in 1909, the most remarkable academic empire in Imperial Germany, the Institute for Cultural and Universal History at the University of Leipzig. The institute was a celebration of his own vision of history. It was staffed by a team of devoted young assistants, who provided instruction to the hundreds of students who passed through its doors. It was also the only place in Germany where one could study the history of the non-Western world, for upon completion of his German history, Lamprecht's interests turned naturally to the only broader fields that remained, to world history, in the belief that the historical development of every culture on earth moved lawfully through his five epochs.[18] In order to demonstrate this truth, the curriculum of his institute featured offerings in the history of the United States, Japan, China, India, and the so-called primitive peoples.

In 1910 the historian was elected rector at the University of Leipzig. He proceeded to raise more money from private sources in order to establish a complex of research institutes in the humanities at his university. These he conceived as an answer to the Kaiser-Wilhelm Society in Berlin, and he proposed to model them after his own institute. Then, on the eve of the war, Lamprecht became an advisor of sorts to Theobald von Bethmann-Hollweg, the German chancellor, with whom he had gone to boarding school. Now Lamprecht's project was to advocate a "cultural foreign policy," which would serve the interests of German power by promoting an appreciation abroad for the fruits of German culture, foremost among them a Lamprechtian vision of history.[19]

He died several months after the war broke out, still the most famous academic historian in Germany. He lived his autobiography until the end. To Beethoven's accompaniment he went to his grave the hero, who had, in his own eyes, transcended his tragic interlude to enjoy vindication and fulfillment. The historian's historian may resist this framing of the biography. Yet the biography cannot end in 1900, at the conclusion of the *Methodenstreit*. The string of achievements and triumphs that followed were not those of a fool; and they betrayed a degree of courage and indomitability that begs to be called heroic.

The reviews have been mixed. Only one observer has attempted to portray the historian on the terms that he himself prescribed. Herbert Schönebaum, who was Lamprecht's last assistant in the Institute for Cultural and Universal History, spent his life as the custodian of the Lamprecht shrine. His full-length biography was an exercise in hagiography; but in part for this reason, it was never published.[20] One can identify two other, more representative schools of thought on Lamprecht. The verdict of the one inclines toward tragic heroism. It emphasizes the bold design, the pioneering attempt to open the study of history to new fields and to an alliance with the social sciences—as well as the narrow-minded resistance of the historian's opponents, who frustrated the grand project and confined the discipline to political history for the next half-century. This view of the hero has been popular on this side of the Atlantic, but it also informs a number of recent German studies that have attempted to cleanse the historian's work of some of its flaws.[21]

The other school of thought is headquartered in Bielefeld. It casts Lamprecht as the fool, whose confusion, grandiose ambition, and feckless advocacy of a broad vision of history set a good cause back fifty years. The classic statement of this view is the article that Hans-Josef Steinberg wrote for the series on German historians that Hans-Ulrich Wehler edited several years ago.[22] The reasons for the hostility of contemporary German social historians to Lamprecht are several, but it is enough to emphasize that Wehler and his colleagues owe a profound debt to Max Weber and that they have tended to take over the great sociologist's verdict on Lamprecht.

The biographer thus confronts a rich variety of possibilities for setting the historian's history: the historian as fool, the historian as tragic hero, the historian as superhero. The remarkable thing about these interpretive schemas, though, is that they all testify to the lingering power of the historian's vision of his own life. Every one of them is compelled to judge him on his own terms, by his success or failure to live his own autobiography. It is difficult to escape the thrall of this historian, this remarkable, powerful, foolish, tragic hero. The fact that he played all these roles calls in the end for a biographical framework that accommodates every one of them while it submits to none. It is a formula for paradox. But how else should the biographer frame the history of the historian who, from the perspective of another era, posed the right questions of the German past with such power and flare and then, with no less power and flare, proffered the wrong answers?

NOTES

1. Universitätsbibliothek Bonn, Nachlass (hereafter cited NL) Karl Lamprecht (M6), Karl Lamprecht zum Gedächtnis. Begräbnis in Schulpforta bei Naumburg, 14.5.14. This chapter represents a substantially revised version of remarks delivered in Leipzig in October 1991, at a conference to commemorate the centenary of Lamprecht's call to the university there: "Ein schwieriges Heldenleben: Bekenntnisse eines Biographen," in *Universalgeschichte—gestern und heute (1): Zum 100. Jahrestag der Berufung Karl Lamprechts an die Universität Leipzig*, ed. Gerald Diesener and Monika Gibas (Leipzig, 1991), 113–23.

2. Karl Lamprecht, *Deutsche Geschichte*, 12 vols. (Berlin, 1891–1909), 8:695.

3. Roger Chickering, *Karl Lamprecht: A German Academic Life (1856–1915)* (Atlantic Highlands, N.J., 1993).

4. See Georg G. Iggers, *The German Conception of History: The National Tradition of Historical Thought from Herder to the Present*, 2d ed. (Middletown, Conn., 1983); Henrich Ritter von Srbik, *Geist und Geschichte vom Deutschen Humanismus bis zur Gegenwart*, 2 vols. (Munich and Salzburg, 1950–1951).

5. Theodor Schieder, "Die deutsche Geschichtswissenschaft im Spiegel der Historischen Zeitschrift," *Historische Zeitschrift* 189 (1959): 1–73.

6. Adolf Kuhnert, "Der Streit um die geschichtswissenschaftlichen Theorien Karl Lamprechts" (Diss. phil., Erlangen, 1906); Friedrich Seifert, *Der Streit um Karl Lamprechts Geschichtsphilosophie* (Augsburg, 1925); Ernst Engelberg, "Zum Methodenstreit um Karl Lamprecht," in *Die bürgerliche deutsche Geschichtsschreib-ung von der Reichsgründung von oben bis zur Befreiung Deutschlands vom Faschismus*, ed. Joachim Streisand (Berlin, 1965); Karl H. Metz, " 'Der Methodenstreit in der deutschen Geschichtswissenschaft (1891–1899)': Bemerkungen zum sozialen Kontext wissenschaftlicher Auseinandersetzungen," *Storia della storiografia* 6 (1984): 3–20; Lutz Raphael, "Historikerkontroversen im Spannungsfeld zwischen Berufshabitus, Fächerkonkurrenz und sozialen Deutungsmustern: Lamprecht-Streit und französicher Methodenstreit der Jahrhundertwende in vergleichender Perspektive," *Historische Zeitschrift* 251 (1990): 325–63.

7. Franz Mehring, "Deutsche Geschichte," *Die Neue Zeit* 12 (1893–1894): 443–48; cf. Mehring, *Gesammelte Schriften*, 15 vols. (Berlin, 1980), 7:496–510.

8. Karl Lamprecht, "Was ist Kulturgeschichte? Beitrag zu einer empirischen Historik," *Deutsche Zeitschrift für Geschichtswissenschaft* (n.F.) 1 (1896–1897): 75–150.

9. Hermann Oncken, "Zur Quellenanalyse modernster deutscher Geschichtsschreibung," *Preussische Jahrbücher* 89 (1897): 83–125.

10. Wolfgang Weber, *Priester der Klio: Historisch-sozialwissenschaftliche Studien zur Herkunft und Karriere deutscher Historiker und zur Geschichte der Geschichtwissenschaft 1800–1970* (Frankfurt am Main, 1984).

11. Roger Chickering, "Young Lamprecht: An Essay in Biography and Historiography," *History and Theory* 28 (1989): 198–214.

12. Lamprecht, *Deutsche Geschichte*, 5:134.

13. Ibid., 5:133.

14. Hayden White, *Metahistory: The Historical Imagination in Nineteenth-Century Europe* (Baltimore and London, 1973).

15. *Jahrbücher für Nationalökonomie und Statistik* 68 (1897): 901–2.

16. Felix Rachfahl, "Über die Theorie einer 'kollektivistischen' Geschichtswissenschaft," *Jahrbücher für Nationalökonomie und Statistik* 68 (1897):674.

17. See Max Weber, "Roscher und Knies und die logischen Probleme der historischen Nationalökonomie," in *Gesammelte Aufsätze zur Wissenschaftslehre*, ed. Johannes Winckelmann (Tübingen, 1982), 24–25, 48. See also Sam Whimster, "Karl Lamprecht and Max Weber: Historical Sociology within the Confines of a Historians' Controversy," in *Max Weber and His Contemporaries*, ed. Wolfgang J. Mommsen and Jürgen Osterhammel (London, 1987), 268–83.

18. Roger Chickering, "Karl Lamprechts Konzeption einer Weltgeschichte," *Archiv für Kulturgeschichte* 73 (1991): 437–52.

19. Rüdiger vom Bruch, *Weltpolitik als Kulturmission: Auswärtige Kulturpolitik und Bildungsbürgertum in Deutschland am Vorabend des Ersten Weltkrieges* (Paderborn, 1982).

20. Herbert Schönebaum, "Karl Lamprecht: Leben und Werk eines Kämpfers um die Geschichtswissenschaft 1856–1915" (Ms., copies in the university libraries of Bonn and Leipzig).

21. Luise Schorn-Schütte, *Karl Lamprecht: Kulturgeschichtsschreibung zwischen Wissenschaft und Politik* (Göttingen, 1984); Peter Griss, *Das Gedankenbild Karl Lamprechts: Historisches Verhalten im Modernisierungsprozess der "Belle Epoche"* (Bern, 1987); Karl J. Weintraub, *Visions of Culture: Voltaire, Guizot, Burckhardt, Lamprecht, Huizinga, Ortega y Gasset* (Chicago, 1966).

22. Hans-Josef Steinberg, "Karl Lamprecht," in *Deutsche Historiker*, ed. Hans-Ulrich Wehler, 9 vols., (Göttingen, 1971–1982), 1: 58–68.

5 "Der Bund für Bürgerrechte": Transnational Relations and the Problem of Democratization in West Germany, 1949–1954

Hermann-Josef Rupieper

When on 20 September 1949 a German "civil liberties union" was founded in Frankfurt am Main, Wilhelm Sollmann, the former minister of interior in the Stresemann government of 1923 who had become an American citizen after his immigration to the United States, gave the key note address in which he compared his experiences in Weimar politics and those in the United States. One year later, on 8 September 1950 the first president of the Federal Republic, Theodor Heuss, together with Roger Baldwin, the president of the American Civil Liberties Union (ACLU), addressed a meeting of the first German civil liberties assembly in the historic *Paulskirche*, the cradle of German parliamentarism and liberalism. Among the nearly fifteen hundred guests were four hundred delegates from "civil liberties unions" and about one hundred journalists. With this meeting an organization made its first public appearance in postwar politics. The new organization was sponsored by the ACLU, by General Lucius D. Clay and the U.S.–Military Government (OMGUS), as well as by the High Commission (HICOG) under John J. McCloy and the various German interest groups involved in establishing the concept of civil liberties in the young Bonn republic.[1]

This chapter will place the foundation of "the Bund für Bürgerrechte" in the context of the system of international relations during the twentieth century. It will also deal with American reform initiatives in occupied Germany, the attitude of German elites, and explain the development of this German-American cooperation as well as its institutional failure.

Traditionally, diplomatic history, or to use the more contemporary term—the system of international relations—has been studied by historians and political scientists as the interplay of states and their official representatives. Only since the second half of the nineteenth century have nongovernmental bodies like the Socialist International, the International Trade Union Organization, industrial and trade organizations, and the World Council of

Churches been examined. On a number of occasions they influenced foreign policy decisions—at the very least their existence could be ignored by politicians no longer. Since the end of the Second World War organizations such as these have started to play an ever increasing role in foreign policy decision making. Nongovernmental actors like trade unions, business organizations, cultural and religious groups, and multinational corporations have formed an important network between themselves or between national governments and interest groups in international affairs. In societies in which the state does not have a monopoly in foreign affairs, that is, Western democracies, these groups have even achieved a relative autonomy in the international system as well and have been described in theories of international relations as important actors, both in domestic and foreign policy. They may form a natural link between the social structure and interest groups and foreign governments.[2]

Political, social, economic, and religious organizations did indeed play an important role in supporting U.S. democratization policy in Germany after 1945. In fact, only after the U.S.–Military Government in Germany under General Clay had opened the U.S.–zone of occupation to private American organizations, did the reeducation and democratization policy begin in earnest. German and American citizens started to meet outside military government circles. True, among the four principal goals of allied policy in Germany—demilitarization, denazification, democratization, and deconcentration—even punitive goals like denazification and demilitarization were necessary elements of the democratization process. They provided the basis for a return to democracy after the Hitler dictatorship as did the rebuilding of parties and organizations starting, in August-September 1945, from the bottom up and on three levels—first local, then county, and finally state (land). The licensing of the press and the writing of new constitutions under allied tutelage further encouraged at the state level, the entire process.

During 1947 there took place a number of developments that proved decisive. In West Germany, the punitive phase of occupation was basically ended when the so-called "Spruchkammern," the denazification process, was turned over to the German authorities. In the summer of that year the U.S. State–War–Navy–Coordinating Committee (SWNCC) decided, after the submission of the George F. Zook report of the previous September, to push to the top of its list of priorities the whole democratization and reeducation policy.[3]

Even more important was a second SWNCC decision. It was obvious that the democratization of society could not be carried through by OMGUS alone, that is, by military decree. Military government and democracy were antithetical: In order to succeed in the long run, the recreation of a democratic society had to be pursued by the Germans themselves, albeit in close cooperation with the nations of the West, the United States most of all. Thus the participation of representatives of the American people became crucial. Moreover, cooperation and contacts between Germans and private American citizens proved of special importance after the beginning of the cold war and the struggle for the political orientation of the defeated country. From late 1947 onward, private American voluntary agencies, organizations, and institutions were allowed, and in fact encouraged, by the Department of State to participate in the reeducation effort. From the American Federation of Labor and the Congress of Industrial Organization to the League of Women Voters, from the American Council on Education to the churches, from the Friends Society to the National Welfare Assembly, from universities to agricultural organizations, from professional groups to the ACLU, American citizens became involved in the restructuring of German society. When the Federal Republic was founded in 1949 more than fifty U.S.-agencies were active in West Germany.[4] Equally important, between 1947 and 1954 these organizations together with the Military Government and the High Commission sponsored 13,354 German exchangees visiting the United States.[5]

The organizations mentioned above did in fact make a significant difference in democratization policy. Besides official policy on the OMGUS and HICOG level, they created a transatlantic network that was crucial for the understanding of U.S. occupation policy and its effect on West German society. Even more important, they became a vital instrument of reform initiatives. As private institutions they dealt with the population on a level different from that of the Military Government. They also cooperated with occupation authorities and thus contributed significantly to the attainment of policy goals. Finally, they influenced public opinion and decision-making processes in the United States as well as in West Germany and in the Military Government. It is from this angle that the activities of the American Civil Liberties Union in the Federal Republic should be seen.

All the same—this point must be stressed—they were only part of a larger story. Similar studies could be made about trade union cooperation, about the relations between churches of different religious faiths, about teachers' organizations, and municipal employees and businessmen, and even about farmers. Each of these would prove to be a vital component of American–West German relations during the early fifties.[6] Obviously, however, contacts were closest between the political elites.

For two reasons the ACLU was destined to play a special role in postwar West Germany. An organization that on the one hand was occupied with the defense of human rights would, of course, want to concern itself with the policy of an American occupation government. Thus the ACLU turned its attention to other theaters of U.S.-occupation or presence—Japan, Korea, and Austria.[7] On the other hand, for the creation of a postwar German democracy, the "reeducation" of German society was also of special interest to the organization. By becoming involved in West Germany the ACLU set its sights on twin aims: (1) control of the Military Government and its activities and (2) support for those liberal reform elites in German society. The latter believed that reform of society must rest not on traditional values but Western political traditions. Though the British Civil Service and constitutional theories played an important role in these deliberations, more often than not, German elites, even outside the American zone of occupation, considered the United States the most compelling model. Whether this was the case because American society had proved to be superior during the war and the United States had become the protective umbrella for European democracies after it, or whether American institutions, personal liberties, individualism, and "the American way of life" proved attractive after total defeat of Germany is a mute question. More important, there was a reform element in West German society that believed that after National Socialism, the Holocaust, and the failure of German parliamentarism, a democratic society could not be rebuilt upon the Weimar democracy, that had existed from 1918 to 1933. As well, under the impact of total defeat the German people, or at least some of them, tried to understand why society had not repudiated a perverted ideology like National Socialism.

Initially the ACLU watched the activities of occupation authorities, reported on developments in the U.S. press, and attacked violations or alleged violations of the law by U.S. military personnel. Of special interest to it were: civil liberties under military rule, freedom of the press, freedom of speech, right of assembly—all rather delicate issues during the initial occupation period. The ACLU, however, also showed interest in the requisition of German property, especially houses for occupation purposes, and the rights of American civilian employees of the Military Government. Later on, the ACLU would defend German employees in American military courts.[8]

Though the interests of the Military Government and the ACLU were not always the same, for a number of reasons, OMGUS was determined to secure ACLU support. This was especially true because of such controversial issues as denazification and the various accounts of Military Government policy that found their way into the columns of the U.S. press. Hot on the heels of these news accounts came a host of other critical events—the onset of the cold war, the failure of the Moscow and London Foreign Ministers Conference of 1947, and the decision of the three Allies to form a West German state. It was at this point that Roger Baldwin, who had earlier visited Japan and Korea, appeared on the scene. In April 1948 he wrote to Under Secretary of the Army William H. Draper to reveal his interest in an ACLU fact-finding mission to Germany and Austria. For the Department of the Army, the State Department, and General Clay this initiative came at a most opportune moment, the occupation having been under attack for some time by important pressure groups in the United States and some American journalists in Europe. The widespread, if untrue, accusation was that denazification was leading nowhere, as the return of former National

Socialist Worker's Party (NSDAP) members into the Civil Service seemed to suggest, brought matters to a head. The onset of the cold war brought about a contest between East and West for German support. The punitive phase of occupation seemed to be over only two years after the end of World War II. In general, important pressure groups in U.S. society were concerned about the development of occupation policy.[9]

Baldwin believed that the American occupation of Germany, Japan, Austria, and Korea was also a test for American democracy: "Democracy, as Americans understand it, is being put to unprecedented tests in the four countries occupied by the United States under Military Government.... The remarkable fact about the occupations is that we should expect an autocratic military machine to act as an agent of democracy."[10] Since Baldwin, after some initial criticism, had praised occupation policy in Japan as an important contribution to overcoming feudal structures and had been impressed by the policy that General MacArthur had followed there, there was no reason to expect that OMGUS would fare worse—both in his opinion and that of the ACLU. After three months in Japan, Baldwin wrote: "I got in Japan a fresh faith in the power of our American democracy to lead peoples on the road to freedom.... Japan is already on the way to becoming one of the great democracies of the world, and a spiritual ally of the American people in the struggle for universal democracy.... The key to the great drama is General Douglas MacArthur.[11] Moreover, OMGUS officials were convinced that the concept of "civil liberties" was underdeveloped in Germany. If society were to change and become Westernized, the fabric of civic culture had to change as well. This could only be done by liberal German elites. Since 1947 this had been official U.S. policy, the result of occupation directives that were formulated in the wake of the visit to Germany after the war by the Zook Commission of the American Council on Education.[12] Clay was also of the opinion that Military Government so far had an excellent record and nothing to hide: "OMGUS has led the way in restoring civil liberties to the German people."[13]

Baldwin and two other officials of the ACLU, Arthur Garfield Hays and Norman Cousins, visited West Germany and Berlin from September 1948 to November 1948 and spent a few days in Austria well. During this first trip and another in 1950, Baldwin met representatives of different organizations: those of trade unions, of churches, and of administrative and political elites. He also visited the British and French zone of occupation. He met General Clay as well as members of the Civil Administration Division (CAD) of OMGUS, with whom he discussed the state of civil liberties and human rights.

After his first encounter with OMGUS Baldwin was, however, fairly skeptical. In contrast to Japan, Military Government seemed to him a "military dictatorship" that had absolute power and ruled without any interference from the indigenous population. Human rights, he felt, had not yet been granted. Military Government was furthermore strictly separated from the Germans. Separate buildings, separate restaurants, hotels, and even restrooms seemed to suggest that American presence should be compared with segregation in the South after the Civil War. To Baldwin OMGUS had set up a "Hans-Crow-system."[14]

These initial negative perceptions were, however, soon to change. After meetings with Clay and his advisors on 5, 6, and 10 October 1948 he formed a different opinion.[15] During these dicussions, which dealt largely with civil liberties, a number of decisions were made that not only changed Baldwin's outlook but drove the Military Government to take several new initiatives. Clay, who convinced Baldwin that he was an ardent supporter of the concept of civil liberties,[16] promised that the CAD would set up a special bureau within OMGUS. This office would deal with Military Government offenses against civil liberties and human rights. Clay announced that activities of American lawyers in the U.S. zone of occupation would be facilitated. German employees of the Military Government would no longer be without legal aid in labor disputes. Once German laws for the licensing of the press had been passed, military decrees would be cancelled. As to the creation of a West German civil liberties union, Clay was skeptical as to British and French support. He was also convinced that the Germans would have to prove themselves capable of developing democratic institutions after National Socialist rule.[17]

Already on 19 January 1949 Clay ordered the necessary organizational changes for the creation of an OMGUS–sponsored civil liberties program. CAD would cooperate, advise, and finance a German civil liberties organization that it would establish.[18] Baldwin was impressed. He wrote to ACLU headquarters: "The direction at the top is certainly liberal, even a bit New Dealish. General Clay is an amazing administrator, quiet, effective, democratic, meeting everybody who wants to see him, with a grasp of factual detail and an over-all policy rare in public life."[19] After his return to Washington, Baldwin informed the Department of the Army and the Department of State: "that they [the ACLU representatives] found Military Government personnel held in general more liberal views than they would expect to find in Washington itself."[20]

This attitude did not last long. When Baldwin visited the Federal Republic again in autumn of 1950 his perception of the U.S. representatives changed drastically. Apparently, he did not get along with U.S.–High Commissioner John J. McCloy. Baldwin believed that HICOG was still meddling in German affairs; still too distrustful of independent activities; moving too slowly toward German self-determination; and basically uninterested in German civil liberties, especially when compared with the record of Clay. One reason for this criticism may have been that McCloy had rejected Baldwin's demand to support a strong national organization, which would have conflicted with McCloy's preference for a weaker, federal one. Nor was McCloy willing to give up HICOG's right to interfere in domestic affairs at a time when the delicate negotiations about a West German defense contribution and contractual relations between the Federal Republic and the Western powers had hardly started.[21] Whatever the basic reason for Baldwin's dissatisfaction, he wrote back to ACLU headquarters: "Most of what we do is 'Made in USA,' and does not reach beyond our zone, and even in it, only a thin layer of Germans,—officials, employees, civil servants. . . . General MacArthur once said that an Occupation tends to defeat its own purposes after a few years; it becomes a machine living for itself. Germany proves this point and, despite our earnest missionary effort to 'reorient, re-educate, and democratize' the Germans, it is we, not they, who are getting most of the re-education."[22]

This criticism was, however, wholly unjustified. Baldwin neglected to take into account the development of civil liberties unions since 1948.

When the president of the ACLU left West Germany at the end of 1948 civil liberties organizations did not yet exist. However, after his arrival, he had met a number of "liberally minded" German citizens interested in the formation of one. We do not know how this came about. Apparently CAD played a role. American lawyers, already active in West Germany, either by representing American clients, or by handling lawsuits in Military Government courts, might have taken a hand. Another important person in this developing network of contacts was Wilhelm Sollmann, who now called himself William. The former minister of interior in the Weimar Republic, editor of the social democratic *Rheinische Zeitung*, Sollman had immigrated to the United States after 1933, had become an American citizen in 1943 and was, during the summer of 1948, teaching political science at Cologne University. Sollmann seems to have been instrumental in establishing contacts with Social Democrats. Baldwin also met a number of representatives of the pre-1933 German League for Human Rights. He sought out and found persons belonging to different political parties. However, most of his contacts were Germans, who had either been forced to emigrate under National Socialism or had returned in the meantime—for example: Prinz Hubertus zu Löwenstein, Willy Brandt, Ernst Reuter, and trade union leaders Ludwig Rosenberg and Fritz Tarnow. Others had been members of the resistance against National Socialism and had survived prosecution and concentration camps—people like Theodor Stelzer, Dr. Hermann Brill, Social Democratic Party (SPD), Hans Lukaschek, Christian Democratic Union (CDU), and Annedore Leber, widow of trade unionist Julius Leber, murdered by the National Socialists in 1944. Still others belonged to the democratic elites of the Weimar Republic—Professor Dr. Gustav Radbruch (SPD), Minister of Justice in the Stresemann and Wirth Cabinets, and the Heidelberg sociologist Professor Adolf Weber (SPD). Others were just beginning their professional or political careers: the political scientist Theodor Eschenburg, the publicist Dolf Sternberger, Josef Gockeln (CDU), the mayor of Düsseldorf, to name only the most prominent. Baldwin also met the leader of the West German Communist Party Max Reimann, and Bernhard Göring of the Soviet Zone trade union organization FDGB.[23]

After Konrad Adenauer became chancellor, Sollmann swung into action. He had known Adenauer from their common Weimar activities in Berlin on behalf of the city of Cologne and immediately succeeded in getting the chancellor's ear. At one point he suggested that the Bonn government create a Federal Committee on Civil Rights within the Ministry of Justice, to be based upon a similar committee created in the United States by President Harry S. Truman.[24] Alexander Böker, who had immigrated to the United States in 1938 and returned to West Germany and who also worked in the chancellor's office may also have aided Sollmann.[25] High-level contacts existed also with the Ministry of Justice, the Office of President Heuss, and other federal agencies.[26]

These people came from a broad strata of political life, but most belonged to the political left and the center. But—the point must be stressed—Baldwin did not intend to restrict his contacts to members of the established political parties and organizations. Quite the contrary. Basing himself upon American tradition he intended to found an organization without any political or religious bias whatsoever. This approach later ran into difficulties, though initially it proved quite successful. Already in early October 1948 a number of persons interested in the foundation of a German civil liberties union met in Frankfurt.

At this point important differences developed between members of the pre-1933 German League for Human Rights, which hoped to continue its prewar activities, and those interested in a civil liberties union based upon the ACLU model. The basic conflict between these two groups had to do with political attitudes and the reputation of the League for Human Rights, which was widely held to be left wing and pacifist. Such an organization, the majority of the middle of the road Frankfurt group believed, would not be attractive to the broader segments of West German bourgeois society. Thus politicians like Carlo Schmid (SPD), Dr. Robert Fritz (CDU, Hesse Minister of Justice in 1946), and the rector of Frankfurt University, Professor Franz Böhm, as well as other local dignitaries rejected cooperation with the League. Members of the league argued, on the other hand, that the founding of a German civil liberties union with U.S. funds would expose the organization to attacks in the existing atmosphere of the cold war. Whatever the validity of these reciprocal accusations, when a civil liberties union was founded, the former members of the League for Human Rights had already pulled out, even though other members of the new West German administrative and political elites had announced their support. Hermann Pünder, (CDU) chairman of the Administrative Council, of the Bizonal Economic Council, approved the initiative wholeheartedly. Pünder believed that the founding of a civil liberties union would lead to the democratization of

German life and suggested this to Harold Landin of CAD. He was convinced also that basic human rights written into the West German Basic Law and into the state constitutions would not be sufficient to develop and secure a democratic society. Instead, each citizen should be responsible for the defense of human rights. H. Graf Posadowsky and Fritz Eberhard (SPD) of the "Büro für Friedensfragen," supported the foundation of the organization as well.[27] During the summer of 1949 a number of civil liberties unions began to spring up, founded by Sollmann, by members of CAD, and by Hermann Heimerich (SPD), former lord mayor of Mannheim, who had been fired by the National Socialists in 1934, who had been appointed the first *Regierungspräsident* in Neustadt an der Weinstrasse by the U.S Army in 1945 and who was now director of the American financed Institute for Public Affairs in Frankfurt.[28]

In most cases, lawyers, civil servants, or university teachers felt attracted to the concept of civil liberties and became involved in the process as well. Local branches were normally created either in administrative centers or university towns like Stuttgart, Heidelberg-Mannheim, Köln-Bonn, Hamburg, Göttingen, Frankfurt, Freiburg, and Berlin. They appeared under different names. Besides "Gesellschaft für Bürgerrechte," they were called "Gesellschaft zur Wahrung bürgerlicher Freiheiten und Rechte," "Vereinigung zur Wahrung staatsbürgerlicher Rechte," "Gesellschaft zur Wahrung der Grundrechte," "Ausschuss für unveräusserlicher Rechte," and "Staatsbürgerbund." In some cities there were ties to womens' organizations that dealt with equality and family law.[29]

Though it is not entirely clear whether the initial concepts were simply adaptions from ACLU charters, the basic goals of the German civil liberties unions had been developed by the end of 1949. The goals of the organizations were to (1) promote understanding for civil rights and liberties, (2) "fight toward the realization of the Bill of Rights as embodied in the Constitutions of West Germany and the Basic Law," (3) "enlighten the Germans about the basic rights and civil liberties which are their just due . . . and show them how to make these rights work in daily life," (4) "denounce publicly serious violations of the basic rights and civil liberties," and (5) "support, in test cases, citizens whose rights have been violated, that means to help them in their fights in the courts against the administration."[30]

The most prominent members of the civil liberties unions were Professor Wilhelm Grewe (Freiburg), Dr. Dolf Sternberger (Heidelberg), Professors Ludwig Raiser (Göttingen), Franz Wiesacker (Freiburg), E. Friesenhahn (Bonn), Erich Kaufmann (Munich), and Dr. Ernst Friedländer (Hamburg, of the liberal weekly newspaper *Die Zeit*), to name but a few.[31]

The list was impressive. But the efforts to create an organization alien to German political culture and dominated by party politics, drew fire. Some of this was simply directed against American reeducation and reorientation policy in general. The sociologist Alfred Weber complained: "The various

Occupations have accomplished absolutely nothing in implanting democracy; that the US methods treat Germans like children; functions like currency reform for which Germans should have responsibility have been assumed by the Occupation."[32] Others—Ludwig Rosenberg and Fritz Tarnow of the German Trade Union (DGB) for example—resented "the US notion that Germans had to be taught democracy and trade unions were too independent to fit that scheme."[33] Though they agreed that the concept of civil liberties was underdeveloped in Germany, they obviously felt that existing parties and organizations were adequate to support the return of democracy after National Socialism.

Other groups in society were also skeptical or resented the founding of civil liberties unions—civil servants, party functionaries, and city officials, to name only three. These groups believed that criticism of administrative decisions should be directed to appropriate local authorities. Others thought that the new organizations represented "superfluous clubs." Still others feared the civil liberties unions would become troublemakers for the local administration. Some lawyers too resented the activities of the organizations. The unions would, after all, also advise their own clientel in legal disputes and therefore might well take away their clients and income.[34]

Others outwardly supported Baldwin and Sollmann and their endeavors, though they were not optimistic about the prospects of success. Ernst Reuter and other Berlin politicians argued that civil liberties could not be built on any German tradition. Reuter noted: "German attitudes in civil rights reflect a long subservience to officials who are expected to act as the experts in the handling of all government affairs. Even the opposition parties reflect the same tendency."[35] The Mayor of Düsseldorf declared in a meeting with Baldwin: "that the Germans have never really learned democratic methods, that the road is difficult and desirable but long, and that an Occupation can do little to teach it."[36] The Cologne judges Paulus van Husen and Hans Lukaschek, (CDU) the latter subsequently Minister for Refugees in the first Adenauer cabinet, argued that the lack of interest in civil affairs resulted from the occupation itself.[37]

Nevertheless, the civil liberties unions got off to a good start. By September 1950, that is, within a year, forty local chapters had been founded. In Bavaria alone there were twenty-six.[38] In April 1952, several weeks before the dissolution of the HICOG Land Commissioners Offices, a total of sixty-three civil liberties unions existed in the Federal Republic. Not only that, the unions were now organized on the regional level. Most of them were active in the former U.S. zone: Bavaria (33), Württemberg-Baden (9), Hesse (4), Bremen (1), Berlin (1), former British zone (11), and French zone (4).[39] Exact figures about individual membership do not exist, but some figures for major cities indicate that overall membership must have been close to thirty-five hundred.[40] Comparing these figures with those for the members of the American Civil Liberties Union founded thirty years before and in 1950 numbering about nine thousand, this was a remarkable success.[41]

With the financial and ideal support of HICOG, the German civil liberties unions were active in five fields:

1. Local organizations held regular office hours to address citizen complaints against the civil service—complaints that had to do with nepotism in controlled housing, the abuse of former members of the NSDAP, election fraud, infringement of the rights of married female civil servants, and police violations of citizens' rights. There were questions as well involving the protection of youth, abortion provisions of the country's fundamental legal document, the Basic Law, and other topics. These services were highly appreciated. In Bavaria alone twelve thousand consultations took place during 1950. However, only fifty-nine cases were brought to court. Apparently most problems either did not justify legal action or were solved without filing a suit.[42] Legal disputes between German citizens and the occupation powers also played a role, but they never reached a level where HICOG felt that occupation was more criticized than the German administration, a fear that had existed in 1949.[43]

2. The local civil liberties unions were also engaged in sponsoring conferences and discussion groups dealing with a number of topics from human rights to equal opportunity. Such meetings were normally organized in cooperation with adult colleges (*Volkshochschulen*) and the so-called "Kreis Resident Officers" (KROs), the lowest administrative level of the American administration. These KROs financed local programs and carefully monitored developments, thus illustrating to the "establishment" the importance of civil liberties programs in democratization policy, even while discussions about a West German contribution to the general Western defense system were under way. Often trade unions, youth, women's, and teachers' organizations, as well as representatives of the churches played a role as well. The Frankfurt civil liberties union, for example, organized in the first quarter of 1950 nineteen public lectures attended by roughly twenty-five persons each. In Munich between two hundred and five hundred persons attended meetings on "The Protection of Human Rights through Constitutional Suits," an unusually interesting topic before the founding of a Federal Constitutional Court. Other lectures dealt with "Women Demand Equality," "Mental Illness and Civil Liberties," and "Intellectual Liberty and the Harmful Publications Act."[44]

Besides the organization of lectures, the Munich civil liberties union, for example, also published information bulletins and pamphlets dealing with topics like "Your Constitutional Rights," "Civil Liberties in German History," "Freedom of Speech and Assembly," "From Subject to Citizen," and "Temporary Arrest, Search, and Seizure."[45] Of special importance was the publication of a journal that appeared from 1950 to October 1953. The first issue was called *Die Bürgerrechte* to be named *Recht und Freiheit*. The journal dealt with the whole spectrum of civil liberties and human rights in the Federal Republic and remains an excellent source for the activities of local organizations.

3. While the activities mentioned above were carried out by the German organizations, HICOG also contributed to the public relations program of the civil liberties unions by producing a number of films dealing with civil liberties issues. These were shown in most movie theaters together with the U.S. newsreel *Welt im Film*. Among such films were *I am a Citizen*, *Equality before the Law*, *Freedom of Speech*, *Equality of the Sexes*, and *Search and Arrest*.[46] It is of course difficult to judge the impact of these pieces on a foreign audience but they must not have been without some success for the themes they addressed found their way into other important media, for example, the press.

4. Besides enlightening the general public, the civil liberties unions also tried to influence legislation. For example, in May 1950, the Mannheim-Heidelberg organization submitted a treatise dealing with the legal claims of German citizens against members of the occupation forces as well as problems of alimony rights. More important, however, was the work of the Frankfurt group which, before the Federal Constitutional Court was founded, produced, together with the members of the Hesse State Court, a brief dealing with individual claims. These suggestions were indeed picked up by the *Bundesrat* and incorporated in the law creating the Federal Constitutional Court in Karlsruhe.[47]

5. Finally, the sponsored visits of German civil liberties unions by members of the ACLU to the United States were reciprocated by those of "visiting experts" from the ranks of the ACLU to West Germany as part of the State Department's exchange program. Complete figures about this exchange program do not exist, but in 1949 only one German civil liberties union representative visited the United States, while this increased to eighteen in 1950 and twenty-two in 1951. Apparently not more than ten U.S. experts visited Germany during this period.[48]

Though, the "Bund für Bürgerrechte" and its local branches, with financial aid from the Civil Administration Division of HICOG, made remarkable strides in popularizing the American concept of civil liberties in West Germany, by the middle of 1952 the civil liberties unions had passed their peak of activity and soon disappeared from public life. The reasons for this development are to be found both in American policy and West German society. With the signing of the General Treaty between the United States, Great Britain, France, and the Federal Republic, the Bonn government gained, with some important exceptions, virtual sovereignty in domestic affairs. The dissolution of the Land Commissioner's Offices of the High Commission meant that a direct intervention in German civic affairs was no longer possible. In anticipation of this development and of West Germany's increasing role as an ally the institution of the Kreis Resident Officer began to dissolve in January 1952. KROs were not replaced once their tour of duty ended. With the abolition of the Land Commissions an already existing financial problem grew worse. Despite several attempts to support itself through the sale of publications, the Bund für Bürgerrechte had never managed to secure a sound financial footing. Last-minute attempts to finance the organization through subsidies from the West German government failed in the end, since the organization could not fulfill the precondition to increase its membership to ten thousand.[49] Perhaps the members of the "Bund" did not understand the irony of such a request: A civil liberties organization deemed it necessary to request funds from the government that it might have to sue in case of civil liberties' violations. In October 1953 the last issue of the civil liberties union magazine *Recht und Freiheit* appeared while some local organizations struggled on for awhile.[50]

Besides the end of American financial support for a Bund für Bürgerrechte there existed indigenous reasons for its disappearance. First of all, there was no German tradition upon which a supraparty organization could be built. Civil disobedience and the accentuation of civil liberties over state rights had not yet developed as far as during the height of student unrest in the late 1960s. In a society in which ideologically oriented parties determined the political culture, there was simply no room for such an organization. Parties as well as churches and other organizations felt threatened or were at least distrustful of a new competitor. The "Chancellor democracy" of the early fifties with its authoritarian structures and its pressure for conformity hindered the development of civil liberties unions probably as much as the anticommunism of the cold war, which did not allow dissenting opinions outside the established political channels. The founders of the local organizations had started their own highly successful careers in government, the universities, and in other institutions. This is not to argue that the concept of Civil Liberties failed, or, that in a broader sense the concept of transnational relations is not a valid point of departure for research in international relations. On the contrary, the transatlantic network that developed between the United States and the Federal Republic of Germany, and of which the cooperation between the ACLU and West German elites was but one excellent illustration, played a major role in shaping postwar society on both sides of the ocean. The study of this concept has only just begun.

NOTES

1. Princeton University, Robert Baldwin Papers [hereafter cited as PU, RBP], Box 15, William F. Sollmann, Report No. II, The "Bund für Bürgerrechte"; Swarthmore College [hereafter cited as SC], William Sollmann Papers, Reel 40.07, Leslie A. Grant–Sollmann, August 29, 1950.

2. See Werner J. Feld, *Nongovernmental Forces and World Politics* (New York, 1972); Samuel P. Huntington, "Transnational Organizations in World Politics,"

World Politics, 25 (1972–1973): 333–68; Robert O. Keohane and Joseph S. Nye, eds., *Transnational Relations and World Polity* (Cambridge, Mass., 1971); Walter L. Bühl, *Transnationale Politik* (Stuttgart, 1978); Werner Link, *Der Ost-West-Konflikt. Die Organisation der internationalen Beziehungen im 20. Jahrhundert* (Stuttgart, 1980). For a recent example see Walter Lipgens, ed., *Documents on the History of European Integration*, vol. 4, *Transnational Organizations of Political Parties and Pressure Groups in the Struggle of European Union, 1945–1950* (Berlin/New York, 1991).

3. James F. Tent, *Mission on the Rhine: Reeducation and Denazification in American-Occupied Germany* (Chicago, 1982), 29, 114.

4. Karl W. Bigelow, Bernyce Bridges, William E. McManus, *The Role of American Voluntary Agencies in Germany and Austria. The Report of a Team of Inquiry that Visited Germany and Austria in October-November 1950* (Washington, D.C., 1951); Ingeborg Koza, *Völkerversöhnung und europäisches Einigungsbemühen. Untersuchungen zur Nachkriegsgeschichte 1945–1951* (Cologne and Vienna, 1987), 8.

5. Henry J. Kellermann, *Cultural Relations as an Instrument of U.S. Foreign Policy: The Educational Exchange Program between the United States and Germany, 1945–1954* (Washington, D.C., 1978), 276.

6. For examples see: Werner Link, *Deutsche und amerikanische Gewerkschaften und Geschäftsleute 1945–1975. Eine Studie über transnationale Beziehungen* (Düsseldorf, 1978); Volker Berghahn, *The Americanisation of West German Industry, 1945–1973* (Lexington Spa, Mass., 1986).

7. PU, RBP, Box 10, Memo Baldwin, Civil Liberties Issues in Occupied Countries, Confidential, November 1946.

8. Ibid., with a wealth of information.

9. National Archives Record Group–OMGUS 260 [hereafter cited as NA RG], Civil Liberties and Democratization Branch, Box 198, Edward N. Litchfield–John Elliott, 30 August 1949; Jean Edward Smith ed., *The Papers of General Lucius D. Clay: Germany 1945–1949*, 2 vols. (Bloomington/London, 1974), 2:642.

10. PU, RBP, Box 12, text of an article for *Corps Diplomatique* (Paris, 1948). Strangely enough, the quasi-official history of the ACLU, Samuel Walker, *In Defense of Civil Liberties: A History of the ACLU* (New York, 1990), does not deal with ACLU activities in the occupied countries.

11. PU, RBP, Box 12, Japan's American Revolution, February 1948; ibid., Victory for Japan, May 1948, Methodist Student Movement.

12. George F. Zook, *The President's Annual Report 1946–1947*, American Council on Education (Washington, D.C. 1948), 336–38.

13. PU, RBP, Box 12, ACLU Press Release, 19 August 1948; NA RG 59, 740.0019 Control (Germany) 12–3148, letter Baldwin–Cousins, Hays–Charles F. Saltzman, Assistant Secretary of State.

14. PU, RBP, Box 12, Facts concerning civil liberties in Germany, September 1948: ibid., Notes on Germany, without date; ibid., Box 13, Arthur Garfield Hays, Civil Liberties in Germany, 10.

15. Ibid., RBP, Box 12, Baldwin, Trip to Germany, Meeting with Clay, 10 October 1948.

16. Smith, *Papers of General Lucius D. Clay*, 2:332.

17. PU, RBP, Box 12, Memorandum of a dinner party by General Clay for Mr. Hays and Mr. Baldwin, 5 October 1948; ibid., 6 October 1946.

18. PU, ACLU Papers, Boxes 1–10, Assignment of Responsibility for Promoting Civil Liberties to Civil Administration Division, 19 January 1949. The material has not been processed. The folders are simply numbered.

19. Ibid., Baldwin-Friends (ACLU), Berlin, 10 October 1948.

20. NA RG 260, Civil Liberties and Democratization Branch, Box 198, Brigadier General G. L. Eberle-Clay, 10 January 1949.

21. PU, RBP, Box 15, Baldwin–Samuel Reber, 20 September 1950; ibid., Baldwin–Shephard Stone, 20 September 1950; ibid., Baldwin–John J. McCloy, 3 October 1950; ibid., McCloy-Baldwin, 14 November 1950; ibid., meetings Baldwin-McCloy 4 October, 1950, November 17, 1950.

22. Ibid., Baldwin-Friends, 30 October 1950.

23. Ibid., Box 12, Trip to Germany.

24. SC, Sollmann Papers, Reel 40.07 Max Adenauer–Sollmann, 26 November 1948; Konrad Adenauer–Sollmann, 27 August 1949; Adenauer-Sollmann, 29 September 1949; Sollmann-Adenauer, 24 November 1949; Baldwin-Adenauer, 10 November 1949.

25. PU, RBP, Box 15 Böker-Baldwin, 17 March 1950; Solmann-Baldwin, 14 July 1950.

26. Ibid., Box 15, Sekretariat der 1. Deutschen Bürgerrechtstagung vom 8.–10.9.1950 in Frankfurt.

27. SC, Sollmann Papers, Reel 40.07, Hermann Pünder–Harold W. Landin, 3 June 1949; ibid., H. Graf Posadowsky–Landin, 3 June 1949.

28. Hermann Heimerich–Eine Freundesgabe zum 21. Dezember 1960, Mannheim 1960, S. 93ff; PU, ACLU Papers, Boxes 28–32, Harold W. Landin, Civil Rights in Western Germany Today, 6.

29. See for example: Frankfurter Gesellschaft für Bürgerrechte (Hg.), Die Gesellschaft für Bürgerrechte, Frankfurt/M. [1950]; PU, RBP, Box 15, Vereinigung zur Wahrung staatsbürgerlicher Rechte für den Regierungsbezirk Schwaben, Sitz Mindelheim–Baldwin, 31 March 1945; NA RG 466, Land Commissioner for Bavaria, Public Affairs and Activities Report, Box 9, Satzung des Staatsbürgerbundes Schwaben e.V.

30. PU, ACLU 1951, Boxes 28–32, Aktionsausschuss für die Gründung eines Bundes für Bürgerrechte, Frankfurt/M. 13 September 1951.

31. For a more complete list see the journal *Bund für Bürgerrechte*, 1950–1953.

32. PU, RBP, Box 12, Baldwin, Heidelberg notes, 20 October 1948.

33. Ibid., German notes, without date.

34. See Karl-Josef Partsch, Bürgerechtsbewegung-wozu? In Frankfurter Gesellschaft für Bürgerrechte, ibid., 5–12; NA RG 59, 762A.07/3–1352, American Consul General Munich Tel. 408, "The Civil Liberties Program in Bavaria"; NA RG 466, Land Commissioner for Bavaria, Public Affairs Activity Report, Box 9, Albert M. Frye–Van Buskirk, 22 December 1950.

35. PU, RBP, Box 15, Meeting with Reuter, Paul Hertz, Dr. Hirschfeld.

36. Ibid., Box 12, Herr Gockeln, Oberbügermeister of Düsseldorf, 18 October 1948.

37. Ibid., 19 October 1948.

38. NA RG 466, Land Commissioner for Bavaria, General Records with Special Reference to the U.S. Zone and Bremen, 1948–1952, Box 19, Survey, 23 August 1950.

39. J.F.J. Gillen, *State and Local Government in West Germany, 1945–1953* (Bonn-Bad, Godesberg, 1953), 120.

40. Ibid.; HICOG Information Bulletin March 1951, Wilfred Saliner, *Germans Guard Civil Liberties*.

41. Walker, *In Defense of Civil Liberties*, 4–15.

42. See the report in *Recht und Freiheit* 2, (15 May 1950): 13–15; ibid., 3 (25 March 1951) with figures for the region Mannheim-Heidelberg.

43. PU, ACLU 1951, William Sollmann, "The Bund Für Bürgerrechte," in Germany, September 1949.

44. Frankfurter Gesellschaft für Bürgerrechte (Hg.), Die Gesellschaft für Bürgerrechte, Frankfurt/M., without date [1950], 8–10.

45. Ibid., 12. See also HICOG, "A Program to Foster Citizen Participation in Government and Politics in Germany," 15 January 1951, 15–16.

46. Gillen, *State and Local Government in West Germany*, 16, 200.

47. *Recht und Freiheit* 2, (15 May 1950): 16. After the foundation of the court, the civil liberties union also established an office in Karlsruhe, to be present at the seat of the court. NA RG 59, 762A.07/11–2051, Linde–E. G. Chapman.

48. HICOG, "A Program to Foster Citizen Participation," 14–15; NA RG 59, 7862A.07/11–2051, Linde-Chapman, Office Memorandum. Information for Reply to State Department on "Conference on Human Rights."

49. See PU, RBP, Box 15, Present and Proposed Funds for Civil Liberties, September 1950; ibid., Anmeldung des Geldbedarfs für die Zeit vom 1.10.1950–20 May 1951; NA RG 59, 762A.07/11–2051, Linde-Chapman. PU, ACLU 1952, Boxes 21–26, Baldwin, German Bund für Bürgerrechte, 11 July 1952; ibid., Baldwin-Kellermann, 31 August 1952.

50. See *Recht und Freiheit*, October 1953. The dissolution of "The Bund für Bürgerrechte" is dealt with in detail in my book *Die Wurzeln der westdeutschen Nachkriegsdemokratie: Der amerikanische Beitrag 1945–1952*, (Opladen, 1993), 281–333.

6 German Unity and Military Professionalism: The Officer Corps of the German Armed Forces Confronts the Legacy of the *Nationale Volksarmee*, November 1989–January 1993

Donald Abenheim

On the morning of 4 October 1990 in Strausberg east of Berlin, a small military ceremony took place on the lawn in front of the defunct Ministry of Defense of the German Democratic Republic (GDR). Here came to life a simple sentence amid the text of the "Second Unity Treaty": "with the entry into force of this treaty, the soldiers of the former Nationale Volksarmee [NVA] become soldiers of the Bundeswehr."[1] Thus ended quietly the armed confrontation in central Europe between NATO and the Warsaw Pact that for over forty years had witnessed two German armies ready to wage an all-out conventional, nuclear and chemical war.

The requirements of demobilization and the assurance of peace that unfolded tested the German soldier's conception of his profession. The ideals of the leadership and command in the Bundeswehr had now unexpectedly to extend to the ninety thousand veterans of the NVA in Bundeswehr uniform. On 4 October 1990 Lieutenant General Jörg Schönbohm assumed command of the Bundeswehr Eastern Command (Bundeswehrkommando Ost). Formerly head of the planning staff at the Ministry of Defense on Bonn's Hardthoehe, Schönbohm had prepared the Bundeswehr for German unity throughout the preceding weeks and months. He had come to Strausberg to oversee the demobilization of the former East German military over the next nine months. Schönbohm announced: "We who have come to you as superiors come not as victors or conquerors. We come as Germans to Germans."

Schönbohm's speech at Strausberg outlined the shape of the challenge to come, a contingency that eighteen months earlier would have seemed utterly a thing of fantasy. This process emerged as nothing less than the "re-foundation of the Bundeswehr" as observers quickly began to describe it. The demise of the Nationale Volksarmee and the extension of the Bundeswehr into the five new federal states subjected the core principles of command and leadership to their most extensive trial since their inception. The present chapter, concerned with the first two odd years of the Bundeswehr in German unity, interprets this development in overview. Though these principles of leadership and morale formed a conscious rejection of the abuse of military command and obedience in National Socialism, the founders of these ideals had never intended to include German officers trained in a Stalinist military ethos. This development became almost a kind of war-in-peace that challenged the officer's self-image and ideals of service of the German soldier. The pages that follow summarize how this challenge emerged and how the leadership of the Bundeswehr tackled the German institutions of the Stalinist military ideal in the first two years after unification. From the perspective afforded by over half a decade of unification, the activities of the Bundeswehr indeed marked the beginning of a process of military reform as central and eastern European armies reoriented themselves to the civil-military fundamentals of the NATO allies.

Like so many other sectors of German state and society at the close of the 1980s, the unification of Germany caught the armed forces of the Federal Republic unprepared for what soon became the most extraordinary phase since its foundation in the 1950s. Indeed, the assertion that the Bundeswehr was surprised by the events after November 1989 understates the situation of those soldiers and civilians who confronted unification. Before the turn of year 1989–1990, when the first reflection began in the Ministry of Defense (MOD) in Bonn about the possibility of unification, the German military leadership concentrated on a daunting set of challenges: the NATO reaction to unprecedented Warsaw Pact arms cuts announced in 1987–1988 that began with the decision to scrap Soviet SS-20s and NATO Pershing–II and Ground Launched Cruise Missiles; future negotiations concerning conventional forces in Europe; the strengthening of German conventional combat power; the maintenance of the peace-time size of the Bundeswehr in the face of a sharp drop of available manpower; and the extension of the term of basic military conscription from fifteen to eighteen months against the wishes of an unmartial population of young men.

Confronted in early 1990 with the possibility of German unification, the strategic planners of the Bundeswehr found no plans locked in a safe on the Hardthoehe that might have formed the basis for such an effort. Three factors limited any MOD preparation for the tasks that loomed rapidly in the latter part of 1990. First, the experience of the military in German unity can be described in Clausewitzian terms as a kind of grand strategic friction. This assertion about a lack of German preparation shocks Americans, however, since the makers of defense policy in the United States have far greater faith in the skill of an exalted caste of strategic planners to anticipate everything. Such faith exists far less in the Federal Republic of Germany (FRG). The U.S.

military has more resources and personnel for such planning than does the Federal Republic. Even though the MOD is the largest section of the German executive branch, it remains tiny in comparison with the U.S. Department of Defense whose rich budgets and legions of defense intellectuals and strategic thinkers dwarf those in Bonn. Second, the existence of a German–German MOD planning cell before November 1989 would have represented a political time bomb. Were such a group the initiative of the uniformed military staff (the so-called *Führungsstab der Streitkraefte*, the command staff equivalent to the US Joint Staff), it would have violated the primacy of civilian control of the military, long the most fundamental strategic principle of the Bundeswehr. If the record of the civil-military relations in the FRG since 1950 offers any guide, then such a group before 1989–1990 would have come to the attention of the German investigative press.

Third, before early 1990, the contingency of German unity and the need to take command of the remnants of the NVA would have struck German military planners as too hypothetical—if not utterly ridiculous—to be of any concern in the year-to-year planning cycles of the Ministry of Defense and NATO. The men who observed the NVA confined themselves to the mundane strategic here and now. The strength of the East German military interested solely intelligence officers and operational planners responsible for the defense of the Federal Republic, who prepared to defeat the NVA on a NATO–Warsaw Pact battlefield. The chief Bundeswehr/NATO emphasis lay upon those things that specialists counted with supermodern intelligence means of the day. This focus meant the regular updating of the East German order of battle in the Warsaw Pact and the analysis of the role of the NVA in the yearly cycle of field and command-post exercises. Here emerged in the eyes of intelligence analysts the pride of place that the Nationale Volksarmee held in the United Forces of the Warsaw Treaty Organization as the most efficient, well-equipped and best-trained army beside the Soviets. The qualities of East German military hearts and minds, however, proved more resistant to enumeration than the panoply of rockets and armor. The institutions of morale in the East German army and the practices of command as they affected military life have long defied the facile efforts of strategic analysts to generalize about them. How would the leaders of the NVA, who gathered in the yearly military parade along East Berlin's ceremonial boulevards, withstand crisis and war? What loomed in the hearts and minds of their troops that marched past them like Hitler's Wehrmacht? How solidly, then, had the Soviets, the Sozialistische Einheitspartei Deutschlands, Socialist Unity Party (SED), and the NVA built the inner structure of the Nationale Volksarmee?

For over twenty years, this Soviet–East German military handicraft appeared to those in the West to be ever stronger. The observers of the NVA in the ranks of the Bundeswehr had scrutinized the institutions of command and morale during the worst days of the cold war. At the time of the Berlin crisis of 1958–1961 as well as the Soviet invasion of Czechoslovakia in 1968, the danger of war in central Europe and the still hostile relations between the two German states made the leadership of the Bundeswehr alert to the durability of command and morale in the Nationale Volksarmee. Such alarm about the threat from the opponent German state came naturally to the first generations of Bundeswehr soldiers, many of whom had been born in the east and fled as the SED regime consolidated itself in the 1950s and 1960s. As time passed, however, the calming of West German external relations with its eastern neighbors led to an atrophy of attention to the heart and soul of the NVA. The dissemination of knowledge about NVA institutions of command, morale, and obedience in the Bundeswehr officer corps slacked off from the middle 1970s, such that by the mid-1980s, this issue played little role in the everyday deeds of West German soldiers.

If Bundeswehr planners, however, were surprised by events of 1990 because of certain habits of mind in the West, then the leaders of East Germany did more than their part to contribute to such wonderment about the nature of East German military power by enshrouding the NVA with a nimbus of Prussian tradition, socialist martial virtue and a cult of secrecy. These principles can be summarized thus: the leadership of the SED was the most vital source of strength and power of the NVA; the struggle for high combat power and readiness for battle formed a central feature of the party labor in the troops; the political-ideological tasks stood at the heart of the party's effort in the ranks.

Analysts in NATO, the citizens of the GDR, and, most important, the soldiers of the NVA confronted a phenomenon described in the publisher's introduction to Thomas M. Forster's widely read work on the East German Army: "It is difficult to receive a valid picture of military structures of communist states, because the communist rulers generally surround everything with a veil of secrecy" (Die NVA: Kernstück der Landesverteidigung der DDR).[2] The central and eastern European regimes based upon the Moscow model inherited the Bolshevist/Russian customs of conspiratorial ways (*Konspiration*), the full dimensions of which only became evident to observers of the NVA after 3 October 1990. Secrecy in all matters of soldierly service was essential to the combat readiness upon which the reputation of the NVA rested in the decades before 1989.

However, the soldiers of the National People's Army who stacked their weapons, furled their regimental standards, and lowered the hammer and compass banner for the last time on 2 October 1990 had long since lost such combat power of the 1970s and 1980s. How did this decline come about? The following pages contain an overview of the developments that undermined the political and social foundations of the NVA in the SED state. This discussion seeks to illuminate the links between state and society and the military institutions of command and morale, all of which bulked large in the military tasks of German unity.

The constant war footing of the Warsaw Pact in its waning years and the civil-military mechanisms of political control sustained ideals of East German military discipline and combat readiness that finally rotted out the army's inner structure. The remote causes of this phenomenon are to be found in the character of the NVA as a party-army subordinate to a senior alliance partner abroad ("army of the socialist type"). All of this was present in the origins of the NVA, which reach back before those of Bundeswehr founded in November 1955. The NVA began as a Stalinist paramilitary police force put in hand by the Soviet occupiers in the late-1940s. In 1943, as the Wehrmacht gave way against the Red Army, the Soviets organized a group of sympathetic German officer prisoners in the *Kommittee Freies Deutschland*, and later in the German Officers' League. Once in possession of the Soviet zone of occupation, the Russians used East German communists to build up a paramilitary police organization, the *Kasernierte Volkspolizei*. In 1952, this KVP provided the basis for the new East German army, which only officially came into existence four years later. After 1956 the Soviets anchored the NVA far more firmly into the command and control mechanisms of the United Armed Forces of the Warsaw Pact than did the United States, the United Kingdom and France with the Bundeswehr in the echelons of NATO. By the same token, the mechanisms of Soviet–East German civil-military integration within the GDR were far more redundant, complex, and complete than the civil-military controls crafted by the founders of the Bundeswehr in the West German parliament. Despite Warsaw Pact propaganda to the contrary, the Bundeswehr enjoyed more autonomy at all levels of the Atlantic alliance and within the West German state; further, despite the Americanized appearance of the Bundeswehr soldier, the West German army also retained far more elements of Prussian-German military custom and practice than did those of the NVA.

The civil-military lines of command and control in the NVA ran from the Central Committee of the SED through the semisecret National Defense Council (*Nationaler Verteidigungsrat*) down through the district and county leadership of the SED and into the ranks of the military itself. Ninety-eight percent of the officers of the NVA held a SED membership book, and of these a very high percentage had administrative functions within the party itself in addition to their military tasks. Central to the entire system of party control in the NVA had been the so-called Main Political Administration (*Politische Hauptverwaltung*), which exercised command and control through its "political officers" at subordinate echelons. These men, together with line specialist officers, functioned according to the system of divided command begun under the Bolsheviks with the Red Army of the 1920s. This institution of leadership and morale represented a radical exception to the theory and practice of Prussian-German command and obedience.

These line and political officers were but part of an enormous Soviet/SED/NVA/MfS (Ministry for State Security) readiness and mobilization system that kept the NVA soldier prepared for a war "expected to come at any hour," even on Christmas Eve. This trend resulted from a Soviet/GDR conventional military build-up over the two decades before 1989. Such efforts prepared a bolt-from-the-blue strategic and operational onslaught to annihilate NATO forward defenses. This readiness for an offensive blow required, however, the Main Political Administration to keep the ranks on a war footing. As the political officers warned their recruits, the NVA and its Soviet partners had to resist a NATO attack with the Bundeswehr and the U.S. Army in the lead. This state of readiness permitted the soldier to leave the barracks once a week, in contrast to Bundeswehr soldiers, who could sleep at home with their families or girlfriends if geography permitted. One-third of the air defense forces in the NVA stood constantly at the ready. The units of the land forces similarly kept their equipment and vehicles combat-loaded with live ammunition and follow-on supply so they could deploy from their barracks within two hours. If need be, NVA units were prepared to defend their barracks from the perimeter against a NATO assault or a rebellious citizenry.

The leadership of the NVA spared no expense for the command and maintenance of weapons and equipment so as to strike instantly against the West. These strategic and operational goals meant, however, that scant resources remained to house and feed the draftee decently. Indeed, the contrast in East German garrisons between the shelters for aircraft, armored vehicles, and equipment of all kinds and the housing for the common soldier reflected the hierarchy of priorities the military assigned to the human and machine elements in war.

NVA officers and soldiers who stood on the verge of war in the dreariness of their barracks and the sandy-dustiness or forest-dankness of their training areas often saw this state of war in peace ruin their professional and personal existence. The burdens of readiness inspections, frictions with the party cadres, and the psychological collapse of home and hearth made the military an all-encompassing world. Professional officers as well as recruits lived in a space demarcated by the barracks square, the training area, and the vehicle park. Once in uniform, the contact of the soldier with civilian society was limited or nonexistent. The double hammers of party and military discipline pounded the army into line; this generalization applied to recruit as well as officer, with the exception of the general officers. They enjoyed the *faux petit bourgeois demi-monde* of the SED nomenklatura. The restrictions on public information, the weight of party indoctrination, and the rigidly enforced prohibition on all contacts with westerners rendered the military rank-and-file an instrument of the SED. In return for the army's role as the steel-backbone of the party/state Nomenklatura, the regime provided the officers of the NVA with social prestige, high pay, and material comforts that drew the resentment and even hatred of the common citizen. The regime recruited young men for the career of officer around the age of 15 or 16; this choice of calling brought early advancement and benefits in a society of scarcity. The draftee who experienced the NVA ideals of command often returned to civilian life with memories of a military caste system marked by poor, or at best, indifferent leadership from his company-grade officers, the hazing by elder conscripts of new arrivals, as well as unkempt quarters and lousy food.

During the middle 1980s, the collapsing economy of the GDR required an increased temporary deployment of troops into the energy and manufacturing sectors. For instance, soldiers of one unit named themselves "the coal division" in honor of their additional duties in the lignite mines of East Germany's most stricken industrial areas. As many as fifty-five thousand troops performed such duty, without, however, any decision by the national command authority to reduce the high state of military readiness; indeed, in some cases, two battalions out of three in a regiment would march off to the mines or the production line, while a third stood ready for war. This widespread emergency industrial use of soldiers in jobs often considered too dangerous for civilians cast the wisdom of the SED leadership into doubt and hastened the collapse of morale.

The growing public anger with the leviathan of party-state power overwhelmed the self-defeating hypertrophy of SED control in the second half of 1989. With the ham-fisted attempt by the regime in May 1989 to falsify the GDR local elections and with the Hungarians opening their Austrian border in the same month, tens of thousands of East Germans rebelled in the course of the summer against Erich Honecker's regime. As summer turned to fall, East Germans in the thousands climbed into little plastic cars and drove off to a new life in the West. Others remained at home to fill the streets of Leipzig, Dresden, and Erfurt. They bellowed at and taunted their secret police oppressors holed up amid the files and eavesdropping devices of their concrete beehives.

The NVA's German/Stalinist inner structure with its worn-Prussian facade had grown as enfeebled as the party and state the NVA had sworn to defend. As did the party leadership, the border fortifications, and the industrial plants, this military inner structure collapsed in 1989–1990. The NVA thus followed the fate of armies in the European past weakened by revolutionary changes in politics and society and by the incompetence of their leadership. As this edifice crumbled, it shook the core beliefs and ideals of military service that had brought soldiers to arms against NATO. "We stand," as one of the leading instructors at the Military Academy of NVA in Dresden put it in the late summer of 1990 reflecting upon the past year, "before the junk heap of our values, our professional careers and our personal existence." "Nearly all my comrades and I," as one political officer of the NVA described his emotions of the time, "honestly believed that we served the people of the GDR as well as peace. It was and is a very painful realization for us that for all these years of military duty, we trusted a leadership that revealed itself as corrupt and incapable of guiding and leading this state. Many have fallen apart as a result of this bitter realization and see no way out of this situation; they are either resigned [to their fate] or have given up."[3] Those NVA officers who had grown doubtful about the wisdom of the SED regime now confronted public protest, especially in Saxony. The NVA units stationed in Leipzig and Dresden faced the civil unrest that led to the collapse of the SED in October-November 1989.

The SED-PDS (Partei des Demokratischen Sozialismus) regime stumbled into its twilight phase between November 1989 and March 1990. Beginning in December 1989, an NVA high command purged of the most notable of the old guard by the Hans Modrow government explored a kind of "third path" of military reform in the GDR. The Modrow military leadership sought to preserve the NVA (within a reformed GDR) according to what appeared to be the civil-military code of the Bundeswehr. But very little of this reform-from-above to fashion a new NVA made much difference to the common soldier. While noble intentions of a sort stood behind this military reform, certain NVA organizations tried quickly to reinvent themselves to please the new West German masters. These principles of civil-military reform were embraced after 18 March 1990, in turn, by the popularly elected Christian Democratic government of Lothar de Maizière, which extolled German unity as its central goal. De Maizière appointed the dissident clergyman Rainer Eppelmann as Minister of Disarmament and Defense. The latter was to perfect the democratization of the NVA on the West German model as well as eradicate the most onerous SED elements of the military inner structure. This task was without precedent in the German past. Eppelmann went about it in a manner befitting his person and his office. He alternated between the extremes of extending his protective hand over what was left of the officer corps, while at the same time he dismantled the NVA communist leadership mechanisms.

His enterprise was ill-fated from the start. The institutional psychology and bureaucratic habits of Teutonic-Stalinist state power defied the few months of idealistic, but ill-focused labor by the de Maizière government, not the least because all concerned worried that to plunge the military elite into poverty and despair might create the potential for an armed uprising. This anxiety, while never articulated openly before October 1990, lurked in the back of the minds of those who presently had to deal with the legacy of the NVA. Political forces beyond Eppelmann's control in Bonn, Moscow, Washington, and Strausberg, presently robbed him of initiative and made his programmatic decisions about the endurance of the NVA appear dubious to West Germans.

In the spring of 1990, few observers of the gathering process of German unity were prepared to believe that the Soviets, even under the apparently enlightened leadership of Gorbachev, would give up their ally and allow their alliance to collapse. As one American strategic analyst had wrongly argued in the fall of 1989, the size of the Soviet infrastructure investment in its East German military glacis alone prohibited such a move. Many East Germans believed that, even in a unified Germany, the Warsaw Pact and NATO might continue to function in some kind of grand strategic cohabitation, and that there would be two German armies, as well. The NVA could become a kind of national guard with territorial duties in an eastern zone under a special military status. This development recalled the alliance disengagement plans of the era 1957–1958 for central Europe and would have preserved most of the structures and functions of the NVA. This ideal of two German armies filled the hearts and minds of many East German officers who traveled west in the early weeks of 1990 to meet Bundeswehr soldiers in polite circumstances for the first time. Simultaneously, however, waves of desertions and mutinies struck certain units of the NVA leaving a shaken cohort of officers with ever fewer troops to command. The process of unity advanced with quickening speed. This pace was set chiefly by the Kohl-Genscher government (with U.S. support), whose diplomacy in the course of mid-1990 overturned the hopes of the NVA professionals for the endurance of their institution and for the efficacy of their neutralist and "third-path" solutions to the strategic future of East Germany.

On 27 April and 28 May 1990 Minister of Defense of the FRG Gerhard Stoltenberg and Eppelmann held the first ever German–German defense ministerials in Cologne and Strausberg. The 27 April meeting at the Holiday Inn at the Cologne-Bonn airport (Eppelmann refused to go up to the MOD on the Hardthoehe) produced an agreement that a united Germany should retain NATO membership. The two men agreed further that areas of cooperation in the near term include mutual exploration of the legal fundamentals of the armed forces and the theory and practice of *Innere Führung*. This untranslatable phrase describes the institutions of leadership, command, obedience, and morale in the Bundeswehr as well as the integration of the West German soldier into the spirit and letter of the constitutional Basic Law. The ongoing, uncontrolled process of unofficial military tourism made up of thousands of Bundeswehr and NVA members in mufti should give way to official contacts. The second meeting on 28 May led to the signing of an agreement that permitted staff-to-staff talks as well as official exchanges between institutions of the Bundeswehr most concerned with education, training, and *Innere Führung*. This effort got underway on 1 June 1990.

Throughout the weeks from mid-March until mid-July 1990, the "Two-Plus-Four" negotiators had struggled with the external modalities of unification and the Soviet acceptance of its strategic consequences. The future of Germany and the efficacy of NATO hung like vast question marks over events. Having faced many crises since 1949, the Atlantic Alliance had the mechanisms and practices in place in July 1990 to adapt the famous Harmel Doctrine of collective defense and dialogue (1967) to the present. The London Declaration of the North Atlantic Council on a "Transformed North Atlantic Alliance" (6 July 1990) embraced cooperation with the nations of the disintegrating Warsaw Pact and offered an olive branch to the leadership of the beleaguered Soviet Union. A few days thereafter to the surprise of all concerned (and to the anger of some Americans anxious about German "assertiveness"), on 16 July 1990, Mikhail Gorbachev and Helmut Kohl agreed at a meeting in the Caucasus that a united Germany could remain in NATO. The last hurdle to German unity fell. Germany would reduce its military from 495,000 (plus the remnants of the NVA) to 370,000 by the close of 1994 and thus pose no numerically superior armed threat to any of its neighbors. Kohl and Gorbachev also agreed that until the Soviets completed their withdrawal from eastern Germany at the beginning of 1995, only national German armed forces outside the integrated military structure of NATO's Allied Command Europe would be stationed in eastern Germany; neither would the stationing of nuclear weapons nor troops from the NATO allies be permitted in the former GDR. The Federal Republic and the USSR would sign a transitional treaty to regulate their relations, and the FRG would become host country to the Soviet Western Group of Forces during these next five years. As a result, the Bundeswehr was about to inherit over 500,000 Soviet and Soviet-style troops (380,000 USSR plus 170,000 GDR), who would have to adjust to the civil-military relations of the FRG. Not only would the Bundeswehr inherit and dismantle the legacy of the Nationale Volksarmee, it would have to reduce its own strength drastically. These events in their sum represented the shape of things to come for NATO in the new decade.

The Kohl-Gorbachev meeting had laid down the strategic parameters for German unification and freed the Ministry of Defense to begin detailed planning for the role of the Bundeswehr in this effort. Until the Kohl-Gorbachev meeting, Stoltenberg had prohibited the MOD from such moves. The makers of German unification statecraft feared that any appearance of secret general staff work on the details of unity might harm the "Two-Plus-Four" negotiations or be seen as a military attempt to undermine unification. A similar prohibition had been in effect on military preparation during the armament of the FRG and the struggle for full sovereignty in 1950–1955. A bit more than two months separated the Kohl-Gorbachev meeting of 16 July and the hoisting of the German flag before the Reichstag on 3 October. The Hardthoehe planners had assumed that they would have until December to prepare the Bundeswehr for its role in unification.

No sooner had this MOD effort begun, however, than the leadership of the Bundeswehr confronted the reaction of a fraction of the officer corps of things to come. Günter Gillessen of the *Frankfurter Allgemeine Zeitung* threw a bomb into the march toward military unity with a lead article of 25 July 1990. He argued for a radical answer to the problem of the East German army. "What should be done with the NVA?" he asked. "There is only one solution: it should be disbanded without a trace." The officers of the NVA and the Bundeswehr, according to Gillessen, had "two, fundamentally different careers," that defied combination. Whoever attempted to merge the two would endanger "the best thing about the Bundeswehr, its morale as the army of another Germany [of the anti-Nazi conspirators of 20th of July 1944]." The editorialist suggested that the NVA was little better than the Waffen-SS, a "party army" compromised by a criminal political ethos. The Bundeswehr should accept nothing more than NVA lieutenants; they should be treated as the FRG dealt with company-grade Waffen-SS officers in the mid-1950s by means of a rigid process of examination that accepted only a handful.[4]

These were strong words. Gillessen attacked the planning assumptions of the MOD. In doing so, he no doubt echoed the views of many Bundeswehr professionals at odds with the perceived details of German unity. As the MOD staff looked closer at the NVA, the more they realized how much East German professional military aid was needed to dismantle and to convert existing organizations and structures; such a demobilization of so many dissimilar military institutions, forces, bases, and facilities required skilled aid and council. This help could only come from those East German officers, soldiers, and civilians willing to cooperate.

Gillessen's assertion, however, that German unity would gut the professional ethos of the Bundeswehr, if the MOD made any compromise with the remnants of the NVA, resonated particularly with veteran Bundeswehr officers as yet innocent of real conditions in the east. Many Bundeswehr officers quite naturally believed that NVA officers deserved to be booted out. The latter, it had long seemed to the generation of officers reared in the crises of the 1950s and 1960s, luxuriated in their hatred of the Bundeswehr. The chief strategic-operational task of the NVA officer had been to blast his way into the Federal Republic along side the Western Group with all barrels blazing. As if Gillessen's broadside was not enough, Eppelmann declared before the press in Bonn on 2 August that he would reduce the 170,000 regulars of the NVA to 98,000; but at the same time, he insisted that the NVA should continue to exist as an independent army, which could grow together with the Bundeswehr after unity—a process that could last until the late-1990s.

In the second week of August, Stoltenberg together with the leading figures of his ministry made five key decisions concerning the Bundeswehr and German unity. Pragmatism triumphed over cold war rhetoric. As has so often been the case with the governance of the FRG, the makers of policy chose a middle path. Stoltenberg's decisions represented a synthesis between the extremes of policy symbolized by Gillessen, on the one hand, and by Eppelmann, on the other.

First, the NVA would cease to exist with unity, and the soldiers of the NVA on hand would become provisional soldiers of the Bundeswehr according to the dictates of the Soldiers Law, the portion of the Basic Law that regulated the conditions of military service in the FRG. Second, Bundeswehr commands in the east would demobilize and dismantle existing NVA units in a staged process. New units would, in turn, be raised with mixed personnel from east and west. Third, twenty thousand career and term soldiers of the NVA could, after a probationary period, become term soldiers in the Bundeswehr for two years (*Soldat auf Zeit [SaZ]* 2). To this number would be added five thousand soldiers of the Bundeswehr dispatched from the west to serve in the east as well as twenty-five thousand eastern draftees, most of whom would enter the barracks on 1 September. The total number of soldiers in East Germany would be fifty thousand. Fourth, the training of draftees inducted on 1 September 1990 would be carried out according to Bundeswehr practice and FRG law. Fifth, the MOD would create a temporary organization, Bundeswehr Eastern Command, as the forward element of the Ministry of Defense in the five new federal states. This headquarters in Strausberg would assume command and control of the torso of the NVA; disband its units step-by-step; release from service the vast majority of former NVA troops; concentrate the storage of what soon proved to be an utterly enormous quantity of weapons and equipment; raise new Bundeswehr troop units according to future force structure plans, as well as maintain liaison with the Soviet armed forces as well as support their orderly withdrawal until late 1994. The Bundeswehrkommando Ost would go out of existence in the middle of 1991. It would be succeeded by the headquarters of the three armed services in the east raised according to the new force structure. The planners intended to consolidate higher-headquarters and reduce to cadre certain units according to the dictates of 370,000 strong Bundeswehr planned for the end of 1994.

Uphill work this was. The makers of German defense enacted these plans quickly during August-September 1990. The effort undertaken between the Hardtberg and Strausberg represented the best of German general staff work, in which the skill and genius of very capable men surmounts the frictional course of events. The responsible figures, however, knew in their hearts that the task at hand was, as one semiofficial observer reflected in November 1990, "more an intellectual-psychological challenge than one of organization." These programmatic choices indicated the way forward into a military world in which former opponents reoriented their concept of professionalism, training, and military operations. The architects of military unity had drafted a series of new organizational diagrams and dispatched liaison officers eastward to transform the forces and facilities of the vanishing NVA into what would now be called Bundeswehr-Ost (in contrast to Bundeswehr-West). If anything, the speed of the bureaucracy only amplified the imponderables made up of the union of mentality, ethos, and self-image. As Schönbohm wrote in 1992, "The central problem after the take-over of the NVA has been to promote a change of consciousness and establish the ideals of the citizen-in-uniform."[5] The fate of democracy in Germany in the twentieth century had been closely linked to such changes of consciousness visible in the link between the state and military power after 1918, 1933, and 1945. While observers of 1990 made facile comparisons to the transition from Wehrmacht to Bundeswehr of 1945–1955 with what stood ahead in the late summer and early fall of 1990, the case of the NVA in the GDR was *sui generis*. The NVA was neither the Reichswehr, nor the Wehrmacht nor, as in Gillessen's mind, the Waffen-SS. It represented something unique, a communist German imitation of the Red Army that had neither developed an effective bond with the average East German citizen, nor had it enjoyed the institutional freedom within its alliance system to nurture its own style of command or what its own officers called a national "military doctrine"; rather quite the opposite had been the case. Although the Bundeswehr had never enjoyed much popularity in the FRG, since the early 1960s it had developed a measure of popular respect and a bond with West Germans by means of effective parliamentary control, the perfection of the ideal of the citizen in uniform, and a rather humane treatment of draftees. The course of unification revealed how the FRG had fitted its strategic interests into those of NATO to the benefit of both. The senior officers of the Bundeswehr of 1990 had inherited from the founding generation, and adapted in turn, effective principles of leadership as well as fostered an institutional flexibility to master the challenge of this unique set of military and social tasks.

All of this had made up the experience of the so-called "white generation" that included Schönbohm and the fourteen general officers and twenty-nine full colonels seconded to the east to take command of units fated for disbandment and reorganization. These men recalled clearly how the effort to make *Innere Führung* a living force in the Bundeswehr of the 1950s and 1960s had faced the skepticism, and at times, the open opposition of military men trained in an earlier political system. The present challenge of the GDR/NVA appeared to be far graver still, and might lead, in the worst case, to disastrous results for the efficacy of unity overall. The Bundeswehr was to be a highly visible test case of unity; it was to be the first, most prominent, and powerful federal institution in the five new states, whereas nearly all the other cases of institutional transition were to take place on the level of the revived *Länder*.

In the first instance, the ghosts of the NVA "Feindbild" and "hate-training" against "Nazis, Nukes, and NATO" in the Bundeswehr could reappear with unpredictable consequences for those in command. If the officers from the west failed to win over the NVA professional for this transitional phase, then units might disintegrate, their equipment fall into dangerous hands, or form the basis for some kind of Werewolf/Rote Armee Fraktion organization to endanger the Federal Republic. There also existed the danger that the Bundeswehr would fail to build a working relationship with the Soviet Western Group of Forces, where civil-military frictions over maneuver rights, low-level flights, free-fire zones, and the details of withdrawal bulked as potential difficulties.

In the second instance, aside from official anxiety about desperate East German men with guns, the observers of military professionalism within the Bundeswehr worried that the "Gillessen phenomenon" would dissolve the cohesion of the officer corps. This worry remained an issue beyond the 1992–1993 permanent commissioning of a few thousand former NVA men as career officers. The conditions of military unity, in their view, posed the danger that, despite de jure equality between soldiers of east and west, the Bundeswehr might cleave into two groups for years to come: the self-confident officers of Bundeswehr-West versus those of the shaken and anxious Bundeswehr-Ost. The latter group, eager to remain soldiers, might become second-class men in their own eyes and those of their new West German peers. Having seen themselves forced to give up old patterns of thought and behavior under the trauma of collapse, revolution, unity, and military probation, their sole imperative was to adapt as quickly as possible to the political, legal and ethical world of the Bundeswehr.

As the Bundeswehr dispatched its first liaison officers in August-September 1990 to prepare for unification, these men found that fears about active or passive resistance were groundless. As they appeared at various bases and headquarters in September and October, no one lurked with pistols drawn to pepper the official Bundeswehr Opel with a volley. The shaken leadership of the NVA looked hopefully to the Bundeswehr as the only competent authority to determine its fate. To be sure, many of those who might have offered resistance of whatever kind for whatever reason resigned before 2 October, and many more were to leave within a quarter year. The senior officer cadres of the NVA who remained in September-October 1990 accepted their former opponents, because nearly all NVA officers had long since lost faith in the political leadership. Eppelmann's myth of two German-armies-in-a-single-state came as a second bitter disappointment after the revelations of SED incompetence and corruption. The Bundeswehr in the process of negotiation for the second unity treaty became the sole lobby the NVA veterans might find to advance their case in a united Germany; the NVA leadership also knew that the surrounding civilian population, long weighted down with military burdens, had no love for them. Many civilians saw the cohort of NVA officers, rightly or wrongly, as yet another tentacle of the SED/Stasi octopus. These men had

German Unity and Military Professionalism 117

been young, arrogant, jackbooted opportunists who stepped on others to gain cash, automobiles, and western goods. This generalization, however, failed to take account of the ambiguities of life and social progress in the GDR; nor did such a judgment recognize the variety of motives that drew young men to a military career. Such minute distinctions, however, were difficult to make in the rush to unification amid the popular revulsion with the personnel of the party colossus.

The ideal of military honor in defeat played a crucial role in the cooperation of many NVA officers with the Bundeswehr. To describe this process as having simply been opportunism visible in other sectors of GDR society after November 1989 overlooks the comradely bonds that link one soldier with another, despite profound differences of world-view and experience. Like other defeated German armies in the twentieth century, the beleaguered officers of the defunct NVA fostered a kind of unifying myth of defeat. This phenomenon is common enough in conquered armies and has been visible, under different circumstances, among the U.S. veterans of Vietnam. This East German quasi-Frederickian bearing (*Haltung*) impressed those newly arrived western commanders shocked by the psychological, physical, and administrative tasks before them. Lieutenant General Werner von Scheven, in remarks made in 1992 to a Bundeswehr commander's conference, paraphrased this code of "honor in defeat" thus:

We [NVA officers] have fulfilled our duty toward the preservation of peace and have also honored our responsibility to the German people. We were professionally good. The German people can thank us that weapons and hazardous material were kept out of malevolent hands and that blood-shed was prevented. Out of our sense of duty we have endured humiliations and taken over the tasks of NCO's and other ranks, in order to make the transition to the Bundeswehr under orderly conditions. But our experience since 9 November 1989 disappointed our trust in the political and military leadership.[6]

The ghost of "hate-training" vanished to leave behind a kind of German–German community of military fate. This process loomed large in the experience of those senior officers dispatched to the east. These men recognized the historical gravity of the moment and its implications for their profession; for many senior Bundeswehr born in eastern Germany before 1945, their service symbolized a return to *Heimat* as well as the chance to master an unprecedented professional challenge. New commanders in the east were generally moved by a feeling of responsibility and kinship for their eastern comrades that Schönbohm captured in his phrase of "Germans coming to Germans." Although these assertions might strike the outside observer as a soppy kind of official German–German military pathos, one would do ill to underestimate the bond of mutual cooperation and respect that arose in many cases.

Kinship between easterner and westerner was all the more astounding when one considers that few of these East German officers had much hope of a permanent position in the Bundeswehr. The ground troops in the east after 3 October were to be organized during 1991–1992 as a combined field/territorial force, concentrated in so-called home-defense brigades. These brigades were to be raised in the garrisons of old NVA troop units; in addition, a small air force and navy presence would round out the new eastern command. The navy, in particular, capitalized on the base infrastructure of the Baltic coast. The strategic idea behind these forces aimed to create a modern structure of forces outside of the NATO integrated command that would pose no threat to any of Germany's eastern neighbors. The first phase required the dissolution of NVA units, while the second phase foresaw the organization of new units in sufficiently habitable NVA facilities. Within this process, the Bundeswehr reduced the officers of the NVA in a staged process that left only a few thousand with any prospect of long-term service; but at the same time, this arrangement provided a form of transitional support to many other younger officers not immediately let go. This effort has been quite complicated, and defies a complete reconstruction here, but its major features included the following.

NVA draftees on hand on 2 October became Bundeswehr regular conscripts (*Grundwehrdienstleistende-GWDL*), but would serve out their term and be paid according to GDR law. This provision meant that easterners of all ranks received far less pay than their western brethren (about 60 percent). The Westerners seconded to the east received very generous tax-free allowances as well as free flights back to western Germany. The so-called term soldiers (*Zeitsoldaten*) and career soldiers (*Berufssoldaten*) in the East depended essentially on the MOD decision whether a given NVA unit or facility would continue to exist. These term soldiers were further broken down into so-called (1) "Further-Employed" (*Weiterverwender*), who retained their NVA rank and remained with an existing unit; examples of such officers included commanders of units slated to be disbanded over the mid-term as well as men with particular skills, for instance, a specialist in Soviet-made rocket fuel, for which no western expertise could be found; (2) "Soldiers in Holding," (*Soldaten im Wartestand*) in case a unit or position was to continue to exist in an altered or reduced form; (3) "Term Soldiers for Two Years" (*Soldat auf Zeit [SaZ]* 2) who were entitled to submit a request for extended service up to two years at a grade determined by the MOD; this provision meant that officers often lost rank by one or even three grades once accorded this status; (4) Term Soldiers and Career Soldiers, who would be drawn from the pool of term soldiers described above. According to demonstrated capabilities, accomplishments, and the needs of the service, these men could receive a limited or permanent position during their two-year term. Officers were to be examined by an independent commission, not unlike the Personnel Screening Committee of 1955–1957 that had vetted colonel and generals. All of the above received lower pay than their western counterparts, an issue that quickly sparked resentment as the cost of living matched or exceeded that of the west.

The number of NVA veterans who might fill these latter categories shrank quickly after 3 October. Eppelmann had already reduced the NVA from over 170,000 to about 100,000 by 2 October. He had fired all general officers, officers over the age of 55, as well as the officers of the abolished Main Political Administration. In addition, because the Bundeswehr employs only a handful of women (chiefly as doctors and musicians), Eppelmann had ejected the NVA women regulars, many of whom transferred into civilian billets. Some 65,000 term service soldiers had already left the ranks by unification. Under Lieutenant General Schönbohm, the cohort of 32,000 officers taken over on 3 October had shrunk to 10,500, that is to say, 70 percent had been let go. Older-aged officers had the chance by 31 December 1990 to make use of their NVA pensions, such that practically all officers over 50 left the ranks by the close of 1990, as well as a great number in the year-groups between 40 and 50. The "Two-Plus-Four" stricture of 370,000 imposed a limit of 50,000 troops in the five new states, of whom 25,000 were to be made up of longer-serving ranks. By the end of 1991, some 18,000 spaces were filled as Two-Year Term Soldiers out of some 26,000 applications. The German army in the East placed 4,031 officers, 5,144 senior NCOs, and 2,371 junior NCOs in this category of service. The contingents for the air force and navy were correspondingly smaller. The army, however, had only need of 2,671 officers, 5,988 senior NCOs, and 5,019 junior NCOs. The eastern army, in particular, had offered a temporary haven to a large number of junior officers, who nonetheless faced the stiff, even unpleasant, competition for a single billet. The smaller number of billets and the early choices made by the navy and air force leadership meant that such competition did not exist in these units on the same scale.

The above numbers reflected a major challenge of military unification connected with the inner structure of the eastern Bundeswehr; further, this problem typified the institutions of command and obedience of all the armies of the Warsaw Pact with which NATO forces cooperated during the 1990s. While there were too many Army officers, there were far too few men for the new NCO corps. The sergeant and corporal had long been the backbone of the Prussian-German armies, a tradition that the Bundeswehr carried forward after 1955. This institution was, by contrast, utterly absent in the *Nationale Volksarmee* as it had been in the Soviet military. Whereas 7.4 percent of the Bundeswehr before 1990 consisted of line and staff officers, 37.3 percent of the NVA had been officers; NCOs had made up 35.4 percent of the Bundeswehr, as opposed to only 24.3 percent of the NVA. These eastern NCOs had none of the esprit de corps visible in the West, where senior sergeants dominate much of garrison life and enjoy status and respect that has long gone with the rank. The eastern NCOs had been specialists without any leadership function at all; as with other tens of thousands they had stood ready to carry out a single function swiftly like some kind of spring-loaded chess piece. The MOD sought to fill the eastern NCO deficit by ordering career senior sergeants from disbanding western garrisons to the east. Granted the primitive conditions in the five new federal states, such moves had proven unpopular with NCO ranks unsettled by the rapid pace of German disarmament and troubled by the personal difficulties of displacing men who had long since put down family roots in a very Federal German manner.

As a result of the above process, the prospect of a permanent commission lay in store for only a small group of younger NVA officer veterans. The rigors of probation and examination imposed on westerners the need to understand fully the institutions of command and morale in the NVA. As the number of officers on hand declined through the first half of 1991, some four thousand army officers of the former NVA applied for two-year positions. Of these, thirty-six hundred sought career and long term service positions, of whom about 65 to 70 percent were to be taken over in the course of 1992–1993. Crucial to this process was an examination of secret police files, the scrutiny of military counterintelligence (*Militaerischer Abschirm Dienst*), and the final judgment of an independent board of examiners about a candidate's performance before and after 3 October 1990.

How can one generalize about these young officers who remained in the Bundeswehr after successful vetting? As von Scheven observed in 1992, "the identity of the NVA officer has resulted from two to three generations of life in a closed society, in which the SED did everything in its power to distance these men from the western world."[7] Candidates for a permanent commission often admitted in command interviews that they knew no one outside the military as a character reference; their entire circle of friends and acquaintances was in uniform. But the camaraderie encountered in the Bundeswehr was no where to be found in the stratified hierarchy of the NVA, not the least, because open talk about life and family might draw the unwanted attention of the Administration 2000, the Stasi branch in the NVA. On reflection, candidates spoke bitterly about a "stolen life," wasted in the night and fog of a Christmas eve alert, awaiting a NATO assault that never came. The former officers remained convinced that they "served peace in an internationally recognized state, that expounded the ideals of anti-fascism."[8] The encounter with the full amibiguities of the German past began for these men in the additional education in *Innere Fuehrung* that included segments on history and politics. This effort brought to light the intellectual damage of NVA maintenance of tradition based on a compact, ideologically vetted "image of the past" that made nonsense out of history to underscore the party's claim to power. Stripped of the unifying ethos of party and state, the former NVA officers retreated to core ideals of discipline, duty, and service. To bark orders, to salute superiors smartly, to click one's heels, and to nod sharply while carrying out commands all enjoy rather less pride of place in the Bundeswehr than in the NVA. The young former-NVA officer learned this difference in the classroom and on the job as he observed his western comrades' methods of command in garrison life. Yet these young NVA officers generally demonstrated a greater endurance and tolerance for hardship than did certain of their western counterparts; this willingness to endure strengthened, in turn, the bond many western commanders felt for their junior eastern officers. This phenomenon showed itself particularly during the German logistical support of Operation "Desert Shield/Storm" in 1990–1991, where NVA veterans served through the Christmas holidays as part of the "out of area" support offered by Atlantic allies to the anti-Iraq coalition. Certain West German–based air force units had deployed to eastern Turkey during "Desert Shield" under the NATO flag. Near-battlefield conditions in Anatolia prompted a handful of soldiers to complain bitterly to the German press, although the electronic media overlooked the far greater number of volunteers for service in Turkey. The sight of German soldiers doubting the efficacy of their service on television struck many NVA veterans as odd.

During 1991, those junior officers who seemed suited to a permanent billet went through a number of assignments in the Bundeswehr schools, temporary duty with units in the old Federal Republic that supported the new eastern ones (*Coleurverbände*), as well as further training in their new units. The theory and practice of *Innere Führung*, and advanced tactical training loomed large in these endeavors. Particular emphasis in the first case fell upon the role of the soldier in a democracy, as well as the professional ideals of the officer and NCO in a state founded upon the rule of law. All of these activities aimed to provide the independent screeners, who would make a final judgment, with as many evaluations possible.

In the course of this process of 1991–1992, a growing number of Bundeswehr professionals encountered the physical and psychological legacy of the NVA first hand. The full dimensions of the professional gulf between the two German armies became obvious to Bundeswehr officers detailed to the east or who served with easterners in the west. Although Schönbohm had been quite right that "Germans had come to Germans," many of the officers of the Bundeswehr who had gone east had underestimated or misunderstood the professional-psychological dimensions of their tasks. The image of Prussian-German military discipline and efficiency nurtured in the martial displays before the *Neue Wache* masked psychological and moral deformations of a Stalinist system that had poisoned the minds and souls of hundreds of millions of Europeans. Behind this facade stood, to the shock and disgust of those westerners who found them, the serried rows of heated vehicle shelters from whose floors one could eat. Near these buildings were the moldering barracks in which recruits had lived in filth and squalor reminiscent of a nineteenth-century slum. Many West German officers had believed that, once they removed the "corset stays" of the communist organizations in the army, the remainder of NVA line officers would quickly reach the professional level of their western counterparts. Here generalizations apply very poorly, because the nature of individual military careers defies any kind of formulaic statement, but this adjustment has not taken place as quickly or as effectively as many had hoped. At the same time, however, the vast majority of the young NVA veterans showed a general willingness, even eagerness, to learn. But they understandably faced great difficulties to adjust fully to the liberality and "torture of choice" inherent in a Bundeswehr that exalts an officer and NCO capable of independent judgment in the garrison and the field.

West Germans seconded to the east found how physical conditions reflected the old spirit behind the barracks gate. The Bundeswehr planners had overlooked the total absence of NVA officers' clubs, for instance. These places form a focal point for young Bundeswehr officers to eat, drink, and smoke socially with their superiors. The NVA, instead, had a series of dining rooms for the senior leadership that were separated from the rest of the officers. A collegial discussion between senior and junior ranks happened very seldom, if at all. The daily contact between officers and the rhythms of their official lives were reduced to empty externals determined by one's position in the hierarchy. The shadow of the secret police further darkened life in the ranks. In many cases, the Administration 2000 (Stasi) fitted listening devices in the officers' apartments; until June 1989, regulations forbid access to West German television; the secret police enforced this ban by regularly questioning officers' children about what they had seen the night before. Purchase of such modern amenities as refrigerators, televisions, and even automobiles went through the hands of commanders, who bestowed these privileges on the "best" of their subordinates. Company-grade and field-grade officers generally turned a blind eye to the hazing of recruits. The harshness and arbitrariness of party control meant in certain cases that officers routinely lied to cover up infractions and bought the loyalty or silence of subordinates with cash bonuses. These means of control warped a young officer's sense of self and poisoned the cohesion of the military whole. The chief task of the practitioners of *Innere Führung* in the new Bundeswehr has been to overcome this professional and psychological legacy.

Upon learning all of the above, many West Germans, conscious of how many of their parents had reacted to National Socialism, asked themselves whether they might have not "made do" at the age of 15 or 16, had they been born in the GDR and failed to get out before 13 August 1961. Perhaps they too would have accepted their teachers' enticements of a snappy uniform and heroic excitement. The western sense of bafflement with the conditions of military life in the former GDR grew even more intense after a more thorough examination of the files of the former Ministry of State

Security under the custodianship of Pastor Joachim Gauck. These documents all too often revealed that a capable and efficient young officer in his probationary two-year term had failed to mention his role as an "unofficial informant" for the Stasi in the initial personnel questionnaire; often times, the MfS had extorted such men into service in their late teens after an infraction of some kind. Despite such mitigating conditions, the Bundeswehr dismissed these officers, not the least out of fear that NATO allies would mistrust them, as would civilians in the five new states.

One might easily suggest that the foregoing has been something less than a process of German-German integration. A procedure that ejected 70 to 80 percent of the NVA leadership has been little more than a purge. This generalization, however, grossly oversimplifies the case. The treaty obligation to reduce the Bundeswehr to 370,000 by the end of 1994, insisted upon by the former Soviet leadership, doomed the command cadres of the NVA; also problematic had been the ideals of command and control of the Warsaw Pact. Despite the exhortation of Günter Gillessen to raze the structures of the NVA and purge all of its personnel, the MOD leadership and the men and women in the east sought a middle path that offered limited hope to some of permanent service, as well as support and retraining to many more for as much as two years. The permanent commissioning of NVA veterans signified a small step forward in the process of German unity and a confirmation that the ideals and methods forged by the founding generation of the Bundeswehr had withstood an unexpected trial. Although a generalization of civil-military studies asserts that armies are inherently conservative and loathe to innovate, the experience of German unity suggests that modern German military institutions accustomed to the need to train large numbers of men and organized to respond to the uncertainties of war might have been better suited to the tasks of postcommunism than other sectors of state and society. The dearth of flexibility among other institutions of German state and society in unity only lends further weight to this generalization.

It is commonplace to recall that the German past contains repeated instances of military collapse and renewal. These episodes stand like milestones along the path from Prussia, to the German Reich, and onto the catastrophes of the twentieth century. The route of march from the Frederickian army to that of the Prussian military reformers and the ensuing reaction after 1819 is familiar enough, as is the way from the old armies, to the Reichswehr and thence to the Wehrmacht. Less well known in the English-speaking world has been the course from defeat into the cold war traveled by the remnants of the military in the Third Reich; for some it led to the gallows and prison, while for others it led to pacifism, the clergy, and professions in trade and education. For others still, this path led to the ranks of NATO and the Warsaw Pact. In view of all this, perhaps one expects too much, amid the turmoil and confusion of the post-1989 world, to offer any historical generalization about the path of the German military out of the cold war.

The tension between the requirements of military effectiveness and the imperatives of democracy long plagued German politics and society. Many outside observers of German unity after 1989 asked anxiously whether the new Germany might pose a threat to its neighbors. These fears increased sharply in 1992 as the flames of neo-Nazi pogroms lit memories of the years before 1939. Those outside Germany had generally forgotten how the disaster of the Weimar Republic, the Third Reich, and the Wehrmacht in National Socialism had required military reform once the Federal Republic began to arm in the early 1950s. The GDR, by contrast, had received Soviet military institutions dressed in a Prussian tunic that cloaked a Stalinist heart and soul. The military experience of the FRG, unlike that of the GDR, fostered what can only be described as more effective and durable military institutions based upon the ideals of the Basic Law and the Atlantic Alliance. The officers of the Bundeswehr, who had grown to professional maturity in these institutions, confronted unexpectedly the collapse of the Soviet empire and the sudden unification of their country. They had to adapt the principles of civil-military integration that, in the first two decades of the FRG, had spared the Bonn republic from the failures of the army and the democracy of 1919–1933. The passage from NVA to Bundeswehr encourages the hope that the civil-military mechanisms crafted in the post-1945 FRG might withstand the trials of post-1989 Europe. The reform of the Bundeswehr to the dictates of unity unfolded while the traditional causes of war reasserted themselves in Europe.

The story of German soldier coming to German soldier related here affects more than merely Germany itself. Events of 1990–1992 beyond Germany's borders indicated that the requirement of the FRG of the early 1950s to fashion a "good army, a good democracy, and a balanced relationship between the two" concerns Europe as a whole.[9] A continent struggling to unite faces the specter of integral nationalism and instability in the international system of states. The danger of militarism arising from the failure of communism became more acute in the war of Yugoslav succession, which resulted in a German role in NATO "crisis reaction" operations according to the alliance's "New Strategic Concept" of November 1991. This transformation of NATO resulted in the dispatch of German logistics contingents to Croatia within the Implementation Force (IFOR) that reached Bosnia-Herzogovina in December 1995.

The return of war to Europe in the 1990s added further importance to German initiatives within NATO's North Atlantic Cooperation Council (NACC–1991) and within "Partnership for Peace" (PfP–1994). These efforts oversaw a growing range of military-to-military and civilian education programs for the so-called "Partners" to accede to the Atlantic Alliance or to forge a network of military cooperation with the West. Central to this enterprise has been interest in *Innere Führung* and the citizen-in-uniform. The Bundeswehr, long depicted in the propaganda of the Warsaw Pact as field-gray villains in swastikas and dollar signs beneath the NATO compass, now appears to central and eastern Europeans as an example of a successful military transformation from the scourge of totalitarianism and defeat.

NOTES

1. "Vertrag zwischen der Bundesrepublik Deutschland und der Deutschen Demokratishcen Republik über die Herstellung der Einheit Deutschlands," *Bulletin des Presse- und Informationsamtes der Bundesregierung* no. 104 (Bonn, 1990), 1011.
2. Helmut Bohn, introduction to Thomas M. Forster, *Die NVA: Kenrstück der Landesverteidigung der DDR*, 6th ed. (Cologne, 1983), 13–14.
3. Wolfgang Scheler, "(Ost-) Deutsche Soldaten im geistigen Umbruch," *Interdiziplinärer Wissenschaftsbereich Sicherheit: Arbeitspapiere, Mititärakademie 'Friedrich Engels'* 3 (1990): 7–19.
4. Günter Gillessen, "Auflösen—ohen Rest," *Frankfurter Allgemeine Zeitung*, 25 July 1990, 1.
5. Jörg Schönbohm, "Deutschen Kommen zu Deutschen," *Ein Staat, Eine Armee: Von der NVA zur Bundeswehr*, ed. Dieter Farwick (Frankfurt Main/Bonn, 1992), 34.
6. Werner von Scheven, "Bundeswehr, Nationale Volksarmee und die Vereinigung Deutschlands," n.d., speech manuscript, p. 11. For the full text of Scheven's speech see "Die Bundeswehr und der Aufbau Ost," in *Von Kalten Krieg zur deutschen Einheit*, Militärgeschichtlsches Forschungsamt (MGFA), eds. (Munich, 1995), 473–503.
7. Ibid.
8. Ibid.
9. Donald Abenheim, *Reforging the Iron Cross: The Search for Tradition in the German Armed Forces* (Princeton, 1988), 227. For more on NATO reform since the advent of "Partnership for Peace" in January 1994, see NATO Office of Information and Press, eds. *NATO Handbook* (Brussels, 1995) and idem. *NATO at a Glance: Factual Survey of Issues and Challenges* (Brussels, 1996). The reorientation of German security and defense since 1990 is in Bundesministerium der Verteidigung eds., *Weissbuch, 1994: zur Sicherheit der Bundesrepublik Deutschland und zur Lage und Zukunft der Bundeswehr (Bonn,* 1994) and *Force, Statecraft and Unity: The Struggle* to *Adapt Institutions and Practices*, ed. Thomas Durrell Young (Carlisle, 1996).

7 Reflections on the German Question
Gaines Post, Jr.

In May 1966 I drove through a thunderstorm to Obergruppenführer Paul Hausser's apartment near Stuttgart. Former commander of a Waffen-SS division in Hitler's Third Reich, Hausser had agreed to talk with me about my doctoral dissertation in German history. As the interview drew to a close, I tried to measure this man who had worn the black uniform of the fighting arm of the Nazi organization that implemented the Final Solution. He had already taken my measure: "You could have been in Sepp Dietrich's division," he said, referring to the most famous Waffen-SS leader. Hausser meant that as a compliment, for he admired my height—Dietrich accepted no one under six feet in the "Leibstandarte Adolf Hitler"—and assumed that I had "German blood." On the way back to my pension, I stopped my VW and took a long walk, the sky clear now but my nerves shaken by imagining what kind of German I might have been. I still look at Germany through subjective and subjunctive lenses, and this chapter is about the interplay between German history and personal experience.

German unification has humbled whatever faith historians had in their predictive powers, and has also upset their sense of time and their understanding of the "German question." The speed and nature of change in central Europe suggest that history is capricious, less amenable to rules of causation and continuity than the word "discipline" implies, and more open than we thought to memorial connections between the present and the past, especially when the future arrives without warning. Or so it has seemed to me since I visited Berlin in June 1990 for a conference on German unification. Overpowering the meeting's focus on the present was the cumulative effect of reminders of my past encounters with German history: the bust of Theodor Mommsen, the great Roman historian, in the garden on the west side of Humboldt University; the vanishing Berlin Wall; the plaque in the courtyard of the former War Ministry in the Bendlerstrasse (now Stauffenbergstrasse) commemorating martyrs of the abortive plot to assassinate Hitler in July 1944.

Images like these haunted preunification discussions of German identity—the *Historikerstreit* (historians' conflict) of the 1980s, the debate over the purpose of a new German Historical Museum, reviews of German films, and many publications and conferences. Arguments and enmities arose over how Germans should remember the Third Reich and the Holocaust as they defined themselves as a nation.[1] Unification has complicated and enriched this ongoing conversation about the interrelationship of history and national identity. "Whose history?" and "Whose identity?" are now questions that must be answered by citizens who recently belonged to two antithetical political cultures and by historians everywhere for whom the future of Germany's past abruptly changed.

Memory can form a bridge between academic and public engagement with these questions. Memory is not the same thing as history. History means the plausible and verifiable reconstruction of a collective past, usually along a linear and sequential axis of time. Memory recalls highly personal episodes, often at random, without much regard for empirical evidence, social significance, or linearity, at least not until we try to join our personal recollections with those of the community. Yet history and memory have much in common. Both employ imagination and experience to look into the past, both undergo changes over time, both juxtapose past and present, both intermix personal and public consciousness, both confront us with ironies.

As we merge our own memories with history, the fusion and separation of past and present "are in continual tension," as David Lowenthal puts it; the past is "both historical and memorial." Charles Maier notes that memory "mingles private and public spheres . . . [and] conflates vast historical occurrences with the most interior consciousness." Anton Kaes sees a "link between public memory and personal experience," and admires Rainer Werner Fassbinder's films for telling public history with "private stories." David Carr draws a parallel between a community's history and an individual's autobiography; both seek a "unifying structure for a sequence of experiences and actions."[2] History and memory thus are indispensable for knowing one's personal and national identity, although identity involves more than history and history more than memory.

One reason the unification of Germany offers a unique opportunity to explore these linkages, especially the usefulness of memory, is that two generations, broadly speaking, are still alive who remember Nazi Germany and the Second World War. Both differ from succeeding generations in having witnessed the most disturbing period of German history, in formulating the German question, and in relating national identity to individual experience. I belong to the younger of these two generations. We were born shortly before or during the war, too young to have fought in it but old enough to have absorbed it as the central political and moral reference point of our lives.

I cannot separate contemporary Germany from intersections of Germany's past with my own. By recalling these, my purpose is not to gratify nostalgia, advocate atonement, define posttraditional narratives, nor analyze theoretically the interrelationship of history, memory, and time. I wish to exemplify that interrelationship by exploring how the German question—or indeed the "question" for any nation—breaks down into small personal stories that assume large public significance over time. I write as both historian and witness, believing, with Thucydides, that two kinds of experience deepen historical consciousness: actual participation in the events under consideration and participation at one remove through oral testimonies, memoirs, autobiographies, and imagination. Both kinds of experience obligate historians to mediate between history and public memory, in order to show how memory and historical reconstruction shape each other.

During the Second World War, boys on West Lawn Avenue in Madison, Wisconsin, were just as eager to play Rommel as Patton and just as likely to fly a Messerschmitt as a Mustang in mock combat. My brother and I rehearsed double-bunk tactics for defending our bedroom against German invaders, not knowing whether to expect the brutal or the laughable stereotypes that we saw in cartoons at the Orpheum Theater. We and our friends imitated Hitler, the goose step, and anything else that we thought silly about the Germans. I coveted the German army's insignias in neighborhood bartering, but I blamed Germany for starting the war, committing atrocities reported by *Life* magazine, and upsetting my parents. I listened patiently as my father tried to explain why the neighborhood bully called anyone whom he wished to insult "kike," and how this behavior had something to do with why we must win the real war. I knew that our side was right and would triumph. There was no German question in my mind, no thought of an ambiguous German identity. I was certain that Germans liked violence, caused wars, hated Jews, and deserved to be punished for a long time.

My undergraduate advisor at Cornell in the late 1950s was Theodor Ernst Mommsen, a medieval historian who wrote about St. Augustine and Petrarch. Mommsen struggled to overcome deep feelings of inferiority in comparison with illustrious forebears—notably his grandfather, the Roman historian whose namesake he was, and his maternal uncles, the sociologists Max and Alfred Weber. He had received his doctorate at the University of Berlin in 1931 and had taken refuge in Florence when the Nazis seized power in 1933. A Protestant, a liberal, and a humanist, he was profoundly offended by Nazi anti-Semitism and other policies "about which you can't make any compromise," as he wrote to his friend, Felix Gilbert, in April 1933.[3] His funds for research in Italy had been shut off in 1935. Unable to obtain an immigration visa in Britain, he had immigrated to the United

States, where he taught at Yale, Groton School, and Princeton—with Gordon Craig—before moving to Cornell in 1954.

The tips of Mommsen's starched shirt collars curled up, and he could not coordinate the swing of his furled umbrella with an awkward gait. Although shy, he liked to talk with students and could usually be found in his office beyond his scheduled office hours. He was a fine teacher, erudite but not stuffy, demanding but not intimidating. He invited small groups of students to his bachelor apartment on Stewart Avenue in Ithaca, where he played phonograph records of Wagner, chain-smoked cigarettes, and labored nervously, with thick accent, to generate conversation among undergraduates who had never known a Central European intellectual or listened to "Lohengrin" straight through. He never spoke of Germany as his true *Heimat*, with that word's comforting connotations of rootedness and identity. He was a lonely man.

Mommsen remains my ideal as an academic advisor. He guided me into German language, art history, and ancient Greek literature and urged me to read fiction—"historians should read novels," he declared. When I saw him for what I could not know would be the last time, at his office in Boardman Hall in June 1958, he gave me an uncharacteristic pat on the back as he wished me a fruitful summer. A month later he committed suicide. When I heard the news, I knew instantly that he had been telling me a final goodbye.

Mommsen's advice to me, combined with the life and death he chose, remains indelible in my thoughts about Germany. Why did so few Gentile intellectuals leave Nazi Germany? What defense can humane letters muster against inhumane policies? What price must one pay for renouncing, or tolerating, or adopting the Nazis' racist portrayal of German identity? Can an expatriate from such a regime ever go home again? Who is a good German? In military service after leaving Cornell, I requested assignment to Germany partly in order to seek answers to these questions, to which Mommsen's example gave predominantly moral overtones.

During my tour of duty in 1959–1961, central Europe was the hottest spot in the cold war. Relations between West and East went from bad to worse, marked by the shooting down of the American U-2 spy plane over the Ural Mountains during the last year of Dwight Eisenhower's presidency and, in the first few months of John Kennedy's, the Bay of Pigs fiasco in Cuba in April 1961, and the abortive Vienna summit meeting of June. In Vienna, Nikita Khrushchev threatened to conclude a separate peace treaty with East Germany if no international agreement were reached—by the end of the year—making West Berlin a free and demilitarized city. France was still a full-fledged partner in NATO, Britain was not a member of the European Economic Community (EEC). American foreign policy struggled somewhere between George F. Kennan's idea of containing the Soviet Union within its spheres of influence and John Foster Dulles' more belligerent hope of rolling back Soviet hegemony in central and Eastern Europe. With

Kennedy's election, American military strategy began to shift from "massive retaliation" to "flexible response."

The wartime Big Four—Britain, France, the United States, and the Soviet Union—had never negotiated a final postwar settlement regarding Germany's borders, its political and economic system, or the status of Berlin. Using a symmetrical calculus, NATO and the Warsaw Pact had each incorporated half of Germany early in 1955, without publicly admitting that neither side wanted the two halves to reunite as one nation. Each side claimed it saw the dark, totalitarian half of Germany's split personality on the other side. The East-West divisions of Germany and Berlin symbolized the larger dilemma of how two irreconcilable ideologies could prevent Europe from becoming the battleground for a third world war in less than half a century.

I was stationed in Giessen, a drab university town on the Lahn River about forty miles north of Frankfurt and twenty miles downstream from the picturesque medieval town of Marburg. Most of Giessen's old buildings had been demolished in December 1944 during Allied bombing raids. In March 1945, after a fierce battle around Wetzlar, forward elements of the U.S. First Army's III and V Corps had occupied Giessen while on their right flank the Third Army swept northeast toward Kassel. By early 1960, Giessen had rebuilt most of the downtown area in utilitarian concrete and glass, and West Germany's "economic miracle" was conspicuous in new automobiles, highways, houses, radio-phonographs, and clothing stores.

I was assigned to an "Honest John" rocket battalion under the command of V Corps. My battery was responsible for maintaining the warheads, most of them nuclear. At Fort Sill, Oklahoma, a course on nuclear warheads—light on theory, heavy on practice—had taught me how to twist a crank in a socket on the side of the warhead. If the green light flashed, the warhead was ready to deliver to the firing battery. If the red light shone, and if a few remedial measures did not change it to green (sometimes a hard slap on the side of the mechanism did the trick), I had to call the battalion's "special weapons" expert. The procedure was "idiot-proof," as a West Point graduate in my unit liked to say of anything made easy for liberal arts majors commissioned through ROTC.

At staff meetings, we rarely discussed the division of Germany, the volatility of Berlin in cold war politics, the limitations imposed on the Federal Republic's sovereignty, the widespread opposition among West Germans to the presence of nuclear weapons on their soil, or the fact that some Germans still regarded us as an occupying power rather than an ally. We presumed that the Soviet Union might upset the European status quo, that NATO's forces must cooperate against a common enemy, that the United States must remain the dominant member of the alliance, and that we might have to use tactical nuclear weapons. We drove northeast from Giessen in private automobiles and civilian clothes—passing a large sign that said "Germany divided in three parts? Never!"—to inspect the secret positions assigned to us opposite the "Fulda Gap," the most likely route of a Soviet assault. Gap was a misnomer. It referred to an area of valleys between middling massifs, extending northeast from Frankfurt toward Kassel, Bad Hersfeld, and Fulda. If a land war broke out, NATO commanders expected the Soviets to pour armor through this area, their objective to split NATO's forces and drive V Corps across the Rhine. Acknowledging that contingency, our battalion convoyed south to practice moving west across the Rhine, upstream from Mainz and a stone's throw from Oppenheim, where General Patton's Third Army had crossed in the opposite direction in March 1945. In our case, boats were provided by a German engineer battalion.

On 13 August 1961, the East Germans closed the border between East and West Berlin. On the 15th, they erected barricades. The Berlin crisis escalated sharply. Mayor Willy Brandt of West Berlin urged President Kennedy to take strong action, and East Germany threatened to blockade Berlin if West Germany imposed economic sanctions. NATO governments sent protests to Moscow, calling the barricades illegal and accusing the Soviets of violating four-power agreements on Berlin. President de Gaulle ordered a number of French units to be shifted from Algeria to France. The Pentagon announced that extensions of active duty and other measures recently taken by Kennedy were not merely a response to the Berlin crisis, but part of a general buildup in military strength "to meet the world-wide threat." Soviet army units reinforced positions in the East German countryside outside West Berlin. Kennedy decided to send an American battle group from West Germany to West Berlin, to reinforce the Berlin garrison and reaffirm Western rights of access. An American political mission arrived in West Berlin on Saturday the 19th, headed by Vice President Lyndon Johnson and including General Lucius Clay, a hero to Berliners for defying the Soviet blockade of 1948–1949. The East Germans closed all but a handful of crossing points between East and West Berlin, and their barricades grew into a wall.

Early on the morning of Sunday the 20th, the 1st Battle Group, 18th Infantry Division, crossed into East Germany at the Helmstedt checkpoint on the autobahn, bound for West Berlin. My battalion had just completed its annual training test at Grafenwöhr, an old training ground near the Czech border in northern Bavaria where one could still find shrapnel from German exercises as far back as the Second Empire under Kaiser Wilhelm II. We were exhausted, many of us not having slept for three days, and thus the unprecedented stand-by alert put all the more strain on the battalion. We stayed close to our vehicles all day that Sunday. There was little griping; we knew that if the East Germans or Soviets fired on the battle group "the balloon would go up" and our commander would open the white envelope containing top secret orders for our deployment in combat far from Giessen and the Fulda Gap. The atmosphere was much more tense—and the risk of war greater—than most scholarly accounts of the Berlin crisis suggest.[4] One of several rumors flying around the battalion referred to Dresden, but I did not know whether that meant an objective for a NATO advance or, more likely, one of the enemy's points of concentration for an offensive and thus a likely target for American nuclear weapons.

The mention of Dresden and the white envelope caused a chain reaction of memories and reckonings. I associated Dresden not only with Allied saturation bombing during the Second World War, but with my paternal grandmother's Meissen tea service, long a symbol to me of delicacy and refinement in the parched landscape of West Texas. In a secluded storage area at Grafenwöhr two weeks before our training test, I had sat atop crates containing our nuclear warheads, peeling an orange and swinging my legs as I enjoyed the sunshine during a break for lunch. Now I estimated that the number of kilotons on which I had perched far exceeded the combined power of the atom bombs dropped on Hiroshima and Nagasaki and the conventional ones that devastated Dresden early in 1945. I thought about the annihilation of civilian life and the loss of my own, in Germany but not for Germany. The battle group reached Berlin without incident, and, as I learned a few years later from Professor Hans Herzfeld of the Free University of Berlin, West Berliners cheered the troops as if they were liberators, the same spirit that greeted President Kennedy's famous speech there in June 1963.

Because I knew German, I received various liaison assignments: with the German engineer battalion during the river-crossing exercise; on joint maneuvers with the German III Korps in the Westerwald (a heavily forested region northeast of Koblenz where the wind did indeed blow cold, as in an old German army song); with III Korps headquarters in Koblenz; during a major NATO winter exercise in Bavaria called "Wintershield II." Relations between the two armies were good. After the war, the U.S. Army had pushed harder than the State Department for arming Germany, and American commanders admired former Wehrmacht generals like Hans Speidel, Erich von Manstein, and Adolf Heusinger, welcoming their views on how to delay a Soviet assault. After 1955, American military advisory groups had helped train the first divisions of the new West German force, the Bundeswehr. Americans and Germans soon cooperated in staging maneuvers, patrolling the inter-German border, and gathering intelligence.

Like the majority of officers in the Bundeswehr, most of the officers I met in III Korps had served in the Wehrmacht and seen action in the war. Some of them complained about the uneven quality of their recruits, but I was impressed by what I saw. During a coffee break one morning in Koblenz, I walked over to the window to watch a platoon march by below. A German major came over and asked me how long I thought those soldiers had been in the army. "About three weeks," I guessed, thinking back to ROTC summer camp at Fort Bragg, North Carolina. "Three days," he said, smiling at the implicit contrast between national learning curves.

A unique German institution had opened a few years earlier on a hill across the Rhine from Koblenz. The "Schule für Innere Führung" (school for "leadership and character training," to translate freely) instructed officers and NCOs in democratic values, the compatibility between democratic citizenship and military service, and the subordination of the military establishment to civilian control by the defense minister and the Bundestag. The school's founders wished to prevent the Bundeswehr from becoming an undemocratic "state within the state" like the Reichswehr in the Weimar Republic. They also sought to overcome the strong anti-military sentiment among young Germans who reacted against Germany's militaristic past. Had I canvassed officers at III Korps, some would have objected to wasting the Bundeswehr's time on teaching citizenship at this school. Even more would have blamed the Social Democratic Party (SPD) for weakening the nation's will to rearm. Perhaps all of them would have dismissed the SPD's charge, in August 1960, that the leaders of the Bundeswehr were interfering in politics when they issued a memorandum stating that the defense of the Federal Republic required universal conscription, continued membership in NATO, and the acquisition of nuclear weapons. Whatever our disagreements, I found West German officers hospitable, cooperative, and sensitive to the political implications of military affairs. I respected them as allies and friends.

Social protocol in the U.S. Army neither prevented nor fostered associations with German civilians, many of whom whetted my interest in German history. Dr. Fritz Ernst, Rector of Heidelberg University, knew my father and had visited us in Madison when I was in high school. Ernst took me several times to his *Stammtisch* at a *Weinstube* on the Heiligenberg across the Neckar River from the city. There I met German academics of many backgrounds and disciplines, including a gentle botanist with a heavy Swabian accent and deer-horn snuffbox, who, unlike most of his colleagues, treated politics with a light touch and disarming sense of humor.

General (ret.) Hermann Flörke had been decorated personally by Hitler in August 1944 for exceptional valor during the unrelenting Soviet offensive of that summer. He had finished the war commanding a corps against the U.S. First Army as it pressed eastward from the Rhine bridgehead at Remagen. Born in Hannover, compassionate, modest, cultivated, a gentleman in every sense of the word, Flörke forced me to rethink Germany's past while I prompted him to reexamine his career. We began to disagree over topics that we would debate for many years to come. He emphasized a nation's freedom from international pressures, claimed that his units in Poland and Russia had no connection with the Final Solution, blamed Hitler for bad military decisions, and criticized the opposition movement against

Hitler for betraying the state while it was at war. I dwelt on personal freedoms, indirect connections, military advisors, and higher laws.

I ran into old German stereotypes. There were unrepentant anti-Semites, such as the family that proudly used china embossed with the swastika. Refugees and others criticized Chancellor Konrad Adenauer for insisting on peaceful means for regaining the lost territories east of the Oder-Neisse line. Devotees of the Teutonic Knights and geopolitics blamed the United States for not joining Hitler in 1945 to defeat Slavic bolshevism. A veteran with sunken eyes gave me a steel-grey look that said, "we could have won, we should have won." Most Germans I met, however, were willing to accept the subordinate role that recent history and cold war politics gave their country. They admired American ideals of freedom and self-rule, and many of them, particularly from my generation, critically examined the Nazi period. In the spring of 1961, the opening of the trial of Adolph Eichmann in Jerusalem caused Germans to remember and talk about the Third Reich more than they had done before. Adenauer welcomed the trial of Eichmann so that truth and justice would be served, and he stated that nearly every German felt ashamed of the Nazis' crimes. The *Giessener Freie Presse* followed the trial. The city government of Frankfurt published a booklet refuting claims that most Germans knew nothing about Nazi brutality against the Jews. As West Germans wrestled with their consciences, feelings of both guilt and persecution heightened their suspicions that the United States opposed German reunification and might abandon West Berlin.

My experiences and friendships in Germany added new dimensions to the German question. More than ever before, I tried to think of Germany as if I were German. I imagined serving as a lieutenant under Flörke on the eastern front in the Second World War, wondering whether our unit could separate military operations from racial policy, and whether we would disobey any orders to treat Slavs and Jews as "subhumans." In Flörke and the Bundeswehr, I saw examples of *Treue* (loyalty) and *Tapferkeit* (courage) that did not point toward blind obedience or mindless brutality. The Federal Republic generated an "economic miracle" while tying itself to democratic institutions and allies. Thus, I thought, perhaps democracy could for the first time in history become a German habit of mind. Membership in NATO provided security and interdependence, allowing Germans, if they would, to redefine *Macht* (power) so as to renounce unilateral hegemony, and to redefine *Recht* (right) so as to disclaim the territories lost to Poland and the Soviet Union. Whether citizens of the Federal Republic could craft a national identity out of such materials in a divided Germany remained to be seen. The German question had grown more complex than Mommsen's moral personification of it. It had also to do with timeless values exploited by the Nazis, with the relationship between institutions and ideals, and with a nation's international accountability. Coming to terms with the Nazi past would have to take place while Germans weighed eventualities.

When I returned to Germany late in 1965 as a Stanford doctoral candidate in history, I had decided to examine foreign policy and military planning in the Weimar Republic. Some British and American historians tended to treat the republic as a German experiment with democracy that was doomed to fail, an interlude during which the antidemocratic, racist, and expansionist excesses of imperial Germany awaited revival by a new Barbarossa.[5] I wanted instead to give the Weimar Republic a chance to succeed, or at least to state the German question in its own terms. Above all, I wanted to find out just what were Germany's sentiments, actions, and aims during the period of relative political and economic stability, 1924–1929.

My research included interviews and correspondence with about twenty former officers of the Reichswehr (the armed forces of the republic), most of whom became leaders of the Wehrmacht under Hitler.[6] I asked them about Germany's secret rearmament (violating both the Treaty of Versailles and the Weimar Constitution), war games, collaboration with the Foreign Office, the problem of recovering the territories lost to Poland and Czechoslovakia at the peace conference, and relations with the Soviet Union, which shared Germany's animosity toward the West and the new Polish state. Inevitably, their replies alluded also to the Third Reich and Germany after 1945. I used chronological and factual filters to determine the accuracy of their testimony. At the time, I trusted documents more than memories, although I soon found the latter valuable for recapturing personal attitudes. As I reconstruct the notes I took thirty years ago, I feel less inhibited about using memory as evidence and more skeptical of the notion that historical time requires linear thinking and division into discrete periods. As a witness, I am more interested in how memory—theirs and mine—moves us back and forth, shaping and contrasting history, present, and future.

General Flörke considered the Polish Corridor the most invidious and unjust creation of the Versailles treaty. If peaceful diplomacy failed to regain the corridor, then war would be justified. Flörke cited Clausewitz on war as a means of policy, to be used if necessary and in favorable circumstances. Regaining the lost eastern territories from Poland would improve Germany's strategic position, and trebling the size of the one hundred thousand-man army would fill the "military-political vacuum" in central Europe that endangered peace far more than would a rearmed Germany.

General Adolf Heusinger's slight stature and lisp did not diminish his strength of personality or sharpness of mind. He had been one of the brightest members of the army's operations staff in the republic (serving under Erich von Manstein in 1930–1932) and in the Third Reich, rising to the position of chief of operations in the OKH (army high command) late in the war. Living in Cologne after his retirement from the Bundeswehr, he recalled how Hitler's seizure of power had boosted morale in the army by promising to cast off the shackles of the Treaty of Versailles. In the same spirit, I thought, he admired Charles de Gaulle for seizing the requisite freedom of movement (*Bewegungsfreiheit*) for France to act independently in the "world-political constellation" instead of staying in the rut caused by the cold war.

I interviewed Admiral Karl Dönitz on the morning of 4 July 1966, without either of us calling attention to the anniversary of American independence. In the German archives a few months earlier, I had read a strategic paper he wrote while on the naval operations staff in the early 1930s, when the republic's military weakness did not prevent him from thinking ambitiously about Germany's future naval power, freedom, international prestige (*Geltung*), and success in war. He now lived in a modest rooming house near Hamburg, his eyesight, hearing, and memory failing. Although he reiterated the importance of freedom and prestige, he had none of the pent-up energy of that paper and none of the charisma I had expected of the man who succeeded Hitler after the Führer's suicide on 30 April 1945. His good wishes for my career "in a free country" were on my mind later in the day as I watched a demonstration by students at Hamburg University protesting U.S. policy in Vietnam. The students unanimously approved a motion to oppose their government's support of that policy, but hooted when a leader of a left-wing organization accused the United States of warmongering and thwarting social progress everywhere. America's founding fathers, I thought, would have applauded the distinction between these two positions.

General Gotthard Heinrici grew up in Gumbinnen and Königsberg. In our conversation at his home near Stuttgart, he praised the East Prussian values that he himself had exemplified—bravery, loyalty, orderliness, and efficiency. He viewed secret rearmament in the Weimar Republic—including plans to treble the size of the army—as a legitimate breach of national and international law because of the injustice of the Treaty of Versailles. He neither liked Poles nor trusted Social Democrats any more in 1966 than he had forty years earlier. Commander of the Fourth Army and First Panzer Army on the eastern front, and of German forces in the last-ditch defense of Berlin early in 1945, Heinrici hoped I would become a better historian than Cornelius Ryan, who had interviewed him and then, apparently, distorted his testimony in *The Last Battle*.

General Hubert Lanz in many ways confirmed the stereotypical contrast between the extroverted Bavarian, which he was, and Heinrici the stolid East Prussian. He rushed to his home in Munich from his brother's farm "so as not to leave you standing at the door." Portly, jovial, patriotic, and a lover of the outdoors, Lanz regretted that two wars had turned Germany into a rump state, blamed Hitler for Germany's downfall, and regarded the loss of territories after both conflicts as "unjust." He had fought in the Kharkov area, commanding a mountain division in the crushing victory of May 1942 and "Army Detachment Lanz" against the Soviet counteroffensive early in 1943. Having later withdrawn through the Balkans, Lanz told me that, in reply to Tito's postwar indictment of the Wehrmacht for inhuman treatment of Yugoslav partisans, he had used the same terms to describe the partisans' treatment of German soldiers.

Army Detachment Lanz had included Obergruppenführer Paul Hausser's II SS Panzer Corps. Hausser had served as chief of staff of the Second Division (Stettin) in the 1920s, helped organize and train the Waffen-SS in the 1930s, and commanded the SS Division "Das Reich" early in the war. As I drove to our interview, I thought of unconvincing attempts by him and other Waffen-SS veterans to acquit this organization of complicity in the Final Solution and other atrocities. They praised the "European" ideology and *"Soldatengeist"* of the Waffen-SS, in which troops from many countries fought for the construction of a "New Europe" to ward off bolshevism.[7]

Hausser served me tea in his spare apartment in Ludwigsburg, where he lived frugally on his Reichswehr pension, the Waffen-SS having been denied such state support after the war. His face bore the marks of some of his many war wounds as he proudly declared that he had commanded troops at the front instead of sitting at a desk in Berlin. He regretted that Churchill and Roosevelt had not had enough sense to join Hitler against Stalin, the real enemy of all. Silesian by birth, he was glad I had no "Polish blood," yet he denied that the Waffen-SS was a racial elite: "If you take the cream of the crop of volunteers, you are bound to get many tall, blond men." As his guest, I decided not to remind him of the racist content of the curriculum at the SS cadet school in Bad Tölz. Nor did I thank him for considering me SS material when I stood up at the end of the interview.

General Hans Speidel, a Württemberger, had served as chief of staff of Army Detachment Lanz in 1943 and as Rommel's chief of staff in France in 1944. After the First World War, Lieutenant Speidel had written his doctoral dissertation at the University of Tübingen comparing Prussia's recovery after 1807 for its war of liberation (*Befreiungskrieg*) against Napoleon with the situation of the Weimar Republic.[8] He had been disheartened then by the republic's powerlessness, encirclement (*Einkreisung*), weak political leadership, and lack of national will, all of which denied Germany freedom. Germany had a right to regain the lost territories, and right depended on power. He returned to these themes in an interview at his home in Bad Honnef in June 1966, three years after retiring from his command of NATO Land Forces, Central Europe. I had met Speidel at exercise Wintershield II in January 1961, where we briefly discussed our mutual interest in history. "Nun, wir sind Kollegen!" (Well, we are colleagues), he had said. Now he nodded as I told him I had read his dissertation. In the 1930s, he affirmed, Hitler had impressed the officer corps by pledging to restore Germany's freedom through rearmament, a strong foreign policy, decisive leadership, and a united people. Our talk ended before I could ask him what he thought would make the Federal Republic truly free.

I met Ambassador Eugen Ott at the railroad station in Murnau on 23 June. He wore tweed knickers, a white cotton jacket, and a brown beret, and I could feel his pale blue eyes quickly sizing me up as we greeted each other on the platform. We walked up a hill to a small park with a view of the Staffelsee to the northwest and the Bavarian Alps to the south. A thunderstorm soon drove us inside the station's restaurant. Ott had been Kurt von Schleicher's chief military advisor in the early 1930s, when Schleicher made and broke chancellors until his own brief chancellorship fell to other schemers in January 1933. According to Ott (whose memory of events easily passed an unobtrusive test I had devised), Schleicher accepted the chancellorship in November 1932 reluctantly and fatalistically, telling Ott, "he who is about to die salutes you," for Schleicher "knew that his path would lead to his demise." In June 1934, Schleicher was assassinated in the "night of the long knives." Ott became Germany's military attaché in Tokyo (1934–1938) and then ambassador to Japan (1938–1943).

Ott told me that the idea of a *Befreiungskrieg* provided an explicit psychological lift for war games immediately after Hitler became chancellor in January 1933. I had called Ott's attention to Major Alfred Jodl's guidelines for the annual commanders' war game that spring. These included an unusually bold hypothesis that had only been implied in Germany's eastern policy during the Weimar Republic: in the struggle for "the recovery of its complete freedom," Germany concluded a secret treaty with the Soviet Union that would restore Germany's old eastern borders in an eastern European war while Italy held France in check in the west.[9] Jodl would later use the even more flamboyant Nazi language of *Lebensraum* as a member of Hitler's military staff and was executed at Nuremberg after the war. Ott attributed Hitler's popularity not just to the Germans' desire for freedom and rights, but also to their historical craving for release or deliverance (*Erlösung*). He saw these emotions in Ludwig Beck, whom he described as extraordinarily civilized and intelligent. Beck had told Ott that Hitler's seizure of power was cause for celebration because Hitler could free Germany, release it from burdens and doubts, and put it on the map again.

Beck's name had come up a month earlier when I visited General Max von Viebahn and his wife in their home on a hillside in a village on the northeastern edge of the Black Forest. They and their daughters, one of whom had learned English in Cambridge (England) and the other in New Jersey, were most hospitable, and Frau von Viebahn proudly showed me fledglings in a nest outside the sitting-room window. The Viebahns asked me to sign their guest book and said I should feel free to look at its earlier pages. On one of these, I found the firm signature of General Beck, who had arranged for Viebahn's appointment in February 1938 as chief of the operations staff in the newly formed OKW (armed forces high command). Viebahn had suffered a nervous breakdown in March, when he concluded that Hitler's determination to annex Austria meant war. Jodl had replaced him, eager to support Hitler's designs for German expansion against the moderate counsel of generals like Beck. Beck resigned as chief of the general staff in August 1938 over disagreement with Hitler's plan to seize parts of Czechoslovakia, by force if necessary, as a preliminary step toward acquiring *Lebensraum* in the east. My host said wistfully, "Beck was the finest mind in the German Army."

As I drove back to my small hotel near Freiburg, I wondered why Beck applauded Hitler's accession in 1933; why eleven years later he died as a leader of the plot against Hitler; and why my friend General Flörke, decorated in August 1944 by Hitler whose arm was in a sling from the concussion of the bomb meant to kill him, still condemned the plot as treason even though he rejected the policy of *Lebensraum* and abhorred the crimes committed by the Nazi state. I also thought of Theodor Mommsen, whose love for Germany had made him leave it, and whose cousin had recently told me he could not understand why Theodor said after the war that he could not return to Germany because he "owed America too much."

Because of these interviews, the German question had for me become deeply imbedded in layers of time. The recollections of these men informed my study of the Weimar Republic and suggested parallels between it and the Federal Republic. I argued that, in its calmest years, Weimar Germany combined democracy with authoritarian tendencies that could have prevailed even without the Great Depression or the rise of Hitler. The Weimar Republic also mixed international cooperation with national objectives—particularly rearmament and recovery of the eastern territories—that would have shaken the European territorial status quo, through war if peaceful means failed, as soon as the government deemed the international climate favorable. I knew the dreadful future of Weimar politics and foreign policy, and this knowledge surely influenced my depiction of a Germany poised somewhere between the inevitability of Nazism and the likelihood of democracy and peace over the long term.

In spite of the Federal Republic's much greater stability and its membership in NATO and the EEC, I was made uneasy by familiar references—largely, but not only from these older Germans—to power, right, freedom, unpatriotic Socialists, lost territories, "Polish housekeeping" (*polnische Wirtschaft*), deliverance, and *Bewegungsfreiheit* (e.g., in the event of a Sino-Soviet conflict). Using such language, the officers whom I interviewed implicitly wrote Germany's history and charted its future. Many of them used memory to justify personal experience, a process that breeds certitude in looking back and ahead. A witness at one remove from their past, my self-consciousness as a historian made me want to understand that past, not to justify it, although General Hausser's placing me in the Waffen-SS nearly stripped away that remove and yanked me, momentarily, into his realm of self-justification. Although I did not know this republic's future, I thought I knew enough about its historical inheritance to assume that West

Germans needed at least another generation before they would think democratically by habit, and that German unification would either cause or follow war. For the next two decades, my memory of an older generation's reminiscences sustained my perception of powerful continuities in the German question. From the Second Empire to the present, I concluded, Germany had tried several variations on the theme of national identity, all without genuinely embracing democracy or effectively mastering power.

Not my judgment, not even my most hopeful dreams, prepared me for what I witnessed in Berlin in June 1990. On the 22nd, our small group of American educators had lunch with members of the Democratic Republic's first democratically elected *Volkskammer* (parliament). The day before, the parliaments of both Germanys had approved the treaty for economic union. Today, Checkpoint Charlie would be hoisted from the Friedrichstrasse before the eyes of the foreign ministers of the "2 plus 4" nations—exactly forty-nine years after Nazi Germany invaded the Soviet Union, nearly twenty-nine years after the construction of the Berlin Wall put my artillery battalion on alert, and twenty-four years after East German border guards frisked me as I crossed into East Berlin to talk with East German historians at the German Academy of Sciences.

I sat with two of the delegates at lunch in the Volkskammer dining room, overlooking the massive Berlin minster built at the turn of this century. Vera Wollenberger had joined the opposition movement about ten years earlier, and was dismissed from her teaching position in philosophy. She was among the demonstrators arrested in January 1988 for demanding freedom of assembly and freedom of the press. Her imprisonment, exile, and return to East Germany on 9 November 1989 (when the Berlin Wall opened) made her one of the heroes of the revolution, although she was too modest to see herself in such a light. She told me that among her own heroes were the student members of the "White Rose," who, along with their philosophy professor at the University of Munich, were executed by the Gestapo in 1943 for defying the Nazi dictatorship. She expressed two fears: that her small and idealistic party (Alliance 90/Greens), which had reaped tiny electoral rewards for its major role in the peaceful revolution, would be crushed as the Christian Democratic Union and Social Democratic Party consolidated their power in East Germany and merged with their western counterparts; that the principles and spirit of political opposition would fade as the Federal Republic absorbed the smaller, newer democracy. After her election in December 1990 to the first all-German Bundestag, Wollenberger supported the peace movement, a liberal asylum policy, and unrestricted access to the Stasi (security police) files of the former GDR, in which she discovered that her own husband had informed on her.

Dr. Eberhard Brecht, a physicist by training, represented the Social Democratic Party. His family tree, which includes civil servants, mayors, pastors, scholars, and artists, had been nourished by liberal democratic ideals since before the German revolution of 1848. His great-uncle, Arnold Brecht, a prominent government official in the Weimar Republic, had left Nazi Germany on 9 November 1933, precisely fifteen years after the proclamation of the republic, for New York City, where he joined many other German exiles on the faculty of the New School for Social Research and, in 1946, became a U.S. citizen. About twenty-five years ago, reflecting on his experiences in Weimar Germany and the United States, Arnold Brecht wrote: "For democracy to function properly it is a necessary condition that a broad majority of the people appreciate democratic ideals and earnestly want to see democratic rules of the game obeyed, whether out of romantic enthusiasm for the will of the people, or because of a firmly held trust in the ultimate wisdom of the common man in fundamental questions of policy, or simply out of fear that uncontrolled autocratic power will be misused."[10]

Eberhard Brecht told me that his uncle's correlation of function and ideals had influenced him greatly, as had the "Prague Spring" of 1968 and Vera Wollenberger's example of protest. Like her, he believed that East German representatives in the future all-German Bundestag could help shape German foreign policy by reassuring countries in central and Eastern Europe and pressing for East-West reconciliation. He seemed readier than she to make compromises with other parties, but no less troubled by the problem of how their democracy ought to go about protecting itself against its internal enemies, who could still be found in the Volkskammer and bureaucracy. Reconciliation and compromise soon colored Brecht's work as an SPD deputy in the all-German Bundestag, where he warned against paternalistic attitudes in western Germany and antidemocratic sentiments in the eastern states.

Berlin's atmosphere was exhilarating, charged with freedom, fellowship, and expectation. The German question suddenly meant the immediate process and future effects of unification. Yet I also found myself tugged backward by memory and history. The Mommsen sculpture recalled his grandson and the anguish of expatriation. Harmless traces of the Berlin Wall, resembling ancient foundations on the Athenian acropolis, evoked explosive realities of the cold war. As I stood in the courtyard of the former War Ministry, a middle-aged woman placed white roses beneath the plaque that reads "HERE DIED FOR GERMANY ON 20 JULY 1944. . . ." She paused for a minute with head bowed, then left as purposefully as she had entered, her manner suggesting a long-standing and deeply felt ritual. Among the names immortalized there is that of Ludwig Beck, whose autograph I had seen many years before while engrossed in the oral history of Weimar and Nazi Germany.

When I returned to Germany in February 1996, history and memory again created ironies. In Heidelberg, the headquarters of USAREUR (U.S. Army Europe) was still located at Campbell Barracks, which had been constructed in 1937 as the *Grossdeutschland-Kaserne* to accommodate the Wehrmacht's 110th Infantry Regiment. The carved swastikas beneath the two stone eagles flanking the front gate were still covered by the USAREUR shield that preserves the flaming sword of liberation from the wartime insignia of SHAEF (Supreme Headquarters Allied Expeditionary Force). Of the sharply reduced American forces in post–cold war Germany, many had been sent to Bosnia, where they cooperated with Russian troops. Only a handful of American soldiers remained in Giessen, none of them in combat units. Garrisons once full of Americans now formed small ghost towns, their silence accented by a light snowfall.

On the way to my old base on the eastern outskirts of Giessen, I passed the Volkshalle. I had attended a speech there by Willy Brandt in October 1960, shortly before the Social Democratic Party named him its candidate for chancellor in the next general election. Party officials distributed a leaflet entitled, "Go with the times, go with the SPD." It contained a short biography of the mayor and a statement of his principles. On the cover was a photograph of Brandt taken in February 1959 at a dinner in Springfield, Illinois, commemorating Abraham Lincoln; behind Brandt was a large banner quoting Lincoln, "A house divided against itself cannot stand." In his statement, Brandt affirmed that democracy was neither guaranteed by a constitution nor handed over like an invoice; it required incessant care and striving. In his speech, he asked Germans to stand united against communism and declared that German freedom and democracy needed "the energies of the younger generation."

In February 1996, Brandt was dead, and Helmut Kohl had been chancellor nearly as long as Adenauer held the office. Brandt's innovative "Ostpolitik," which improved relations with East Germany and the other Warsaw Pact countries, earning Brandt the Nobel Peace Prize, had been overshadowed by Kohl's adroit accomplishment of German reunification following the collapse of the Iron Curtain. The German government was trying to send recent immigrants back home, and it limited the influx of ethnic Germans from the former Soviet Union whom West Germany had given the constitutional right in 1949 to acquire German citizenship. Germany's younger generation was struggling to find work in a country where economic growth stagnated, and the rate of unemployment stood at 10 percent. I saw few cheerful faces and no quotes from Lincoln as Germans tried to define what they were united for and against.

Visiting Germany since 1989 has made me see German unification as an immense historical divide where memory will shape the future while reshaping the past. Germans on both sides of the former Iron Curtain have a new *Stunde Null* for working out their common identity. As they do, knowing that memory recognizes no zero hour, how will they remember their history?[11] We now know that Germany united through largely democratic means, without exploiting or threatening war, and renounced its lost territories. Are Germans and historians therefore likely to accentuate those heartening elements of Germany's past that point to this future and to give commensurately less attention to authoritarian, aggressive, arrogant, and exclusionary tendencies? (Would I, for example, now write a different book on Weimar military and foreign policy?) Or will they warn that such tendencies can resurface under prolonged economic and social stress, as has happened in the outburst of extremist violence against guest workers and asylum-seekers?

Both approaches—sometimes called "positive" and "critical"—have survived the historians' debate of the 1980s. The latter course, especially for non-Germans, risks adopting an apocalyptic double standard. Americans, in particular, may pose the German question as if the worst of German history could repeat itself whereas the best of ours is yet to come. Moreover, we expect Germans to define their national identity at a time when large-scale immigration stretches our own social fabric and when the spiteful epithet "un-American" has outlived communism. The greater risk, however, lies in using the "positive" course for recreating the past largely to convince ourselves that as individuals we did not or would not have behaved badly, or that as a nation we were only temporarily misled by demons not of our own making. When we employ history for this purpose, often to deny or expiate guilt that we either feel or resent being told we should feel, we stop conversing with the past or with ourselves. We alter the past. We cease to acknowledge that, quite apart from the problem of guilt, history gives us moral dilemmas bound up with personal choices.

Although this didactic power of history is universal, there is something singularly compelling about the German question. Twentieth-century Germany has come to symbolize matters of the heart that define what it means to be human. These things make historians uneasy, persuading many of us to stick to projects that have little impact on public consciousness while prompting a few of us to enter the marketplace only because we suspect each other of misleading the public for political ends. What are historians to do? Richard Evans observes that, "in the postmodern world, history plays an increasingly important role in political culture." But what role can historians play if, as David Lowenthal laments, "the consensually shared past shrinks to a thin media-dominated veneer" in literate societies where knowledge is fragmented? Maybe historians should tell stories, drawing upon their own memories of having engaged questions of personal choice and national identity in their study of history and in their observation of unfolding events. Using personal memory to mediate between history and public recollection, the historian can help guide collective memory along both positive and critical avenues of historical reflection by finding national and transnational values of the best quality and developing a meaningful narrative that traces continuity and change.[12]

Using my own history as an example, I have shown that the German question has visceral, moral, imaginative, temporal, and memorial qualities. Reflecting on real and imagined encounters with German history, I view German unification with mixed feelings—anxious that the generals' nationalistic reminiscences in 1965–1966 might reemerge in German policy today, yet more confident than ever before that democracy and internationalism have taken firm root there. Asking myself whether I would be a good German now makes me wonder whether I would have emulated Mommsen, Flörke, Beck, Hausser, or Wollenberger then. I suppose I would have wanted to be either as good an officer as Flörke or as courageous an opponent of tyranny as Wollenberger. But of one thing I am sure: For Germans and non-Germans alike, every generation's private memories offer public evidence for what it means—or might mean—to be German. Unification has given Germans the unparalleled opportunity to sift through this evidence to identify Germany's better nature.

NOTES

This chapter substantially revises and expands my "German Unification and Historical Memory" article that originally appeared in *The Historian* 58, 2 (Winter, 1996): 473–86.

1. For good summaries, see Peter Baldwin, ed., *Reworking the Past: Hitler, the Holocaust, and the Historians' Debate* (Boston, 1990); Richard J. Evans, *In Hitler's Shadow: West German Historians and the Attempt to Escape from the Nazi Past* (New York, 1989); Charles S. Maier, *The Unmasterable Past: History, Holocaust, and German National Identity* (Cambridge, Mass, 1988). See also Anton Kaes, *From "Hitler" to "Heimat": The Return of History as Film* (Cambridge, Mass., 1989); Saul Friedlander, ed., *Probing the Limits of Representation: Nazism and the "Final Solution"* (Cambridge, Mass., 1992).

2. David Lowenthal, *The Past Is a Foreign Country* (New York, 1985), 186–87; Maier, *Unmasterable Past*, 149; Kaes, "Hitler" to "Heimat," 83, 198; David Carr, *Time, Narrative and History* (Bloomington, Ind., 1986), 163.

3. Felix Gilbert, *A European Past: Memoirs, 1905–1945* (New York, 1988), 144. For sketches of Mommsen, see also Norman F. Cantor, *Inventing the Middle Ages* (New York, 1991), 371–74, 397–402, 404–7; Robert E. Lerner, "Ernst Kantorowicz and Theodor E. Mommsen," in *An Interrupted Past: German-Speaking Refugee Historians in the United States after 1933*, ed. Hartmut Lehmann and James J. Sheehan (New York, 1991), 200–205; Frederick G. Marcham, introduction to Theodor E. Mommsen, *Medieval and Renaissance Studies*, ed. Eugene F. Rice, Jr. (Ithaca, 1959). I am indebted to Professor Karl F. Morrison for his recollections in a personal letter.

4. See, for example, Robert M. Slusser, *The Berlin Crisis of 1961* (Baltimore, 1973).

5. To name a few examples: A.J.P. Taylor, *The Course of German History* (London, 1946), chaps. 11, 12; Winston S. Churchill, *The Second World War*, vol. 1, *The Gathering Storm* (Boston, 1948), bk. 1, chap. 4; Koppel S. Pinson, *Modern Germany* (New York, 1954), chaps. 14–20. None of these books had as much impact on

American consciousness of German history as did William L. Shirer's *The Rise and Fall of the Third Reich* (New York, 1960), in which most of Germany's earlier roads lead to Hitler.

6. For biographical information on most of the officers discussed on the following pages, see Correlli Barnett, ed., *Hitler's Generals* (New York, 1989); Peter Hoffman, *The History of the German Resistance, 1933–1945*, trans. Richard Barry (Cambridge, Mass., 1977); B. H. Liddell Hart, *The German Generals Talk* (New York, 1948); Klaus-Jürgen Müller, *Das Heer und Hitler: Armee und nationalsozialistisches Regime, 1933–1940* (Stuttgart, 1969); Robert J. O'Neill, *The German Army and the Nazi Party, 1933–1939* (London, 1966).

7. Paul Hausser, *Waffen-SS im Einsatz* (Göttingen, 1953); Felix Steiner, *Die Freiwilligen* (Göttingen, 1958); idem, *Die Armee der Geächteten* (Göttingen, 1963).

8. Hans Speidel, "1813/1924: Eine militärpolitische Untersuchung," Ph.D. diss., University of Tübingen, 1925.

9. Gaines Post, Jr., *The Civil-Military Fabric of Weimar Foreign Policy* (Princeton, 1973), 329–30.

10. Arnold Brecht, *The Political Education of Arnold Brecht: An Autobiography, 1884–1970* (Princeton, 1970), 185.

11. See Konrad H. Jarausch, *The Rush to German Unity* (New York, 1994), 197–210; James J. Sheehan, "National History and National Identity in the New Germany," *German Studies Review* (special issue, Winter 1992): 163–74; Rudy Koshar, "The Shock of 'It Was': Memory and Germany Unification," in *German Unification: Problems and Prospects*, ed. Gaines Post, Jr. (Claremont, Calif., 1992). I am grateful to Professor Koshar for his comments on an early draft of this chapter.

12. Evans, *In Hitler's Shadow*, 135; Lowenthal, *The Past Is a Foreign Country*, 238; see Charles Maier's discussion of Jürgen Habermas' "postconventional identity," in *The Unmasterable Past*, 151–55.

Afterword: Gordon A. Craig and the Old-Fashioned Way of Doing History

David Wetzel and Theodore S. Hamerow

The reader of the preceding seven chapters will by now be so deeply aware of the influence that Gordon A. Craig has exercised over their respective authors that he might want to know a little more about Gordon Craig's own background and outlook. This is not an easy topic. Gordon Craig's scholarly output has been both high in quality and broad in scope. He has also played a considerable part in public affairs for more than fifty years. He has instructed us on matters as diverse as the diplomacy of the Helsinki Conference of 1975 and the genius of Theodor Fontane. His powers have never shown any sign of fading. There is therefore no reason to apologize for being fascinated with his life and to end our volume with a chapter about him in his own right.

Gordon Craig has been a man of letters, a consultant to various branches of the U.S. government, adviser to prime ministers of Great Britain and Germany, as well as a historian. A portrait of him that left out any of these aspects would be a misleading one. For instance, though most of the public know Gordon Craig as an author and an authority on the modern history of Germany and international relations, something needs to be said about Gordon Craig the teacher. No one ever knew better how to stir the excitement of history. Behind the lectern Craig displayed an amazing knowledge of his subject and the ability to present it with extraordinary cogency and clarity. His lectures were remarkably compact, beautifully organized, and elegantly phrased. Moving with ease from one topic to another, he exhibited analytical power honed to razor sharpness. Always careful, precise, and thorough, he instilled an eradicable sense of the importance of those qualities. In his graduate courses his students received training so rigorous that they could never again look at a source without thinking of him. Quite palpably, therefore, they carried into their own work as historians the imprint of what he taught them.

In the meanwhile, his reputation as a scholar grew thanks to a succession of outstanding publications. He wrote several books and edited several others, including, in 1953, a coedited collection, *The Diplomats, 1919–1939*, to which a sequel, a book with the same title dealing with the period 1939–1979 and coedited by his friend, Francis L. Loewenheim, appeared forty years later.[1] Over the years, at home and abroad, a number of honors have come his way of which one, the presidency of the American Historical Association in 1982, was the most conspicuous, but by no means the only, example.

But to go back. Gordon Alexander Craig was born in Glasgow, Scotland on 26 November 1913. He showed from the outset a predilection for German and international history. To this predilection a trip to Germany in 1935, where he did work on "The Rise and Fall of the Weimar Republic," his honors thesis which he completed and submitted the following year to Princeton University, as well as a two-year sojourn to Oxford as a Rhodes Scholar from 1936 to 1938 contributed significantly. Craig became interested in Weimar and in important diplomatic questions of the nineteenth century. He gave each of these a good deal of attention while he was abroad. On his return to the United States he continued to ponder them while he did graduate work at Princeton, from which he received his B.A. five years earlier. There, in 1941, when he was twenty-eight, he earned his Ph.D. after writing a thesis that marked the beginning of his career as a diplomatic historian. The subject of his dissertation was "Britain and Europe, 1866–1869."

He would return repeatedly to diplomatic themes during the next four decades when he taught first at Princeton from 1941 to 1961 and, afterwards, at Stanford and the Free University of Berlin. But like so many other people from various walks of life, he became increasingly absorbed after the end of the Second World War with the German problem. Indeed his preoccupation with diplomatic history dovetailed with this interest and reinforced it. Inevitably, therefore, he found himself drawn into the controversy over what to do about the country that produced Hitler and that launched, in the space of twenty years, two world wars. Many historians in the 1940s and 1950s, both in the United States and Europe, were inclined to believe that there was something peculiarly wicked in the German character that by nature made Germans uniquely subservient to aggression, militarism, and tyranny. In the eyes of these historians the Germans were inherently anti-democratic; their former enemies could do no more than see to it that the Germans did not solve their problem at others' expense, and in practice this meant doing everything that was possible to keep Germany divided. As A.J.P. Taylor put it in 1961: "Only a divided Germany can be a free Germany. A reunited Germany would cease to be free: either it would become a militaristic state in order to resume the march toward European domination, or its power would be compulsorily reduced by foreign interference if the allies had the sense to come together in time." And he added with characteristic *gemainerie*: "It was no more of a mistake for the German people to end up with Hitler than it is an accident when a river flows into a sea."[2]

This attitude has not died away with the passage of time. On the contrary, it has a genuine contemporaneity on both sides of the Atlantic—the sensation created by Daniel Jonah Goldhagen and his book *Hitler's Willing Executioners* (1996) is but the most recent example. The very title of the book reveals its thesis. One observer noted: "Goldhagen has revived the notion that there is something indelibly spooky about the Germans—a gene in the culture that outsiders cannot detect and that gets passed from generation to generation."[3] This comment was a plausible deduction from a book that indicted a nation and that implied, if it did not explictly assert, that most Germans were, all along, covert Nazis and could become Nazis again. All the same, the thesis was not all that new. A.J.P. Taylor had been playing this tune for forty years.

To Gordon Craig the views of Taylor and Goldhagen are no more than facile attempts to peer into the German mind and character. Any reading of his work on the modern history of Germany will underscore this. That the German record was marked by some of the most dreadful episodes in recorded history Craig readily accepts; that there was something inherently defective in the German character he flatly denies. On the contrary, he sees German life and political action in the nineteenth and twentieth centuries as the record of attempts to create a viable democracy. The attempts failed. But that did not make them any less important—or even noble, as he wrote in 1978:

The darkest pages of history are also the most instructive. The brief history of united Germany, which lasted seventy-five years and died in the ruble of Berlin, demands the attention of reflective men, not only for what it has to teach about the role of fear and cupidity and obtuseness in human affairs, about the seductions of power and the consequences of political irresponsibility, and about the limitless inhumanity that man is capable of inflicting upon his fellows, but because it also has much to say about courage and steadfastness, about devotion to the cause of liberty, and about resistance to the evils of tyranny.[4]

These words formed the preface to one of Craig's most famous books, *Germany 1866–1945* (1978), but they may also be viewed as the guiding thread running through all of his works on Germany—namely, his belief that whoever studies German history studies the role of individuals in the shaping of it. The Germans are a people whose progress out of darkness has been a painful one, marked by enormous sufferings and devastating setbacks. Yet Craig has, in all his writings, always managed to find Germans whose faith in the dignity and charity of man survived against the winds that tore at it. Even their worst tyrants never lacked opponents and, as he wrote in a passage from the same book quoted above: "There were always men and women who shared the belief expressed in one of Ferdinand Freiligrath's poems—

> Trotz alledem und alledem,
> trotz Dummheit, List und alledem,
> wir wissen doch: die Menschlichkeit
> behält den Sieg trotz alledem—

and who risked their careers and their lives to create the kind of Germany in which this could come true."[5]

This belief has been Craig's for a long time. An early example came with the publication of "Hans Delbrück: The Military Historian" in *The Makers of Modern Strategy*, a book that appeared under the editorship of Edward Mead Earle in 1943. Challenging the earlier historiography that had explained that the military had been immune from criticism of civilians, Craig argued that Delbrück's work proved just the opposite. By writing a steady stream of articles in the *Preussiche Jarhbücher* on whose editorial board he sat from 1883 to 1890 prior to the outbreak of the First World War, Delbrück became a thorn in the side of the German government. In 1899, for instance, as professor at the University of Berlin, he used the columns of the journal to denounce the government's policy of Germanization in Schleswig-Holstein, an offense for which he was hauled before a disciplinary court with a view to dismissal. Delbrück's life and work may, Craig argued, stand as an example of a heroic attempt to secure restraint by civilians over the armed forces and to do so with clear sight and with a mind that was not blinded by the chauvinistic conceit that so pervaded the atmosphere of the time.[6]

Military maneuverings, short term bids for advantage, and the all too frequent miscalculation of politicians and statesmen were at the heart of Gordon Craig's most famous book, *The Politics of the Prussian Army* (1955). Though this great work is now over forty years old, it still serves as one of the major texts of German history. There can be few works of such breadth that pursue a thesis with such single-minded consistency. In a nutshell Craig argued that in Germany the military establishment has, since the time of the accession of the Great Elector in 1645, tended to become a state within a state, that as such it inhibited social progress and blocked the development of liberal and democratic institutions, and that—in Imperial Germany, the Weimar Republic, and the Third Reich—it either encouraged or condoned the kind of adventurous foreign policy that led to aggressiveness and to the kind of war that was disastrous for the nation. But militarism, aggression, and nazism are not inherent in the German character. In Craig's words: "Rather they are the product of a structure which vitiated the attempts to create a viable democracy." He went on:

Inveterate Germanophobes are apt to forget that such attempts were made. Yet it can scarcely be denied that the reforms inaugurated in Prussia after 1807 represented a comprehensive effort to transform the social and political structure of Prussia and to make this state a constitutional kingdom capable of developing in the same direction as the more liberal states of the West. The revolution of 1848, in Prussia and in the other German states, was an attempt of the same nature. In the constitutional struggle in Prussia in the 1860s, fought out in the years immediately preceding the unification of Germany under Prussian leadership, organized Prussian liberalism sought to restrict the prerogatives of the Crown and lay the foundation for an effective evolution towards parliamentary democracy. Finally, in the catalogue of earnest attempts to secure reform, the strivings of the Progressive and Socialist Parties after 1871 should be mentioned, as should the experiment which was born of the military collapse of 1918 and was finally defeated by Hitler's rise to power.[7]

The most incisive parts of the book come from the portraits he draws of individuals in the years 1862–1864, the period (the first of two, Weimar being the second) when the army was under assault from liberalism. It is well known that Albrecht von Roon, the Chief of Staff, was out to thwart the attempts of the parliament to determine the size and character of the army. Craig showed that Roon was himself threatened from the more extreme of the generals, particularly from Edwin von Manteuffel, who wished to destroy the constitution altogether and establish a dictatorship of the monarchy. Bismarck certainly defeated the chamber but he and Roon also managed to defeat Manteuffel and to remove him from the personal relationship he enjoyed with William I. Bismarck appears in new clothes as the defender of both the constitutional balance against the liberals and generals alike. Indeed, though Bismarck always resisted parliamentary sovereignty, he successfully asserted civilian authority against the Prussian generals. The tangled web of subterfuge and deception that the Prussian generals built up after 1871 was designed to thwart none other than Bismarck. He was too strong for them. It needed the weaknesses of the later chancellors and the frivolity of William II to give the generals the free run they enjoyed in the years before the outbreak of the First World War.[8]

Bismarck was not the only example of those who resisted, though less successfully, attempts by the military to control civilian policy. So was Theobald von Bethmann-Hollweg, Imperial chancellor during the First World War. Craig was decidedly critical of Bethmann's handling of relations with the generals in the period immediately preceding the outbreak of war in July 1914. But as the struggle wore on, he found much to praise in the attitude that he took in the face of what was united military opposition on matters like the introduction of unrestricted submarine warfare and attempts to reach a negotiated settlement. Bethmann, insisted Craig, had beliefs of his own, even though he was hamstrung in his attempts to translate them into policy. Among the deepest of these was his conviction that, in order to effectively prosecute the war, the government had to press ahead with a program of social reform. For this he deserved credit.[9]

The Nazi period was something else altogether. Nowhere did Craig deny that, to the day of his death, Hitler commanded greater popularity and support than any other German has ever had. But Craig showed that Hitler also owed this authority to terror, to cynical calculation, and above all to the army chiefs who had shirked their obligations to the people.[10] Craig conceded that after 1938 army opposition to Hitler may have been moot, given the strength that National Socialism had gathered. But that did not prevent him from delivering a crushing judgment:

The important point . . . is that the great majority of those in a position to take action neither did so nor recognized that they had any obligation to do so; and it is in this failure that the responsibility of the officer corps lies.[11]

Craig also recognized that there were others whose objective it was—in the years before 1939 and after—to save their country from the disaster that Hitler would bring upon it. One of those was Colonel-General Werner Freiherr von Fritsch, Chief of the Army Command from 1934 to 1938. Craig did not make light of Fritsch's shortcomings—his timidity, his reluctance to engage in political affairs, and his general moodiness and penchant for cynicism. But he had no difficulty finding his strengths. Fritsch was, among other things, "before his disgraceful dismissal in 1938," one of a number of officers who were determined to see the army remain as an autonomous force, free from party control, having as its *raison d'être* the protection of the vital interests of the state, and anxious that it not become the passive executor of Hitler's grandiose schemes.[12]

The same was true of Colonel-General Ludwig Beck, Chief of Staff of the German army from October 1933 to October 1938. Craig saw Beck as a political visionary, out of touch with the masses whose support he would have to have if he were to be successful in his efforts to defeat Hitler's aims. But he sympathized with Beck's efforts and particularly with his view, stated repeatedly in his writings, that the German officer corps had to repay the confidence the people placed in them by staving off disaster.[13]

Craig thus explained and added new meaning to the German problem. But his book was more than that. It had genuine philosophical significance. It traced the three-hundred-year ascendancy of the army from the founding of the Hohenzollern military state by the Great Elector and Frederick William I in a straightforward narrative approach and in prose that was sensitive, polished, and, above all, clear. A work of profound learning and beautiful simplicity, it showed triumphantly that the old-fashioned way of doing history makes sense.

The Politics of the Prussian Army is certainly no more illustrative in focusing on what Craig believed to be the essential goodness of the German people than two of his later works, *Germany 1866–1945* (1978) and *The Germans* (1982). The first of these, a magisterial volume in the Oxford

History of Modern Europe, appeared in 1978. His contribution was so basic that no serious student of the subject could afford to ignore it. It was noteworthy for its tone as well as for its substance. Though relentless in its pursuit of detail, it was also a monument of erudition. The arrangement was conventional: one fourth of the book dealt with the Bismarckian era, one fourth with the Wilhelminian, one fourth with the Republican and one fourth with the Hitlerian. Craig's story was, he wrote, a tragic story. The spectacle of immeasurable evil on a mass scale that was part of the period he examined aroused in him pity, horror, and indignation, but never, unlike some writers on the subject, self-righteousness. He declared on the first page: "One runs the risk of being considered old-fashioned if one gives too much preference to personality,"[14] but later registered his agreement with the great Italian historian Federico Chabod: "In a given situation the work of a statesman can intervene decisively in the course of events."[15] This belief was evident when he discussed policy making and the influences that played upon it. He denied the notion, put forward most famously by Fritz Fischer and his followers—that Hitler was a traditional statesman, of limited aims, who carried on, with more brutality, where his predecessors left off.[16] His language was emphatic but eloquent:

The similarities of thought and action that have been adduced to prove Hitler's kinship with other German statesmen or to demonstrate the native roots of his political behavior are too trivial to be persuasive. Adolf Hitler was *sui generis*. . . . Both the grandiose barbarism of his political vision and the moral emptiness of his character make it impossible to compare him in any meaningful way with any other German leader. He stands alone.[17]

Craig tells us that he disagrees with those historians who insist on *les forces profondes*, economic and social. His preference is for individuals. He rejects the concept of forces as identifiable agents creating, controlling, or conditioning historical events and human beings. To him this concept is both unusable and inadequate—unusable in that it provides an abstract and artificially clear-cut abstraction from infinite variety, and inadequate because the description of the past as a pattern eliminates too many ill-fitting particulars and only very rarely assists the discovery and understanding of additional particular events. In a series of lectures at the University of Wisconsin, *The End of Prussia*, published in 1985, Craig briefly refers to the long background of profound cause of the subject he is considering, but swiftly changes gears when, in writing about the Second Empire, he declares:

Those who believe that structures are more important in history than personalities would do well to study the impress that William II put upon every aspect of domestic and foreign policy and particularly the importance of his personal decisions in the fields of naval policy, imperial expansion, war planning (his tacit acceptance of the Schlieffen plan, for instance) and alliance policy (the fateful "Nibelungen loyalty") to Austria.[18]

As for *The Germans*, his most personal book that appeared in 1982: It is a work which, to quote the words on the cover of the dust jacket, "attempts to come to grips with the complex paradoxes at the heart of the German identity." In particular, Craig argued that too much had changed in Germany and the world to permit a return to the habits and thoughts of the bad old past. He asserted that 1945 made a watershed in the history of Germany that was sharper and more decisive than any other break in modern times, "infinitely more decisive, than, to take one example, the so called revolution of 1918."[19]

Craig stated at the outset that it was not his intention to speculate about the Teutonic mind and spirit. "No people," he wrote, "is harder to generalize about than the Germans perhaps because they have been quicker to throw off the laws of logic than have other peoples."[20] His book was intended to prove

> the way in which contemporary attitudes of individual Germans show the effect of old but stubborn assumptions and prejudices: a religious heritage that has always been ambivalent in its simultaneous tendency toward establishmentarianism and revolt; a respect for hard work and the financial rewards that it brings that is combined with the uneasy knowledge, based on traumatic historical experience, that such rewards are apt to be impermanent; a veneration of learning and literature that has traditionally been offset by a disinclination to allow them full freedom of expression; a resistance to change and to nonconformity and to those who represent it, whether they are rebellious students or advocates of women's rights; and—associated with this—an inconsistent attitude toward modernity which, through most of the modern period, has expressed itself in eager adoption of technical and economic innovation and a simultaneous reprobation of its social and moral effects.[21]

All the same, Craig never had trouble finding Germans who had thrown themselves against the outnumbering odds trying to do good in their country and to restrain the excesses of their contemporaries. Take the case of the Germans and the Jews—obviously a sensitive topic. Craig found evidence of toleration—indeed of bravery—from the eighteenth century. Did not the Great Elector give permission for Jewish families who had been expelled from Vienna to take up residence in his lands and grant them privileges that they were denied in other states? Did not Moses Mendelssohn seek to break down the barrier between Gentile and Jew by turning his home into a meeting place for intellectuals and distinguished foreign visitors? Did not Christian Wilhelm von Dohm express the Enlightenment's faith to change the way people thought by calling upon the German governments to undertake steps that would make their peoples cherish the common bond of citizenship which should make out of them a

Afterword

harmonious whole?[22] When it came to what they considered simple goodness and decency, these Germans and others like them did not hesitate to speak out clearly and boldly and to risk their careers and their lives to create the kind of Germany that would embody the spirit of Freiligrath's poem. *The Germans* was a conspicuous success. By means of anecdotes Craig managed to show that history, is in part, a recognition of outstanding personalities—outstanding in position and in personal qualities—and that individuals do indeed affect the fortunes of mankind.

Craig's view of German history has come in for its share of criticism, especially from those historians inside Germany who tended to emphasize the importance of long-term historical forces for "change" and "reform" and who were impatient with historians who call attention to the particular happenings in history, to the role of chance or accident, to the critical importance of individual personalities and unique events, and to the "ups and downs" of politics. It may indeed be true, as one of his critics once pointed out, that Craig never appreciated the movement toward great democracy in the first years after Bismarck's fall, a movement ended only by the alliance between agrarian magnates and industrialists, and by the launching of the World Policy. And while economic statistics are employed in his books, there is little about economic and social developments, especially little about the runaway expansion of German industry or about the consequences that inevitably followed; nothing on the strength of bureaucratic tradition that, as Jürgen Kocka has argued, strongly influenced the course of German history, little on demography or comparative history, few tables, no graphs, no charts.[23]

Yet there is an answer to this sort of charge. For one thing it is important to note that Craig's reminder of the short-term, of the individual, the immediate, the tactical, and the personal *is* a vital point of departure whether it contains the general methodology of German history or the interpretation of specific episodes. For example, the First World War is nowadays seen by many historians as having been caused by a variety of factors, including domestic political and economic causes that might well be described as deep routed and profound; but the short-term conjunction of diplomatic circumstances prevailing in the summer of 1914 surely must be acknowledged as part of the whole story. Similarly about the Second World War. Its origins, too, have sometimes been seen to be the result of structural tensions and crises produced by dictatorships. To quote from T. W. Mason: "A war for the plunder of manpower lay square in the dreadful logic of German economic development under National Socialist Rule."[24] Yet who would deny the importance of the calculating element in Hitler as the irrational fanatic and opportunist; the dreamer of the thousand-year Reich; the purveyor of plans laid down in *Mein Kampf*? To use J. H. Hexter's terminology, most historians are inclined to be either "splitters" or "lumpers."[25] Each has it merits. Each also has its risks. Each is also in constant tension with the other, both correcting and being corrected by its opposite. What we have in Gordon Craig, therefore, simply may be one of those scholars who reminds us of the importance of the particular in history.

If the story could end at this point, with the establishment of Craig's role as the skeptical critic of "profound causes," our analysis also would end. The writing of history must be, after all, an exercise in selectivity and thus (to a greater or lesser degree) in subjectivity. The facts that the historian goes after are like fish in a sea, and as E. H. Carr once observed: "What the historian catches will depend partly on chance, but mainly on what part of the ocean he chooses to fish in and what tackle he chooses to use."[26] According to the historical theme being pursued, writers will tend toward the general or the particular, toward broad changes or specific events. Gordon Craig may be seen as therefore simply an outstanding representative of the latter group.

He has also so often reminded us at other times about long-term trends and general forces in history. In some ways, of course, this is hardly surprising. After all, even the most specific monographs have to say a little about the context within which their study is to be placed. Given the size of Craig's output, generalizations are unavoidable. What seems to us much more important are the instances in which Gordon Craig has offered an analysis of the larger structures in German history, and of the changes that occurred in them over the longer period of time. For example, in the introduction to his book, *The Politics of the Prussian Army*, Professor Craig offered his readers one of the most incisive and penetrating observations of what he viewed as a protracted ordeal:

It is possible in short to view German history in the nineteenth and twentieth centuries as one long continuous constitutional struggle in which the critical battles—those of 1819, 1848, and 1918—were followed by uneasy truces in which the opposing forces recovered their strength and prepared for new encounters.[27]

Or take the penultimate page of *Germany, 1866–1945* where Craig approvingly quotes Meinecke's judgment that

the roots of Germany's recent experience lay in the inadequacies of Bismarck's work when he created the national state, and that throughout the short history of united Germany, the emphasis on power at the expense of the spirit . . . corrupted the values and stunted the growth of the German people.[28]

Finally, *The Germans*, though a masterly example of the use of stories of important persons and significant incidents to shed light on a nation's history, can also be seen as an attempt to portray West Germany as a model for the institutionalizing of a modern democracy. Indeed, Craig's model suggests that the course of events there from 1945 to 1980 has a larger significance than the Third Reich whose history was admittedly more compellingly melodramatic. And this is not without implications for the unification of 1990.

> [1945] was not a time that was conducive to nostalgia, but rather one in which the Occupying Powers encouraged the Germans to reflect upon the consequences of their past political behavior.... The occupation period which lasted for four years was a hiatus in German political life in which the finishing touches were put to Hitler's destructiveness of the German past.[29]

Craig himself has called for a wider approach to the subject of history in general. This was the thrust of the argument that he gave in his presidential address to the Amercian Historical Association (AHA) in 1982 when he quoted the poet Roy Fuller:

> The treason of clerks is when
> They make a fetish of the pen
> Forget that art has duties to—
> As well as to the "I"—the "You,"
> And that its source must always be
> What presses most, most constantly.[30]

The fact of the matter is therefore that, despite Craig's preference for politics and his skepticism about profound causes, he himself does not ignore them. Indeed in respect of the workings of German history, and particularly in reaching into the background of it from Bismarck to Hitler, it is clear that Craig believes both in specific circumstances and profound causes—a traditionalist who really is concerned with underlying forces as a reality of the past, but who knows that such forces should be treated as a point of departure, as a tool, not a template, as the beginning of research and explanation, not as a substitute for them, still less as the end of a search for cause.

There is a more general point. However well established Craig's writing of history may be, some professional historians nowadays incline to treat it as a manifestly inadequate form. Some think it too easy. It requires none of the sophisticated techniques of the social analyst or the economist, no mathematical statistics, none of the equations and parameters with which the econometrist historian dazzles the understanding. It is accused of being exceptionally unscientific—impressionistic, open to the historian's bias, and lacking the quantifiable detail that allegedly provides sure foundations in social and economic history; it averts its eyes from the explanatory contributions to be made by medical science that might provide guidance to the historian's ascription of motives or his understanding of his characters.

This kind of attitude need not detain us. If the charge against Gordon Craig's kind of history is that it manages without all those graphs and tables, without the abstract vocabulary of the logician or the proliferating prolixity of the sociologist, then there is really no charge at all. Craig manages to get his points across by writing in English not in figures or in jargon. He manages to get them across without behavioral sauce—without producing the kind of history that A.J.P. Taylor, with whom we may here emphatically agree, once descibed as being "ninety perent true and one hundred percent useless."[31]

This is the essence of the matter. The wonderful thing about Gordon Craig's books is precisely that they *are* traditional and that they show that the traditional and mainly political narrative not only is useful but indispensable. Rich in erudition, sharp in insight, overflowing with wit and grace, they reflect how much sharper and brighter and more exciting history can be when told by a master who knows his stuff. They avoid quantification like the plague; they shrink from the languages of the social sciences. As one of us has pointed out: "At a time when historiography is tending more and more towards new interests and emphases, new methods and approaches, sometimes new tricks and gimmicks, he continues to uphold the established tradition of the historian's craft."[32]

Any study of Gordon Craig's history will surely undermine the conviction that the fate of mankind is beyond the influence of the accidental and the personal, that it is shaped by forces beyond the play of human personality. It will encourage the view that things happened because individual and discoverable people did things or decided them. It recognizes that greatness in politics can exist; it refuses to deny that there are overwhelming personalities in history; it understands—it insists—that the activities of a few have been disproportionately important for all. It continuously destroys overready generalization. It rejects faddism and modishness. It teaches that people are vastly different. It deals with matters of enduring importance. Above all, it has the advantage of being interesting, amusing, exciting, and fun—or it can be all of these things when the other forms of historical study find it difficult to come down from the tedious plane of high seriousness. Traditional and even a trifle old-fashioned though Gordon Craig's history may be, dead it is not—and will never be.

NOTES

1. Gordon A. Craig and Felix Gilbert, eds., *The Diplomats, 1919–1939* (Princeton, 1953); Gordon A. Craig and Francis Loewenheim, eds., *The Diplomats, 1939–1979* (Princeton, 1994).

2. A.J.P. Taylor, 1961 preface to the 1946 edition, *The Course of German History* (London, 1946), 7.

3. Richard Cohen, quoted by Peter Schneider, "For Germans, Guilt Isn't Enough," *New York Times*, 5 December 1996, 23.

4. Gordon A. Craig, *Germany 1866–1945* (New York, 1978), viii–ix.

5. Ibid., ix.

Afterword

6. Gordon A. Craig, "Hans Delbrück: The Military Historian," in *The Makers of Modern Strategy*, ed. Edward Meade Earle with the collaboration of Felix Gilbert and Gordon A. Craig (Princeton, 1943), 260–83. This essay has been reprinted in a new edition of the book that appears under the editorship of Peter Paret (Princeton, 1986).

7. Gordon A. Craig, *The Politics of the Prussian Army* (Oxford, 1955), xiii–iv.

8. Ibid., 215.

9. Ibid., 322.

10. Ibid., 497.

11. Ibid., 498.

12. Ibid., 491.

13. Ibid., 409.

14. Craig, *Germany*, 3.

15. Ibid., 302.

16. See the *festschrift* to Fritz Fischer, *Deutschland in der Weltpolitik des 19. und 20. Jahrhunderts*. Immanuel Geiss amd Bernd Jürgen Wendt, eds. (Düsseldorf, 1973).

17. Craig, *Germany*, 543.

18. Gordon A. Craig, *The End of Prussia* (Madison, 1985), 64.

19. Gordon A. Craig, *The Germans* (New York, 1982), 10.

20. Ibid., 11.

21. Ibid.

22. Ibid., 127–31.

23. Jürgen Kocka, "Crisis of Unification: How Germany Changes," *Daedulus* (January 1994): 173–89.

24. T. W. Mason, "Some Origins of the Second World War," in E. M. Robinson, ed., *The Origins of the Second World War* (London, 1971), 124–25.

25. J. H. Hexter, *The History Primer* (New York, 1971), 5–25.

26. E. H. Carr, *What Is History?* (New York, 1961), 26.

27. Craig, *Prussian Army*, xiv.

28. Craig, *Germany*, 763.

29. Craig, *The Germans*, 35–36.

30. Gordon A. Craig, "The Historian and the Study of International Relations," *American Historical Review* 88, 1 (February 1983): 3.

31. Quoted in Adam Sisman, *A.J.P. Taylor* (London, 1994), 37.

32. Theodore S. Hamerow, review of *Germany 1866–1945* by Gordon A. Craig in *Journal of Modern History* 51, 4 (December, 1979): 841.

Selected Bibliography

Abenheim, Donald. *Reforging the Iron Cross: The Search for Tradition in the German Armed Forces*. Princeton, 1988.

Alperowitz, Gar. *Atomic Diplomacy*. New York, 1965.

Arblaster, Anthony. "Taking Monarchy Seriously." *New Left Review* 174 (April 1989): 97–110.

Backerra, Manfred, ed. *NVA: Ein Rückblick für die Zukunft—Zeitzeugen berichten über ein Stück deutscher Militärgeschichte*. Cologne, 1992.

Bald, Detlef. *Militär und Gesellschaft, 1945–1990: Die Bundeswehr der BonnerRepublik*. Baden-Baden, 1992.

―――, ed. *Die Nationale Volksarmee: Beiträge zu Selbstverständnis und Geschichte des deutschen Militärs, 1945–1990*. Baden-Baden, 1992.

Baldwin, Hanson. *World War I*. New York, 1962 ed.

Baldwin, Peter, ed. *Reworking the Past: Hitler, the Holocaust, and the Historians' Debate*. Boston, 1990.

Barclay, David E. "The Soldiers of an Unsoldierly King: The Military Advisers of Frederick William IV, 1840–1858." In *Geschichte als Aufgabe. Festschrift für Otto Büsch zu seinem 60. Geburtstag*, edited by Wilhelm Treue. Berlin, 1988.

―――. "Ritual, Ceremonial, and the 'Invention' of a Monarchical Tradition in Nineteenth-Century Prussia." In *European Monarchy: Its Evolution and Practice from Roman Antiquity to Modern Times*, edited by Heinz Duchhardt, Richard A. Jackson, and David Sturdy. Stuttgart, 1992.

―――. "The Court Camarilla and the Politics of Monarchical Restoration in Prussia, 1848–58." In *Between Reform, Reaction, and Resistance: Studies in the History of German Conservatism from 1789 to the Present*, edited by Larry Eugene Jones and James Retallack. New York and Oxford, 1993.

―――. *Anarchie und guter Wille. Friedrich Wilhelm IV. und die preussische Monarchie*. Berlin, 1995.

―――. *Frederick William IV and the Prussian Monarchy 1840–1861*. Oxford, 1995.

Barnett, Correlli, ed. *Hitler's Generals*. New York, 1989.

Baron, Udo. *Die Wehrideologie der Nationalen Volksarmee der DDR*. Bochum, 1993.

Belous, Richard, and Kelly McClenahan, eds. *Global Corporations and Nation States*. Washington, D.C, 1991.
Benedick, Richard. *Ozone Diplomacy: New Directions in Safeguarding the Planet*. Cambridge, Mass., 1991.
Berghahn, Volker. *The Americanization of West German Industry, 1945–1973*. New York, 1986.
Bieglow, Karl W., Bernyce Bridges, and William E. McManus. *The Role of American Voluntary Agencies in Germany and Austria. The Report of a Team of Inquiry that Visited Germany and Austria in October–November 1950*. Washington, D.C., 1951.
Blasius, Dirk. *Friedrich Wilhelm IV. 1795–1861. Psychopathologie und Geschichte*. Göttingen, 1992.
Blessing, Werner K. *Staat und Kirche in der Gesellschaft. Institutionelle Autorität und mentaler Wandel in Bayern während des 19. Jahrhunderts*. Göttingen, 1982.
Börner, Karl Heinz. *Kaiser Wilhelm I. 1797 bis 1888. Deutscher Kaiser und König von Preussen. Eine Biographie*. Cologne, 1984.
Brecht, Arnold. *The Political Education of Arnold Brecht: An Autobiography 1884–1970*. Princeton, 1970.
Brunner, Max. *Die Hofgesellschaft. Die führende Gesellschaftsschicht Bayerns während der Regierungszeit König Maximilian II*. Munich, 1987.
Bühl, Walter L. *Transnationale Politik*. Stuttgart, 1978.
Bunsen, Marie von. *Kaiserin Augusta*. Berlin, 1940.
Büsch, Otto, ed. *Friedrich Wilhelm IV. in seiner Zeit. Beiträge eines Colloquiums*. Berlin, 1987.
Bussmann, Walter. "Die Krönung Wilhelms I. am 18. Oktober 1861. Eine Demonstration des Gottesgnadentums im preussischen Verfassungsstaat." In *Politik und Konfession. Festschrift für Konrad Repgen zum 60. Geburtstag*, edited by Dieter Albrecht et al. Berlin, 1983.
_____. *Zwischen Preussen und Deutschland. Friedrich Wilhelm IV. Eine Biographie*. Berlin, 1990.
Cannadine, David. "The Context, Performance and Meaning of Ritual: The British Monarchy and the 'Invention of Tradition,' c. 1820–1977." In *The Invention of Tradition*, edited by Eric Hobsbawm and Terence Ranger. Cambridge, 1983.
Cantor, Norman F. *Inventing the Middle Ages*. New York, 1991.
Carr, David. *Time, Narrative and History*. Bloomington, Ind., 1986.
Carr, E. H. *Propaganda in International Politics*. New York, 1939.
Charles-Roux, F. *Souvenirs diplomatiques d'un âge révolutionaire*. Paris, 1956.
Chickering, Roger. "Young Lamprecht: An Essay in Biography and Historiography." *History and Theory* 28 (1989): 198–214.
_____. "Ein schwieriges Heldenleben: Bekenntnisse eines Biographen." In *Universalgeschichte—gestern und heute: Zum 100. Jahrestag der Berufung Karl Lamprechts an die Universität Leipzig*, edited by Gerald Diesener and Monika Gibas, 113–23. Leipzig, 1991.
_____. "Karl Lamprechts Konzeption einer Weltgeschichte." *Archiv für Kulturgeschichte* 73 (1991): 437–52.
_____. *Karl Lamprecht: A German Academic Life (1856–1915)*. Atlantic Highlands, N.J., 1993.

Chou, S. R. *Le côntrole parlementaire de la politique étrangère*. Paris, 1920.
Churchill, Winston S. *The Second World War*. Vol. 1, *The Gathering Storm*. Boston, 1948.
Collmer, Sabine, et al. *Einheit auf Befehl: Wehrpflichtige und der deutsche Einigungsprozess*. Opladen, 1994.
Craig, Gordon A. *The Politics of the Prussian Army 1640–1945*. 2d ed. New York, 1964.
———. *War, Politics, and Diplomacy*. New York, 1966.
———. "The Historian and the Study of International Relations." *American Historical Review* 88 (February 1983): 1–11.
Craig, Gordon A., and Alexander L. George. *Force and Statecraft: Diplomatic Problems of Our Time*. New York, 1995 ed.
Craig, Gordon A., and Felix Gilbert, eds. *The Diplomats, 1919–1939*. 2 vols. New York, 1953.
Craig, Gordon A., and Francis Loewenheim, eds. *The Diplomats, 1939–1979*. Princeton, 1994.
Dillon, E. J. *The Inside Story of the Peace Conference*. New York, 1920.
Engelberg, Ernst. "Zum Methodenstreit um Karl Lamprecht." In *Die bürgerliche deutsche Geschichtsschreibung von der Reichsgründung von oben bis zur Befreiung Deutschlands vom Faschismus*, edited by Joachim Streisand. Berlin, 1965.
———. *Bismarck. Das Reich in der Mitte Europas*. Berlin, 1990.
Ermarth, Michael, ed. *America and the Shaping of German Society, 1945–1955*. Providence and Oxford, 1993.
Evans, Richard J. *In Hitler's Shadow: West German Historians and the Attempt to Escape from the Nazi Past*. New York, 1989.
Farwick, Dieter, ed. *Ein Staat—eine Armee: Von der NVA zur Bundeswehr*. Frankfurt am Main and Bonn, 1992.
Fehrenbach, Elisabeth. *Wandlungen des deutschen Kaisergedankens 1871–1918*. Munich, 1969.
Feld, Werner J. *Nongovernmental Forces and World Politics*. New York, 1972.
Fellmann, Walter. *Sachsens letzter König. Friedrich August III*. Berlin and Leipzig, 1992.
Forster, Thomas M. *Die NVA: Kernstück der Landesverteidigung der DDR*. 6th ed. Cologne, 1983.
Friedlander, Saul, ed. *Probing the Limits of Representation: Nazism and the "Final Solution."* Cambridge, Mass., 1992.
Gaddis, John Lewis. *The Long Peace*. New York, 1987.
———. "International Relations Theory and the End of the Cold War." *International Security* 17, 3 (1992–1993): 5–58.
George, Alexander, ed. *Managing U.S.-Soviet Rivalry: Problems of Crisis Prevention*. Boulder and London, 1983.
Gilbert, Felix. *A European Past: Memoirs, 1905–1945*. New York, 1988.
Gillis, John R. *The Prussian Bureaucracy in Crisis 1840–1860: Origins of an Administrative Ethos*. Stanford, 1971.
Gollwitzer, Heinz. *Ludwig I. von Bayern. Königtum im Vormärz. Eine politische Biographie*. Munich, 1986.

Grew, Joseph. *Turbulent Era: A Diplomatic Record of Forty Years, 1904–1945*. 2 vols. Boston, 1952.

Griss, Peter. *Das Gedankenbild Karl Lamprechts: Historisches Verhalten im Modernisierungsprozess der "Belle Epoche."* Bern, 1987.

Grünthal, Günther. *Parlamentarismus in Preussen 1848/49–1857/58. Preussischer Konstitutionalismus—Parlament und Regierung in der Reaktionsära*. Düsseldorf, 1982.

———. "Bismarck Anticipated? The Manteuffel 'System' and the Politics of Reaction in Postrevolutionary Prussia, 1848–58." Paper presented at the American Historical Association, 107th Annual Meeting, Washington, D.C., 28 December 1992.

Hanisch, Manfred. *Für Fürst und Vaterland. Legitimitätsstiftung in Bayern zwischen Revolution 1848 und deutscher Einheit*. Munich, 1991.

Hanotaux, Gabriel. "L'Europe qui naît." *La Revue hebdomadaire* 48 (30 November 1907): 561–70.

Haus der Bayerischen Geschichte, ed. *König Maximilian II. von Bayern 1848–1864*. Rosenheim, 1988.

Hausser, Paul. *Waffen-SS im Einsatz*. Göttingen, 1953.

Hoffmann, Peter. *The History of the German Resistance, 1933–1945*. Trans. Richard Barry. Cambridge, Mass., 1977.

Hoffmann, Theodor. *Das letzte Kommando: Ein Minister erinnert sich*. Berlin, Bonn, and Herford, 1993.

Hoyau, Georges. *Die Kunst des Arrangierens oder Diplomaten-Brevier*. Vienna, 1973.

Huber, Ernst Rudolf. *Deutsche Verfassungsgeschichte seit 1789*. Vol. 3, *Bismarck und das Reich*. 3d ed. Stuttgart, 1988.

Hull, Isabel V. "Prussian Dynastic Ritual and the End of Monarchy." In *German Nationalism and the European Response, 1890–1945*, edited by Carole Fink, Isabel V. Hull, and MacGregor Knox. Norman, Okla., 1985.

Huntington, Samuel P. "Transnational Organizations in World Politics." *World Politics* 25 (1972–1973): 333–68.

Iggers, Georg G. *The German Conception of History: The National Tradition of Historical Thought from Herder to the Present*. 2d ed. Middletown, Conn., 1983.

James, Harold. *A German Identity*. New York, 1989.

Jarausch, Konrad H. *The Rush to German Unity*. New York, 1994.

Johnson, Paul. *The Birth of the Modern World, 1815–1830*. New York, 1991.

Kaes, Anton. *From "Hitler" to "Heimat": The Return of History as Film*. Cambridge, Mass., 1989.

Keller, Kenneth H. "Science and Technology." *Foreign Affairs* 69, 4 (Fall 1990): 123–38.

Kellerman, Henry J. *Cultural Relations as an Instrument of U.S. Foreign Policy: The Educational Exchange Program between the United States and Germany, 1945–1954*. Washington, D.C., 1978.

Kennedy, A. L. *Old Diplomacy and New*. London, 1922.

Keohane, Robert O., and Joseph S. Nye, eds. *Transnational Relations and World Polity*. Cambridge, Mass., 1971.

Kirchbach, Hans Peter von, et al. *Abenteuer Einheit: Zum Aufbau der Bundeswehr in den neuen Ländern*. Frankfurt am Main and Bonn, 1992.

Kissinger, Henry. *Nuclear Weapons and Foreign Policy*. New York, 1957.

_____. *Diplomacy*. New York, 1994.
Klein, Paul, ed. *Beispielhaft? Eine Zwischenbilanz zur Eingliederung der NVA in die Bundeswehr*. Baden-Baden, 1993.
Knaber, Frithjof H. *Unter der Flagge des Gegners: Wertewandel im Umbruch in Streitkräften—von der NVA zur Bundeswehr*. Opladen, 1994.
Kollander, Patricia. *Frederick III: Germany's Liberal Emperor*. Westport, Conn., 1995.
Koshar, Rudy. "The Shock of 'It Was': Memory and German Unification." In *German Unification: Problems and Prospects*, edited by Gaines Post, Jr. Claremont, Calif., 1992.
Koza, Ingeborg. *Völkerversöhnung und europäische Einigungsbemühen. Untersuchungen zur Nachkriegsgeschichte 1945–1951*. Cologne and Vienna, 1987.
Kroll, Frank-Lothar. *Friedrich Wilhelm IV. und das Staatsdenken der deutschen Romantik*. Berlin, 1990.
Krüger, Peter, ed. *Kontinuität und Wandel in der Staatenordnung der Neuzeit*. Marburg, 1991.
Kuhnert, Adolf. "Der Streit um die geschichtswissenschaftlichen Theorien Karl Lamprechts." *Diss. phil.*, Erlangen, 1906.
Laforgue, Jules. *Berlin, la cour et la ville*. Paris, 1922.
Lamprecht, Karl. *Deutsche Geschichte*. 12 vols. Berlin, 1891–1909.
_____. "Was ist Kulturgeschichte? Beitrag zu einer empirischen Historik." *Deutsche Zeitschrift für Geschichtswissenschaft* (n.F.), 1 (1896–1897): 75–150.
Langewiesche, Dieter. *Liberalismus in Deutschland*. Frankfurt am Main, 1988.
La Roche, Jules. *Au Quai d'Orsay*. Paris, 1957.
Lauren, Paul Gordon. *Diplomats and Bureaucrats: The First Institutional Responses to Twentieth-Century Diplomacy in France and Germany*. Stanford, 1976.
_____. *Power and Prejudice: The Politics and Diplomacy of Racial Discrimination*. Boulder and Oxford, 1996 ed.
_____, ed. *Diplomacy: New Approaches in History, Theory, and Policy*. New York, 1979.
Lerner, Robert E. "Ernst Kantorowicz and Theodor E. Mommsen." In *An Interrupted Past: German-Speaking Refugee Historians in the United States after 1933*, edited by Hartmut Lehmann and James J. Sheehan. New York, 1991.
Liddell Hart, B. H. *The German Generals Talk*. New York, 1948.
Link, Werner. *Deutsche und amerikanische Gewerkschaften und Geschäftsleute 1945–1975. Eine Studie über transnationale Beziehungen*. Düsseldorf, 1978.
_____. *Der Ost-West-Konflikt. Die Organisation der internationalen Beziehungen im 20. Jahrhundert*. Stuttgart, 1980.
Lowenthal, David. *The Past is a Foreign Country*. New York, 1985.
McKay, Vernon, ed. *African Diplomacy*. New York, 1966.
Maier, Charles S. "Marking Time: The Historiography of International Relations." In *The Past Before Us*, edited by Michael Kammen. Ithaca, 1980.
Mansel, Philip. *The Eagle in Splendour: Napoleon I and His Court*. London, 1987.
_____. *The Court of France 1789–1830*. Cambridge, 1988.
Manteuffel, Otto Freiherr von. *Unter Friedrich Wilhelm IV. Denkwürdigkeiten des Ministers Otto Freiherrn von Manteuffel*, edited by Heinrich von Poschinger. 3 vols. Berlin, 1901.
Marshall, Charles Burton. "The Golden Age in Perspective." *Journal of International Affairs* 17, 1 (1963): 9–17.

Maurer, Alfred C., et al., eds. *Intelligence: Policy and Process*. Boulder and London, 1985.
Mayer, Arno. *Wilson vs. Lenin: The Political Origins of the New Diplomacy*. New York, 1964.
Mehring, Franz. "Deutsche Geschichte." *Die Neue Zeit* 12 (1893–1894): 443–48.
Metz, Karl H. " 'Der Methodenstreit in der deutschen Geschichtswissenschaft (1891–99)': Bemerkungen zum sozialen Kontext wissenschaftlicher Auseinandersetzungen." *Storia della storiografia* 6 (1984): 3–20.
Meyer, Georg Maria, et al. *Soziale Deutungsmuster von Bataillonskommandeuren der Bundeswehr*. Wiesbaden, 1992.
_____. *Kolonisierung oder Integration? Bundeswehr und deutsche Einheit—eine Bestandsaufnahme*. Opladen, 1995.
Militärgeschichtliches Forschungsamt, eds. *Militärgeschichte im 19. Jahrhundert 1814–1890*. Munich, 1979.
_____. *Armee für Frieden und Sozialismus*. 2d ed. Berlin, 1987.
_____. *Volksarmee schaffen ohne Geschrei: Studien zu den Anfängen einer "verdeckten Aufrüstung" in der SBZ/DDR 1947–1952*. Munich, 1994.
_____. *Vom Kalten Krieg zur Deutschen Einheit: Analysen und Zeitzeugenberichte zur deutschen Militärgeschichte 1945–1995*. Munich, 1995.
Möckl, Karl, ed. *Hof und Hofgesellschaft in den deutschen Staaten im 19. und beginnenden 20. Jahrhundert*. Boppard am Rhein, 1990.
Mommsen, Theodor E. *Medieval and Renaissance Studies*, edited by Eugene F. Rice, Jr. Ithaca, 1959.
Moynihan, Daniel Patrick. *Pandaemonium*. New York, 1993.
Mueller, John E. *Retreat from Doomsday*. New York, 1989.
Müller, Klaus-Jürgen. *Das Heer und Hitler: Armee und nationalsozialistisches Regime. 1933–1940*. Stuttgart, 1969.
NATO Office of Information and Press, eds., *NATO Handbook*. Brussels, 1995.
Naumann, Klaus, ed. *NVA: Anspruch und Wirklichkeit*. Berlin, Bonn, and Herford, 1993.
Nicolson, Harold. *The Evolution of Diplomacy*. New York, 1966 ed.
_____. *Diplomacy*. London, 1968 ed.
Nincic, Miroslav. "New Perspectives on Popular Opinion and Foreign Policy." *Journal of Conflict Resolution* 36 (December 1992): 772–89.
Nye, Joseph, Jr. *Bound to Lead*. New York, 1990.
Obenaus, Herbert. *Anfänge des Parlamentarismus in Preussen bis 1848*. Düsseldorf, 1984.
Oncken, Hermann. "Zur Quellenanalyse modernster deutscher Geschichtsschreibung." *Preussische Jahrbücher* 89 (1897): 83–125.
O'Neill, Robert J. *The German Army and the Nazi Party, 1933–1939*. London, 1966.
Paléologue, Maurice. *Un grand tournant de la politique mondiale*. Paris, 1934.
Pares, Richard. "Human Nature in Politics." In *The Historian's Business and Other Essays*, edited by R. A. Humphreys and E. Humphreys. Oxford, 1961.
Pflanze, Otto. *Bismarck and the Development of Germany*. 3 vols. Princeton, 1990.
Pinson, Koppel S. *Modern Germany*. New York, 1954.
Ponomaryov, B., A. Gromyko, and V. Khvostov. *History of Soviet Foreign Policy, 1945–1970*. Moscow, 1974.
Post, Gaines, Jr. *The Civil-Military Fabric of Weimar Foreign Policy*. Princeton, 1973.

Pröll, Bernd. *Bundeswehr und Nationale Volksarmee in Staat und Gesellschaft: Legitimation, Motivation, und gesellschaftliche Integration.* Frankfurt am Main, 1983.
Rachfahl, Felix. "Über die Theorie einer 'kollektivistischen' Geschichtswissenschaft." *Jahrbücher für Nationalökonomie und Statistik* 68 (1897): 659–89.
Radowitz, Joseph Maria von. *Aufzeichnungen und Erinnerungen.* 2 vols. Berlin, 1925.
Raphael, Lutz. "Historikerkontroversen im Spannungsfeld zwischen Berufshabitus, Fächerkonkurrenz und sozialen Deutungsmustern: Lamprecht-Streit und französischer Methodenstreit der Jahrhundertwende in vergleichender Perspektive." *Historische Zeitschrift* 251 (1990): 325–63.
Rassow, Peter. *Der Konflikt König Friedrich Wilhelms IV. mit dem Prinzen von Preussen im Jahre 1854. Eine preussische Staatskrise.* Mainz, 1961.
Richert, Elisabeth. "Die Stellung Wilhelms, des Prinzen von Preussen, zur preussischen Aussen- und Innenpolitik der Zeit von 1848 bis 1857." Inaug.-Diss. Universität Berlin, 1948.
Röhl, John C. G. *Kaiser, Hof und Staat. Wilhelm II. und die deutsche Politik.* Munich, 1987.
———, ed. (with Elisabeth Müller-Luckner). *Der Ort Kaiser Wilhelms II. in der deutschen Geschichte.* Munich, 1991.
Rosecrance, Richard. *The Rise of the Trading State.* New York, 1987.
Rühmland, Erich. *NVA, Nationale Volksarmee der Sowjetzone in Stichworten.* Bonn, 1968.
Rupieper, Hermann-Josepf. *Die Wurzeln der westdeutschen Nachkriegs demokratie: Der amerikanische Beitrag, 1945–1952.* Opladen, 1993.
Saint-Aulaire, Comte de. *Confession d'un vieux diplomate.* Paris, 1953.
Sasse, Heinz. "Von Equipage und Automobilen des Auswärtigen Amts." *Nachrichtenblatt der Vereinigung Deutscher Auslandsbeamten* 10 (October 1957): 145–48.
Schieder, Theodor. "Die deutsche Geschichtswissenschaft im Spiegel der Historischen Zeitschrift." *Historische Zeitschrift* 189 (1959): 1–73.
Schmidt-Bückeburg, Rudolf. *Das Militärkabinett der preussischen Könige und deutschen Kaiser. Seine geschichtliche Entwicklung und staatsrechtliche Stellung 1787–1918.* Berlin, 1933.
Schmitt, Bernadotte. *Triple Alliance and Triple Entente.* New York, 1934.
Schönebaum, Herbert. "Karl Lamprecht: Leben und Werk eines Kämpfers um die Geschichtswissenschaft 1856–1915." Ms., copies in university libraries of Bonn and Leipzig.
Schönebaum, Jörg. *Zwei Armeen und ein Vaterland: Das Ende der Nationalenn Volksarmee.* Berlin, 1992.
Schorn-Schütte, Luise. *Karl Lamprecht: Kulturgeschichtsschreibung zwischen Wissenschaft und Politik.* Göttingen, 1984.
Schroeder, Paul W. "Containment Nineteenth Century Style: How Russia Was Restrained." *South Atlantic Quarterly* 82 (1983): 1–18.
Schulze, Hermann. *Die Hausgesetze der regierenden deutschen Fürstenhäuser.* 3 vols. Jena, 1883.
Seabury, Paul. *The Wilhelmstrasse.* Berkeley, Calif., 1954.
Seifert, Friedrich. *Der Streit um Karl Lamprechts Geschichtsphilosophie.* Augsburg, 1925.

Sheehan, James J. "National History and Naitonal Identity in the New Germany." *German Studies Review* (special issue, Winter 1992).
Shirer, William L. *The Rise and Fall of the Third Reich*. New York, 1960.
Siemann, Wolfram. *Gesellschaft im Aufbruch. Deutschland 1849–1871*. Frankfurt am Main, 1990.
Skyelsbaek, Kjell. "The Growth of International Non-Governmental Organizations in the Twentieth Century." *International Organization* 25 (Summer 1971): 420–42.
Slusser, Robert M. *The Berlin Crisis of 1961*. Baltimore, 1973.
Smith, Jean Edward, ed. *The Papers of General Lucius D. Clay: Germany 1945–1949*. 2 vols. Bloomington and London, 1974.
Speidel, Hans. "1813/1924: Eine militärpolitische Untersuchung." Ph.D. diss., University of Tübingen, 1925.
Spender, J. A. *The Public Life*. London, 1925.
Srbik, Henrich Ritter von. *Geist und Geschichte vom Deutschen Humanismus bis zur Gegenwart*. 2 vols. Munich and Salzburg, 1950–1951.
Stamm-Kuhlmann, Thomas. *König in Preussens grosser Zeit. Friedrich Wilhelm III. Der Melancholiker auf dem Thron*. Berlin, 1992.
Steinberg, Hans-Josef. "Karl Lamprecht." *Deutsche Historiker*, edited by Hans-Ulrich-Wehler. 9 vols. Vol. 1: 58–68. Göttingen, 1971–1982.
Steiner, Felix. *Die Freiwilligen*. Göttingen, 1958.
———. *Die Armee der Geächteten*. Göttingen, 1963.
Steiner, Zara. *The Foreign Office and Foreign Policy, 1898–1914*. Cambridge, 1969.
Stoessinger, John. *Nations in Darkness*. New York, 1990 ed.
———. *The Might of Nations: World Politics in Our Time*. New York, 1993 ed.
Stürmer, Michael. *Das ruhelose Reich. Deutschland 1866–1918*. Berlin, 1983.
Sywottek, Arnold. "Wege in die 50er Jahre." In *Modernisierung in Wiederaufbau. Die westdeutsche Gesellschaft in den 50er Jahren*, edited by Axel Schildt and Arnold Sywottek. Bonn, 1993.
Taylor, A.J.P. *The Course of German History*. London, 1946.
Tent, James F. *Mission on the Rhine: Reeducation and Denazification in American-Occupied Germany*. Chicago, 1982.
Tilly, Charles, ed. *The Formation of National States in Western Europe*. Princeton, 1975.
Union of International Associations. *Yearbook of International Organizations, 1995–1996*. Munich, 1995.
United States Advisory Commission on Public Diplomacy. *1991 Report: Public Diplomacy in the 1990s*. Washington, D.C., 1992.
Vansittart, Lord. "The Decline of Diplomacy." *Foreign Affairs* 28 (January 1950).
———. *The Mist Procession*. London, 1958.
Vom Bruch, Rüdiger. *Welpolitik als Kulturmission. Auswärtige Kulturpolitik und Bildungsbürgertum in Deutschland am Vorabend des Ersten Weltkreiges*. Paderborn, 1982.
von Scheuen, Werner. "Die Bundeswehr und der Aufbau Ost." In MGFA eds., *Vom Kalten Krieg zur dentschen Einheit*. Munich, 1995.
Walker, Samuel. *In Defense of Civil Liberties. A History of the ACLU*. New York, 1990.

Weber, Max. "Roscher and Knies und die logischen Probleme der historischen Nationalökonomie." In *Max Weber, Gesammelte Aufsätze zur Wissenschaftslehre*, edited by Johannes Winckelmann, 1–145. Tübingen, 1982.

Weber, Wolfgang. *Priester der Klio: Historisch-sozialwissenschaftliche Studien zur Herkunft und Karriere deutscher Historiker und zur Geschichte der Geschichtswissenschaft 1800–1970*. Frankfurt am Main, 1984.

Wehler, Hans-Ulrich. *Deutsche Gesellschaftsgeschichte*. Vol. 2, *Von der Reformära bis zur industriellen und politischen "Deutschen Doppelrevolution" 1815–1845/49*. Munich, 1987.

Weinberg, Gerhard. *The Foreign Policy of Hitler's Germany: Diplomatic Revolution in Europe*. Chicago, 1970.

Weintraub, Karl J. *Visions of Culture: Voltaire, Guizot, Burckhardt, Lamprecht, Huizinga, Ortega y Gasset*. Chicago, 1966.

Werner, Karl Ferdinand, ed. *Hof, Kultur und Politik im 19. Jahrhundert. Akten des 18. Deutsch-französischen Historikerkolloquiums, Darmstadt vom 27.-30. September 1982*. Bonn, 1985.

Whimster, Sam. "Karl Lamprecht and Max Weber: Historical Sociology within the Confines of a Historians' Controversy." In *Max Weber and His Contemporaries*, edited by Wolfgang J. Mommsen and Jürgen Osterhammel. London, 1987.

White, Hayden. *Metahistory: The Historical Imagination in Nineteenth-Century Europe*. Baltimore and London, 1973.

Willett, Ralph. *The Americanization of Germany: Post-War Culture 1945–1949*. London, 1989.

Wilson, Hugh Robert. *The Education of a Diplomat*. London, 1938.

Wortman, Richard. "Rule by Sentiment: Alexander II's Journeys through the Russian Empire." *American Historical Review* 95, 3 (June 1990): 745–71.

Zechlin, Walter. *Diplomatie und Diplomaten*. Stuttgart, 1925.

Zook, George F. *The President's Annual Report, 1946–1947*, American Council on Education. Washington, D.C., 1948.

Index

ACLU. *See* American Civil Liberties Union
"Addresses to the German Nation" (Fichte), 2
Adenauer, Konrad, chancellor of FRG, 94; criticism of, 135
Administration 2000, 120, 122. *See also* Stasi
AIDS, 52
Ambassadors, 6; in "new diplomacy," 7
American Civil Liberties Union (ACLU): activities in FRG, 89–90, 92, 96, 98; role, in new diplomacy, 9–10
American Historical Association: Craig's presidential address, 157; Lamprecht, 83; members questionnaire, 16
Anderson, M. S., 5
Annalistes, 2, 4, 15, 17
Arbeitsgruppe, University of Marburg, 34
Augusta, wife of William I, 64–65
Austria-Hungary, and Russian revolutions of 1905 and 1917, 31

Balance of power: emergence of, 3; decline of, 30
Baldwin, Hanson, 47

Baldwin, Roger, ACLU president, and German democracy, 10, 87; interactions with: Gen. Lucius D. Clay, 92; U.S.–High Commissioner John J. McCloy, 92–93; Gen. Douglas MacArthur, 91; and the U.S.– Military Government (OMGUS), 90–93
Balkans, 32–33
Basic Law (West German), 95, 97, 124
Beck, Ludwig, 139, 152
Bielfeld School, 84
Berlin: atmosphere of, 1990, 142; Berlin crisis, 132; and Khrushchev ultimatum about, 130; and effects of unification, 127, 142
Berliner Tageblatt, 50
Berufssoldaten, 118
Bethmann-Hollweg, Theobald von: and Karl Lamprecht, 84; Imperial chancellor (World War I), 151
Bismarck, Otto von, 8, 65–66; and German unification, 2, 3; confrontation with William II, 69; defender of constitution, 151
Blériot, Louis, 46
Blasisus, Dirk, 68
Bound to Lead (Nye), 40
Boutros-Gali, Boutros, 54
Brandt, Willy, 132; *Ostpolitik* of, 143
Brecht, Eberhard, 141–42

Brest-Litovsk, peace of, 43
Die Bürgerrechte, 97
Bund für Bürgerrechte (Civil Liberties Union), 10, 87–99
Bundeswehr (West German Army), 133; and the NVA, 103–25; and unification, 10–11; and the "Schule für Innere Führung," 134
Bundeswehr Eastern Command, 114
Burckhardt, Jacob, 80
Butterfield, Herbert, 19

CAD. *See* Civil Administration Division
Camarilla, 64, 68
Carr, E. H., 156
Chabod, Fedrico, 153
China, 45
Churchill, Winston, 47
Civil Administration Division (CAD), 91–92
Clay, Lucius, 90, 92; and Berlin crisis, 1961, 132; head of OMGUS, 87–88
CNN, 50
Colby, Bainbridge, 43
Cold War, 44, 50, 53, 54
Columbia University, 83
Comines, Phillipe de, 6
Comintern, founded by Lenin, 43
Concert of Europe, 23, 24
Congressional diplomacy, 50
Cousins, Norman, 91
Craig, Gordon A., 3, 4, 5; on diplomacy, 43; on First World War, 47; philosophy of, 13

Decolonization, effect on international system, 38–41, 53
De Gaulle, Charles, and Berlin, 1961, 132, 136
Delbrück, Hans, 77, 78, 150
De Mazière, Lothar, forms government in GDR, 110
Desert Shield/Storm, 121
Diplomacy (Kissinger), 2
Diplomacy, and human rights, 7, 52–53; changes in 4–8, 37, 41–43, 45;
new, 39; public opinion and, 51–54. *See also* International politics
Diplomatic history, 20; rise and fall of, 1–14. *See also* International history; International politics
Dohm, Christian Wilhelm von, 154
Dönitz, Admiral Karl, 137
Dulles, John Foster, 48
Dreadnought battleship, launched, 46
Draper, William H., 90
Du Bois, W.E.B., 5
Dynastic wars, political effects, 25–26

Earle, Edward Mead, 150
Earth Summit, 53
Eberhard, Fritz, 95
Economics, and diplomacy, 49–50, 51
Eichmann, Adolph, 135
The End of Prussia (Craig), 153
English Channel, 46
Eppelmann, Rainer, and NVA, 110, 113, 116, 119; meeting with Stoltenberg, 111; minister of defense, GDR, 110
Ernst, Fritz, 134
Europe and the French Revolution (Sorel), 1
Evans, Richard J., 144

Federal Republic of Germany (FRG), and NATO, 115; importance of nongovernmental agencies in, 89
Fichte, Gottlieb (poet), 2
First World War: diplomatic revolution and, 46–47; impact on historians, 1; international system and, 38–43
Fischer, Fritz, 3, 15, 153
Flörke, Hermann: on Hitler, 134–35; on Versailles treaty, 136
Force and Statecraft (Craig and George), 4
Foreign Policy of Castlereagh (Webster), 1
Foreign Service, 54
Forster, Thomas M., 106
France, Second Empire, 60
Francis Joseph of Austria, 60
Frankfurt, 87, 94–95, 97, 98

Frederick William IV, 8; Camarilla and, 64; constitutional government and, 59–60, 65–69; court of, 62–65; Manteuffel and, 69; popularization of the monarchy, 67
Freiligrath, Ferdinand, 150, 155
FRG. *See* Federal Republic of Germany
Fulda Gap, and the Berlin crisis, 1961, 132
Fuller, Roy, 157

Gauk, Joachim, 123
GDR. *See* German Democratic Republic
German Democratic Republic (GDR), and NVA, 107
German Historical Museum, 128
German History (Lamprecht), 76, 80–83
German League for Human Rights, 93–94
"German question," and memory, 127–28, 129
The Germans (Craig), 152, 156
Germany: contemporary historians, 34; historical memory and, 12; non-governmental agencies and, 10; Russian revolutions of 1905 and 1917, 31; unification, 1990, 2, 10–11
Germany 1866–1945 (Craig), 149, 152, 156
George, Alexander L., on the balance of power, 4–5
Gesellschaftsgeschichte, 15
Giessner Freie Presse, 135
Gillessen, Günter (journalist) on the NVA-Bundeswehr merger, 11, 112–13
Goldhagen, Daniel Jonah, 149
Gorbachev, Mikhail, 111–12
Great Britain, and Russian revolutions of 1905 and 1917, 31
Great Powers of Europe: world dominance, 37–38; effects of expansion of international community on, 38–41
Grünthal, Günther, on Prussia, 61, 65, 68

"Hans Crow System," 92
"Hans Delbrück: The Military Historian" (Craig), 150
Hardthoehe, 104
Harmel Doctrine (1967), 112
Hausser, Paul, 127, 138
Hays, Arthur Garfield, 91
Heimerich, Hermann, 95
Heinrici, Gotthard, 137
Herzfeld, Hans, 133
Heusinger, Adolf, 136–37
Heuss, Theodor, 87
Hexter, J. H., 155
HICOG. *See* High Commission
High Commission (HICOG), 87, 89, 91–92, 96–97, 98
Historikerstreit, of the 1980s, 128
Historische Zeitschrift, 77
Hitler, 1, 88; and diplomacy, 44
Hitler's Willing Executioners (Goldhagen), 149
Hofstaat (royal retinue), growth of under Frederick William IV, 63
Honecker, Erich, 109
Human rights, and diplomacy, 7, 52–53
Husen, Paulus van, 96
Hussein, Saddam, 30

IFOR. *See* Implementation Force
IHR. *See* International History Review
Implementation Force (IFOR), 124
Information revolution, 48
Innere Führung: defined, 111; practice of, 115, 120, 122, 125
Institute for Cultural and Universal History, 83
Institute for Public Affairs, 95
International history, 15–20, 23–25
International History Review (IHR), 17
International politics: concept of, 3–4; dynamic, 15–25; eighteenth century and, 25–27; events of 1985–1991 and, 28, 30; expansion of, 5; German historians and, 2, 10–11; institutional integration and, 8, 28; memory and, 12; military power and, 28–30; nineteenth century

and, 23–25; NGOs and, 9; structural change and, 34; trading state and, 28; transformation of, 23–25. *See also* Diplomatic history

Japan, defeats Russia, 1905, 38
Jaurès, Jean, 24
Jefferson, Thomas, 6

Kasernierte Volkspolizei (KVP), 107
Kehr, Eckhart, 15
Keller, Alexander von (Marshall of the Court), and crown budget, 62
Kennedy, John F., and 1961 Berlin crisis, 132; and Berlin speech, 133
Kennedy, Paul, 2, 4
Kissinger, Henry, 2; theoretician, 6; secretary of state, 48–49
Koblenz, court of Prince William of Prussia, 64
Kocka, Jürgen, 155
Kohl, Helmut, and German unification, 112, 143; and Gorbachev, 112
Kommandogewalt, 65
Kommittee Freies Deutschland, 107
Kreis Resident Officers (KRO), 97–98
KRO. *See* Kreis Resident Officers
Kröungs- und Ordenfest, festival of, 67
Kulturgeschichte, 8–9, 15, 76
Kulturzeitalter, 76
KVP. *See* Kasernierte Volkspolizei

Lanz, Hubert, 137–38
Lamprecht, Karl: controversy over *Kulturgeschichte*, 8–9, 15; death of, 75; life and philosophy of, 75–85; relationship with father, 79–80
Landin, Harold, 95
Langewiesche, Dieter, 61
League for Human Rights (German), 94
League of Nations, 39
Lebensraum, 44, 139
Leipzig, University of, 83
Lenin, V. I., founds Comintern, 43; and "new diplomacy," 42
Lenz, Max, 77, 78
Life (magazine), 129

Lloyd George, David, Paris Peace Conference, 1919, 42
London Declaration of the North Atlantic Council on "Transformed North Atlantic Alliance" (1990), 112
London Foreign Ministers Conference, 90
Lowenthal, David, 128, 142
Lukaschek, Hans, 96

MacArthur, Douglas A., 91, 93
Maier, Charles S., 12, 15, 128
Main Political Administration (*Politische Hauptverwaltung*), 107, 119
Makers of Modern Strategy (Earl), 150
Manteuffel, Minister President, 69
"Manteuffel system," 68
Marburg, University of, 34
Mason, T. W., 155
Massow, Ludwig von, Minister of the Royal House (Prussia), 62
McClelland, Charles, 9
McCloy, John J., differences with Roger Baldwin, 92–93; head of HICOG, 87
Media, and international politics, 6
Mehring, Franz, 78
Meinecke, Friedrich, 77, 79
Mein Kampf (Hitler), 44
Memory: and history, 127–29; and national identity, 127–28
Mendelssohn, Moses, 154
Methodenstreit, 77, 79, 82
Military power, decline in value of, 28
Ministry of Defense (MOD), 11, 103; NVA and, 120, 123–25
Ministry of the Royal House (Prussia), 62
MOD. *See* Ministry of Defense (West Germany)
Modrow, Hans, and the NVA, 110
Mommsen, Theodor, 127, 129–30, 140
Moynihan, Daniel Patrick, 40
Munich civil liberties union, 97
Mussolini, Benito, *tono fascista* of, 43–44
Murphy's Law, and history, 29

Index

National Defense Council (*Nationaler Verteidigungsrat*), 107
National Socialist Worker's Party (NSDAP), 90–91, 97
Nationaler Verteidigungsrat. See National Defense Council
Nationale Volksarmee (NVA), 11, 105, 112, 115; becomes *Bundeswehr-Ost*, 115–16; draftees of, 118; during the Cold War, 105–6; effects of unification on, 110–11; merger with *Bundeswehr*, 103, 116–17; origins and nature of, 107–9; physical and psychological legacy of, 121–22; Rainer Eppelmann and, 110, 119; veteran officers, 120–21
NATO: Berlin, 1961 and, 132; FRG and, 111–12, 115, 134, 135; German military reform and, 104, 118, 119, 123, 124; NVA and, 106, 108, 109; Warsaw Pact and, 103, 111, 131–32
"New diplomacy," 39
"New Era," regency (Prussia), 62–63
Niebuhr, Marcus, 64
NGO. *See* Nongovernmental Organizations
Nikisch, Arthur, 75
Nicolson, Harold, 45
Nongovernmental Organizations (NGO): and the "diplomatic revolution," 9–10; growth of, 41, 87; important in FRG, 89
NSDAP. *See* National Socialist Worker's Party
Nye, Joseph, Jr., 40
NVA. *See Nationale Volksarmee*

"Old diplomacy," collapse of, 42
Olmütz Accords of 1850 (Prussia), 8
OMGUS. *See* U.S. Military Government
Oncken, Hermann, critically destroys Lamprecht, 78–79
Ostpolitik (Brandt), 143
Ott, Eugen, 139

Pandaemonium (Moynihan), 40

Pares, Richard (historian), on international history, 19–20, 22
Paris Peace Conference (1919), effect on international system, 39, 42
Partnership for Peace, 124
Persian Gulf War, 48–49
Planet Earth, diplomacy and, 53
Polish Corridor, 136
The Politics of the Prussian Army (Craig), 150–52, 156
Politische Hauptverwaltung. See Main Political Administration
Posadowsky, H. Graf, 95
Pünder, Hermann, 94
Preussiche Jahrbücher, 78
Primat der Aussenpolitik, 3, 15, 17
Primat der Innenpolitik, 15
Prussian monarchy, 7; changes in court life, 60, 62–63, 66; constitutional monarchy in, 59–69; and "New Era" regency, 62–65; political court functions, 64–65; and state, 61–62

Radowitz, Joseph Maria von, 59, 69
Ranke, Leopold von, 1, 3, 8, 15; Lamprecht and, 78, 81–82
Recht und Freiheit, 97
Reichswehr, former officers interviewed, 127, 136–40
Reuter, Ernst, 96
"The Revolution in War and Diplomacy," (Craig), 5
Rheinische Zeitung, 93
The Rise and Fall of the Great Powers (Kennedy), 2, 4
The Rise of Modern Diplomacy (Anderson), 5
Roon, Albrecht von, 151
Roosevelt, Franklin, D., 47
Roosevelt, Theodore, mediates end of Russo-Japanese War, 38
Rosenberg, Ludwig, 96
Russia, defeated by Japan, 38; revolutions of 1905 and 1917, 31

Scheven, Werner von, remarks in 1992, 117; on NVA, 120

Second Empire (France), court life, 60
Second World War, and memory, 12; effect on international system, 39, 50
SCHAEF. *See* Supreme Headquarters of Allied Expeditionary Force
SCHAFR. *See* Society for the History of American Foreign Relations
Schleicher, Kurt von, 139
Schleinitz, Alexander von, 66
Schulpforta, 79
Schönbohm, Jörg, 103, 115, 117, 121
Schönebaum, Herbert, 84
"Schule für Innere Führung," 134
SED (*Sozialistische Einheitspartei Deutschlands*): incompetence and corruption of, 116; and the NVA, 105–6; and the revolution of 1989, 109
Sieman, Wolfram, 61
Society for the History of American Foreign Relations (SCHAFR), 17
Soldier's Law, NVA acceptance of, 114
Sollman, Wilhelm, 87, 93, 94
Sorel, Albert, 1
Soviet Western Group of Forces, and Bundeswehr, 116
Soviet Union, collapse of, 3, 27, 29; in the Cold War, 44. *See also* Russia
Speidel, General Hans, 138
"Spruchkammern," denazification process, 88
Stalin, Joseph, 47
Stasi (Administration 2000), 120, 122, 123
Steinberg, Hans-Josef, 84
Stillfried-Rattonitz, Baron Rudolph von, Prussian Royal Master of Ceremonies, 63
Stoltenberg, Gerhard, meeting with Rainer Eppelmann, 111–14
Strausberg, 1990, Schönbohm oversees demobilization of East German military, 103
Summitry: effect on international politics, 6–7; Second World War and, 47
Supreme Headquarters of Allied Expeditionary Force (SCHAEF), 143

Tarnow, Fritz, 96
Technology, and diplomacy, 45–49, 51–52
Telegraph, and diplomacy, 46
Theory of International Politics (Waltz), 4
Thucydides, 129
Trading state, rise of, 11, 27
The Transformation of European Politics (Schroeder), 4
Trotsky, Leon, Commissar for Foreign Affairs, 43
Truman, Harry, and the Cold War, 44
Truman Doctrine, 44
"Two-Plus-Four" ("2 plus 4"), 119, 141; negotiators of unification, 111–12
Two-Year Term Soldiers, 119

United Nations: Balkans and, 33; birth and growth of, 39–40; "Declaration of Human Rights" and, 52; international integration and, 28; NGOs and, 40
United States: Balkans and, 33; as a trading state, 27–28
U.S. Army Europe (USAREUR), 142
U.S.–Military Government (OMGUS), 87; in FRG, 88–92
U.S. State–War–Navy–Coordinating Committee (SWNCC), 88

Valéry, Paul, 46
Vienna System: European monarchies, 7; revolution in international politics, 4–5, 26–28; unification of 1990 and, 11–12
Volkschochschulen, 97
Volkskammer, 141
Vormärz, 60–61

Waltz, Kenneth, 4; structural realism of, 20
Warsaw Pact, 103; NATO and, 119; NVA and, 105, 107
Weber, Alfred, 95
Weber, Max, 83
Wehler, Hans-Ulrich, 61, 84

Weinberg, Gerhard, 2
"White Rose," 141
William I, court of, 65–66; modernization of the monarchy, 67
William II, confrontation with Bismarck, 69
Wilson, Woodrow, indicts old diplomacy, 42
Wollenberger, Vera, at Volkskammer, 1990, 141
A World at Arms (Weinberg), 2
World Conference on Human Rights, 52
World Conference on Women, 52
Die Wurzeln der westdeutsche Nachkriegsdemokratie, (Rupieper), 9

Yugoslavia, power politics in, 30, 32

Die Zeit, 95
Zeitsoldaten, 118
Zook, George F., report, 88
Zook Commission of the American Council on Education, influence on U.S. policy, 91

About the Editors and Contributors

DAVID WETZEL works in the Administration at the University of California, Berkeley, and is author of *The Crimean War: A Diplomatic History* (1985) and editor of *From the Berlin Museum to the Berlin Wall: Essays on the Cultural and Political History of Modern Germany* (Praeger, 1996).

THEODORE S. HAMEROW is Gooch Professor of History Emeritus at the University of Wisconsin. His books include *Restoration, Revolution, Reaction* (1958); a two-volume work, *The Social Foundations of German Unification 1858–1871* (1969; 1972); *From the Finland Station: The Greying of the Revolution in the Twentieth Century* (1990); and, most recently, *To the Wolf's Lair: German Resistance to Hitler* (1997).

DONALD ABENHEIM is Associate Professor of National Security Affairs at the Naval Post-Graduate School, Monterey, California, and research fellow at the Hoover Institution, Stanford University. He is author of *Reforging the Iron Cross: The Search for Tradition in the West German Armed Forces* (1988).

DAVID E. BARCLAY is Professor of History and Director of the Center for Western European Studies, Kalamazoo College. He is author of *Rudolf Wissel as Sozialpolitiker 1890–1933* (1984) and *Frederick William IV and the Prussian Monarchy 1840–1861* (1995).

ROGER CHICKERING is Professor of History at the Center for German and European Studies, Georgetown University. Among his many books are

We Men Who Feel Most German: A Cultural Study of the Pan German League, 1886–1914 (1984) and *Karl Lamprecht: A German Academic Life* (1993).

PAUL GORDON LAUREN is Regents Professor of History at the University of Montana. A specialist in international relations, his publications include *Diplomats and Bureaucrats: The First Institutional Responses to Twentieth Century Diplomacy in France and Germany* (1976) and *Power and Prejudice: The Politics and Diplomacy of Racial Discrimination* (1988).

GAINES POST, JR. is Professor and Chairman of the Department of History, Claremont-McKenna College. He is author of *The Civil–Military Fabric of Weimar Foreign Policy* (1973).

DIETHELM PROWE is Professor of History at Carleton College, and author of *Weltstadt in Krisen, Berlin 1949–1958* (1973).

HERMANN-JOSEF RUPIEPER is Professor of History at Martin-Luther University, Halle-Wittenberg. He edited, with others, *American Policy and the Reconstruction of West Germany* (1993) and is author of *The Cuno Government and Reparations: Politics and Economics* (1993) and *Die Wurzeln der Westdeutschen Nachkriegsdemokratie* (1993).

PAUL W. SCHROEDER is Professor of History and Political Science at the University of Illinois, Champagne–Urbana. He is author of *Austria, Great Britain and the Crimean War* (1972) and *The Transformation of European Politics 1763–1848* (1994), the last a volume in the Oxford History of Modern Europe.

ISBN 0-275-95749-7

90000>

9 780275 957490

HARDCOVER BAR CODE